BEYOND LISTENING

Children's perspectives on early childhood services

Edited by Alison Clark, Anne Trine Kjørholt and Peter Moss

First published in Great Britain in October 2005 by

The Policy Press
University of Bristol
Fourth Floor
Beacon House
Queen's Road
Bristol BS8 1QU
UK

Tel +44 (0)117 331 4054
Fax +44 (0)117 331 4093
e-mail tpp-info@bristol.ac.uk
www.policypress.org.uk

British Library Cataloguing in Publication Data
A catalogue record for this book is available from the British Library.

Library of Congress Cataloging-in-Publication Data
A catalog record for this book has been requested.

ISBN 978 1 86134 612 4 paperback

A hardcover version of this book is also available

Cover design by Qube Design Associates, Bristol.
Front cover: photograph supplied by kind permission of Elise Sotberg
(elises@broadpark.no).
Printed and bound in Great Britain by Hobbs the Printers, Southampton.

Contents

Foreword

According to a well-known English proverb, children should be seen but not heard and, until the past 20 years or so, it would seem that this maxim has been adhered to by the research and policy-making community, at both the national and international level. Only with the advent of the United Nations Declaration of the Rights of the Child (1979), and the emergence of a new paradigm for social science research with children in the 1990s, did the idea that we might listen to what children have to say begin gradually to gain some credence. However, as this collection rightly demonstrates, the acceptance of such a point of view is, at one and the same time, still less widespread than it should be and less critically considered than it might be. *Beyond listening* therefore opens up a series of debates that have, until now, tended to be swept under the political carpet of a newly awakened interest in children's rights and childhood research.

What *Beyond listening* draws to our attention, quite literally, is the need to move beyond the rhetoric that so easily trips off the tongue when questions are raised about children's participation in policy initiatives and research or when the cry goes out that we need to hear 'children's voices'. By making such clarion calls its starting point, rather than its conclusion, *Beyond listening* therefore identifies clearly the dilemmas and controversial issues that need to be tackled if we are really serious about listening to children.

Thus, a key theme that runs through the book, and one that is revisited in a number of different ways, is the question of power and the ways in which right-minded and kind-hearted attempts to listen to what children say run the risk of transforming into subtle instruments of social control, of promoting rather than playing down inequalities between children and of therefore, ironically, creating new routes for the subjection of children. This is why we have to move beyond simply listening to thinking about what it means to listen and how we might do it more effectively, producing change for and with children rather than retaining the status quo.

These issues are core to this volume, whether in relation to accounts of empirical research or of professional practice, and are all the more refreshing given that the volume centres on early childhood. While it may be becoming more acceptable for policy makers to listen – and even learn – from what older children might have to say about matters that concern them, the idea that young children might also speak out and be listened to represents a far greater obstacle still to be overcome. Traditional developmental models of childhood, translated into and through popular practices, continue to hold sway over public imaginings of what young children can do or say. This often means, in effect, that the younger the child, the less importance and credence their views and opinions are given.

By centering its concerns on younger children, *Beyond listening* challenges such assumptions and, indeed, makes us listen with fresh ears.

But it also does more than that. It argues that we have to learn to listen to children in new ways and to learn the new languages that children speak or, perhaps more correctly, to relearn the languages of childhood that appear new to us, as adult listeners. This is, of course, no simple task and, as the various contributions to this volume show, it requires us, as researchers and as practitioners, to learn new skills – and to apply what we have learnt. And this latter point is of particular importance. We need to do more than listen. *Beyond listening* has the provision of better services for children in its sights, services that, it is suggested, might be improved if we take account of what children have to say about the services that are designed to meet their needs.

Drawing within its remit discussions of childhood services from across the globe – from Norway, Denmark and the UK through to New Zealand – *Beyond listening* therefore makes a timely and powerful contribution to current debates within the fields of social policy, early education and childhood sociology. It is to be hoped that the insights it draws to our attention will have some practical outcomes in spreading ideas about 'best practice' in early childhood services so that children in different communities might experience better service provision.

Allison James
Professor of Sociology, University of Sheffield, England

Acknowledgements

We would like to thank the children, practitioners and parents who have made this volume possible. We are grateful to Michelle Cage at the Thomas Coram Research Institute for her competent assistance in organising a seminar for contributors and for putting together the final text.

List of contributors

Margaret Carr is Professor of Education in the School of Education at the University of Waikato, New Zealand.

Alison Clark is a Research Officer at the Thomas Coram Research Unit, Institute of Education, which is a graduate college of the University of London, England.

Valerie Driscoll is a teacher with an early years specialism in the Fortune Park Children's Centre, London, England.

Brit Johanne Eide is an Associate Professor in the Faculty of Education, Oslo University College, Norway.

Carolyn Jones is the Operations Manager at the Wilf Malcolm Institute of Educational Research at the University of Waikato, New Zealand.

Linda Kinney is Head of Early Childhood and Out of School Care at Stirling Council, Scotland.

Anne Trine Kjørholt is Associate Professor and Director of the Norwegian Centre for Child Research at the University for Science and Technology (NTNU) in Trondheim, Norway.

Wendy Lee is a Senior Research Fellow at the School of Education, University of Waikato, New Zealand, and Director of the Educational Leadership Project, an early childhood professional development programme based in the city of Hamilton and funded by the New Zealand Ministry of Education.

Peter Moss is Professor of Early Childhood Provision at the Thomas Coram Research Unit, Institute of Education, which is a graduate college of the University of London, England.

Carlina Rinaldi is Pedagogical Consultant to Reggio Children and Professor of Education at the Reggio-Modena University in Italy and former Director of the Municipal Infant-Toddler Centres and Preschools in Reggio Emilia, Italy.

Caron Rudge is Head of the Fortune Park Children's Centre, London, England.

Hanne Warming is Associate Professor at the University of Roskilde, Denmark.

Nina Winger is an Associate Professor in the Faculty of Education, Oslo University College, Norway.

ONE

Introduction

Peter Moss, Alison Clark and Anne Trine Kjørholt

Early childhood is increasingly institutionalised, and part of a wider historical process affecting children of all ages (Nasman, 1994). More children from earlier ages spend more time in some form of early childhood service, whether it is a centre of one type or another (nursery, kindergarten, nursery school, playgroup) or family day care. Like any other major social change, this creates both new possibilities and new risks. It also places new responsibilities on adults who, for a variety of reasons, have brought about this change to childhood. Not only do we, adults, need to understand the possibilities and risks, we also need to open up to the experiences and perspectives of the young children who live their everyday lives and large portions of their childhoods in early childhood services. We need, in short, to listen.

This book is about listening to young children, and in particular their perspectives on early childhood services and what goes on in them. (By young children we refer in this book to children below compulsory school age, which in most countries is around six years.) It brings together authors from a number of countries – Denmark, England, Italy, New Zealand, Norway and Scotland – who have been working in this field, to share their experiences and understandings, their hopes and concerns. Through their contributions we consider the rationales for listening to young children, not only the issue of responsibility but also listening as a means of enhancing children's participation in shaping their own lives and environments and listening as a principle and practice in learning. We show how practitioners and researchers have been finding innovative ways to listen to young children – and in the process question the distinction between 'practitioner' and 'researcher'.

But although we look at different approaches to listening to young children, the book is not a handbook on 'how to listen'. We do ask 'why?' and 'how?', but we also ask other questions that arise from entering into a committed but critical relationship to the concept and practice of 'listening'. Two are particularly important. What do we mean by 'listening'? Can it be dangerous? Seeking answers to the former question will take us beyond a narrow idea of listening as hearing one form of language, that is, verbal communication, to an understanding that encompasses relationships, dialogue, interpretation and the hundred languages of children. The latter question makes for uncomfortable, but we believe necessary, confrontation with power relations between children and adults, relations that even the most benign and caring adult cannot stand outside.

But before developing these questions further in this introduction, we want to set this discussion in its historical context. Why is there today a growing interest in listening to children, young and old? Why do we talk so much about it?

Why so much listening?

The impulse to listen more to children of whatever age is coming from several quarters. An international impetus for change has been the rising profile of children's rights. Or, to be more precise, children's voice and participation has come to occupy a central place in the children's rights movement, which was traditionally concerned with child protection: "the modern children's rights movement is distinctive in its emphasis on the child's participation and perspective and the emergence of a number of relatively new organisations to advance their rights" (Foley et al, 2003, p 109). Kjørholt (2001) reminds us that "children's active participation in learning processes has long been a central theme in progressive education" (for example, Dewey and Freire), but identifies a major recent turn in participation discourse: "during the last fifteen years the emphasis on children as social and political actors holding special rights in decision-making processes at different levels has been overwhelming" (pp 67, 68).

This turn to a dominant discourse of voice and participation is epitomised by the United Nations Convention on the Rights of the Child, in particular Articles 12 and 13:

> States Parties shall assure to the child who is capable of forming his or her own views the right to express those views freely in all matters affecting the child, the views of the child being given due weight in accordance with the age and maturity of the child....

> The child shall have the right to freedom of expression; this right shall include freedom to seek, receive and impart information and ideas of all kinds, regardless of frontiers, either orally, in writing or in print, in the form of art, or through any other media of the child's choice.

The notion of rights as participation has intersected with other socio-political concerns, notably about citizenship (Roberts, 2003) and the need to combat a perceived alienation with mainstream institutions. As part of this rights and citizenship discourse, many governments have instigated a search for new practices to involve people, old and young, as citizens and in their communities, including *policy* initiatives at a national level to promote children's participation. One example, referred to in the chapter by Brit Johanne Eide and Nina Winger (Chapter Five), is the requirement in the Norwegian framework curriculum for *barnehager* (kindergarten) staff to take the children's point of view into account in planning and evaluating their work (Norwegian Ministry for Children and Family Affairs, 1996). Another example is the 'Core principles of participation for children and young people' published by the English government in 2001 (CYPU, 2001). These principles are intended to apply across all government departments and all agencies delivering government-funded services. In addition, children and young people's participation has been an explicit element in a wide range of national initiatives and policies in England such as New Deal for Communities, the Children's Fund, Children's Services Planning Guidance and Connexions (Kirby et al, 2003).

A parallel development has occurred in the *academic* world, or at least a part of it, in particular a shift in how children are viewed within sociology. A new sociology of childhood, or childhood studies, has been taking shape in recent years. From this disciplinary perspective, children are seen not as 'becomings' but as 'beings' whose ideas, approaches to life, choices and relationships are of interest in their own right (James and Prout, 1997): interest shifts from what children will become later in life to their childhoods here and now. Recognising children's competencies, that children can be considered experts in their own lives (Langsted, 1994), can help adults reflect on the limitations of their understanding of children's lives (Tolfree and Woodhead, 1999). Researchers are increasingly interested in children's perspectives and committed to children being active participants in research itself (Christensen and James, 2000; Lewis and Lindsay, 2000). This academic turn has contributed to a wider change of perception: that children have to be involved in decision making, that children form a social group, and that children make a valued contribution to society (Kirby et al, 2003).

A third driver has been *economic* change, which has emphasised the primacy of the consumer, and values such as choice, individualism and customer satisfaction. In this context, the construction of the 'participating child' emerges not only from the rights movement and new academic perspectives, but also from the discourse of consumerism, as "children are today increasingly being drawn into economic markets as both consumers and workers" (Kjørholt, 2001, p 75). Children have begun to be seen as customers and consumers, both of products (such as clothing and toys) and services. In England, for example, early childhood services aimed at working parents, termed 'childcare', have been viewed in policy terms as private commodities to be purchased by consumers (parents). The state's role has been to regulate the market, to inject funding in cases of so-called 'market failure' (that is, poor families and poor areas that cannot access the market) and to support market development (Cohen et al, 2004). 'Childcare audits', a policy initiative in the late 1990s for this latter purpose, were expected to include user views, including those of children, on the improvement of childcare services.

Such developments can be seen as surface manifestations of subterranean and seismic shifts in social, economic and political relations. The turn, from the late 1970s, to new (or rather reconfigured) forms of liberalism – advanced liberalism politically, neoliberalism economically – has called for a new subject, discussed by Anne Trine Kjørholt in Chapter Nine: autonomous (in the sense of being not dependent) and self-regulating, flexible and problem solving, ready and able to participate as a consumer in the market and to manage his or her own risks, operating within a network of individual responsibilities and rights, with self-realisation as an overarching value. While established political forms, including identification with mass political parties based on class interest, and confidence in representative democracy have been in decline, other forms of political engagement have emerged, including new social movements and human rights campaigns. A discourse of rights, participation and empowerment has provided a political context for these movements and campaigns and for repositioning many social groups as active subjects rather than passive dependants: not only children but also, for example, people with disabilities.

Young children's participation

Most work on listening to children to date has been concerned with older children and young people. For example, in a recent review of English projects involving children and young people in policy development, service planning, delivery and evaluation the most common age group was 12- to 16-year-olds (Kirby et al, 2003). Or to take another example, this time from Norway, a survey in the late 1990s of participatory projects in Norwegian local authorities found that half reported such projects, but very few were addressed to children under 10, let alone under school age; 60 per cent involved children and young people aged 14 or more (Kjørholt, 2002).

There are several reasons for the under-representation of young children. Lansdowne (2004) has pointed out that many of the key players in the debate on the Convention on the Rights of the Child have been non-governmental organisations (NGOs) whose involvement is predominantly with older children. She further suggests that the lives of young children are managed by a combination of parents, other carers and professionals who have tended to be less engaged and proactive in debates on children's rights. The focus, too, on this youngest age group tends to be promoting development rather than promoting rights.

The dominance of the paradigm of development in early childhood policy, provision, practice and research has a further significance. It produces an image of young children that is not conducive to listening: as a becoming, at the beginning of a process of linear progression from the incompleteness of infancy to the maturation of adulthood, with the value (and feasibility) of listening presumed to increase commensurately. This image, too, is far from the liberal subject of rights and participation, the autonomous citizen and active consumer, rational and calculating. Indeed, as O'Neill (1994) argues, the child is missing in liberal theory, unable to participate in its central mechanism of the contract, which assumes relationships between independent individuals.

Similarly the dominance of certain languages – in particular verbal and written languages – privileges listening to those who are more fluent in these languages.

Rinaldi (2005) relates how the development in Reggio Emilia of the theory of the 'hundred languages of childhood' (discussed further in Chapter Two) grew out of a "wider political and cultural debate, for example the debate about how privileging these two languages [verbal and written] were, how in some way they supported the power, not only of certain knowledges, but also of certain classes" (p 193). Listening to young children requires of adults some revaluing and relearning of other languages, which takes time and effort and presupposes a willingness to be multilingual. It is, in short, difficult for those who by adulthood have lost many of the hundred languages of childhood.

However, the situation has been changing. This book offers a number of innovative and important examples of listening to young children, drawn from a larger field of experience. As in many areas of early childhood, the Nordic countries have led the way, in particular Denmark (for a review of Danish literature in this area see Warming, 2003). But important work on this subject can also be found today in other parts of the world, including Italy and parts of the English language-speaking world.

This work on listening to young children has apparently different rationales: learning (see, for example, Chapters Two, Seven and Eight); improving communication between children and the adults in their lives (see Chapter Six); researching children's perspectives on institutions and institutional life (see Chapters Three, Four and Five, but also Langsted, 1994; Miller, 1997; Daycare Trust, 1998; Dupree et al, 2001); or giving children opportunities to participate in decision making, on a routine daily basis or in connection with some larger-scale institutional change (see Chapter Nine). Prout (2003) takes an ever broader view of this last and most explicitly political rationale when he argues "that one of the most important reasons for hearing children's voice ... [is] making children's interests visible in the social and political process of directing and garnering resources for children" (pp 6-7).

However, to differentiate rationales in this way may be misleading. The work with young children reported here and elsewhere does not necessarily fall neatly into one or other of these categories. For example, research methods may be applied to decision making, while learning and research may also be connected.

More fundamentally, it seems to us that much work on listening, however it may be labelled, is motivated by a broader, underlying approach to early childhood services – and indeed to relationships and life in general. In these cases, listening can be understood as more than just a tool or instrument; it can also be understood as a culture or an ethic, a way of being and living that permeates all practice and relationships. Langsted (1994) made this point some time ago in his groundbreaking study of Nordic children's views on life in kindergarten. Structures and procedures, he argued, are important but:

> ... more important is the cultural climate which shapes the ideas that the adults in a particular society hold about children. The wish to listen to and involve children originates in this cultural climate. This

wish will then lead to structures and procedures that can guarantee the involvement of the children. (pp 41-2)

Carlina Rinaldi (personal communication) takes up the same theme, that listening cannot be neatly confined to particular tasks or procedures but is an approach to life, when she comments that:

> … listening is not only a technique and a didactic methodology, but a way of thinking and seeing ourselves in relationship with others and the world. Listening is an element that connects and that is part of human biology and is in the concept of life itself…. [It] is a right or better it is part of the essence of being human.

Hanne Warming in Chapter Four of this book refers to listening as a 'democratic ethos of giving voice'. Continuing this line of thought – listening as culture or ethos – listening has also been understood as the defining feature of an ethic: 'the ethics of an encounter' (Dahlberg and Moss, 2005). This approach to ethical relationships is associated with the work of Emmanuel Levinas (1906-95), a Lithuanian Jew who made his home in France. Largely ignored until the mid-1980s, today Levinas is considered one of the greatest French philosophers of the 20th century (Critchley, 2001). The ethics of an encounter emphasise the importance of relationships, which respect the alterity (otherness) of the Other and resist attempting to make the Other into the Same. 'Grasping' is Levinas's vivid term for this attempt: it expresses the violence involved in reducing the particularity of the Other when the Other is 'grasped' and placed in the totalising system of the knowing subject by, for example, applying the knower's prefabricated system of understandings, concepts and categories.

Dahlberg and Moss (2005) have argued that the ethics of an encounter opens up for a new and quite different idea of education, learning and pedagogical practice, for "to think an other whom I cannot grasp is an important shift and it challenges the whole scene of pedagogy" (Dahlberg, 2003, p 273). Listening is the ethic and method at the heart of this idea of education. Readings (1996) defines the condition of pedagogical practice as 'an infinite attention to the other' and education itself as 'drawing out the otherness of thought' or 'listening to thought':

> To listen to Thought, think beside each other and beside ourselves, is to explore an open network of obligations that keeps the question of meaning open as a locus of debate. Doing justice to Thought, listening to our interlocutors, means trying to hear that which cannot be said but that which tries to make itself heard. And this is a process incompatible with the production of (even relatively) stable and exchangeable knowledge. (p 165)

Dahlberg and Moss (2005) suggest that an example of education as listening to thought, based on the ethics of an encounter, can be found in the pedagogical theories and practices of the municipal preschools in the northern Italian city of Reggio Emilia. Here has developed what the educators in Reggio call 'a pedagogy of listening', understood as an openness to the other's thought and to the question of meaning:

> If we believe that children possess their own theories, interpretations, and questions, and are protagonists in the knowledge-building processes, then the most important verbs in educational practice are no longer 'to talk', 'to explain' or 'to transmit' … but 'to listen'. Listening means being open to others and what they have to say, listening to the hundred (and more) languages, with all our senses. (Rinaldi, 2005, pp 125-6)

The pedagogy of listening, and the understanding of 'listening' on which it is based, are the subject of Chapter Two.

Reggio is not an isolated instance of listening, in its many forms, being the expression of a culture or ethic. There are other examples in this book, but also elsewhere, of how listening to young children permeates every aspect of the life of particular early childhood services. The significance of such listening – listening as a culture or ethic – goes far beyond these services. We might even say it is potentially revolutionary, for it challenges the whole scene of life and all human relationships. Nothing that Readings or Rinaldi say above can or should be confined to young children.

We should end this section with a note of caution. There is much innovative work on listening to young children, as this book demonstrates. But it is, for the moment, more of the exception than the norm; as already noted, most work on listening has been with older children and young people. Awareness of the importance of listening, and competence in doing so, is patchy among those many organisations and individuals involved in early childhood services. Some professions, for example, are only just beginning to take such ideas on board; while, where there is more familiarity with the idea, there are still many gaps between rhetoric and practice. Policies may be contradictory: promoting listening on the one hand, while at the same time requiring standardisation of practice and outcome that runs counter to listening as a process of openness to thought and difference. It is difficult to see, for example, how listening understood in this way is compatible with detailed and predetermined goals and targets, which are more akin to grasping the child.

Listening to young children has also made little headway in much of the research undertaken on early childhood services, in particular in the English-speaking world where such research has been dominated by one particular disciplinary perspective: developmental psychology. As Bloch (1992) observes, "with rare exceptions, [American] early childhood educators who fail to frame their research or research methods in the largely positivist traditions and theories of child development or developmental psychology find themselves marginalized in their own field" (p 3). Here we still see much research that is *on*, rather than *with*, young children, in which judgements are made about children's experience in early childhood services based on standardised measures and without any attempt made to listen to young children themselves. Given the global dominance and influence of American research, the absence of an American contribution is perhaps the most worrying omission in this volume – although this may say as much about gaps in our knowledge of the American scene and the absence of transatlantic networks as it does about the early childhood research culture of the US. (We do recognise some important relevant work by William Corsaro and Vivian Paley, referred to in a number of chapters in this volume.)

What do we mean by 'listening'?

'Listening' is one of those *zeitgeist* words (others include 'quality' and 'excellence') that get bandied around until it seems to crop up everywhere. Everyone, from banks to politicians, wants to be perceived as listening. But few, or so it seems, want to consider what meaning the word may have. 'Listening' is used as if its meaning and value were self-evident and incontestable.

Several contributors to this book raise questions about meaning. Rinaldi in particular, in Chapter Two, goes deeply and quite openly into the concept of listening and its meaning in a 'pedagogy of listening'. She understands listening as part of a way of relating, just as Langsted saw it as part of a wider culture and Dahlberg and Moss treat it as part of an ethic. She foregrounds listening as emotion and reciprocity, interpretation and meaning making, and openness and sensitivity to connections, difference and change, the importance of doubt and uncertainty. She emphasises, too, that listening involves many senses and many languages: "listening to the hundred, the thousand languages, symbols and codes we use to express ourselves and communicate, and with which life expresses itself and communicates to those who know how to listen" (see page 20, this book).

The question of meaning leads to the relationship between listening and participation. Are they one and the same thing or do they differ in meaning? Participation in the liberal rights discourse is usually associated with influencing change and decision making. Kirby et al (2003) conclude, "it is important that participation activity is undertaken with the specific purpose of enabling children to influence decision making and bring about change" (p 30), while Lansdowne (2004) argues that to be meaningful and effective, children's participation requires four key ingredients including "an on-going process of children's expression and active involvement in decision-making at different levels that concern them" (p 15).

Listening as a method could form part of participation as involvement in decision making. But they are not entirely coterminous. Participation understood in this way may require conditions and methods that go beyond listening, such as voting rights (for example, discussions about reducing the voting age) or the exercise of sanctions (for example, withdrawing labour or taking other industrial action); or, to take a more specific example, the court that the Polish children's rights pioneer Janusz Korczak established in his orphanage in inter-war Warsaw, where children acted as judges (Halpérin, 2004). Listening, too, can go beyond this understanding of participation, when defined as a way or ethic of relating to others that, as we have already suggested, is more than just about decision making, but extends into every aspect of life itself.

Perhaps listening as an ethic sits more comfortably with a rather different understanding of participation, as feeling part of a community and having a sense of belonging (Rinaldi, 2005), an understanding that is less individualistic and more relational than participation as involvement in decision making – it is more 'I want to be part of this', less 'I know my rights'. We want to avoid adopting a dualistic either/or approach; listening can be both a method and an ethic, participation can be both about having influence over what concerns one and about being part of a larger network of relations. But there is at the same time some tension present, between the autonomous subject and the social participant, between listening as self-expression and listening as reciprocity; some of this tension surfaces in Chapter Nine.

Listening is dangerous

The French social thinker Michel Foucault (1926-84) once observed that everything is dangerous. By this he meant to draw our attention to the impossibility of neutral and value-free relationships and practices, and the impossibility of individuals being able to stand outside power relations offering disinterested and benign knowledge and opinions:

> ... in human relations, whatever they are – whether it be a question of communicating verbally ... or a question of a love relationship, an institutional or economic relationship – *power is always present: I mean the relationship in which one wishes to direct the behaviour of another.* (Foucault, 1987, p 11; emphasis added)

What sort of risks does power introduce into listening? Here the field of postcolonial studies, in particular critiques of participatory approaches in Majority World development projects, can inform the field of listening to children. There are useful points of similarity, while the former field has been subject to more critical discussion.

One area of risk concerns *the distorting effect of listening without taking account of power relations and their inequalities.* One result may be to gain an elite perspective and affirm the agenda of the more powerful, for example by favouring elite languages and by not hearing the voice of the marginalised. Inequalities may be hidden behind a mask of apparent unity:

> When voice is 'conferred' upon the 'other', when 'they are given voice', without recognising or attempting to alter the inequities that created the original distinctions, the 'giving of voice' or 'listening to' just becomes another colonizing apparatus.... Allowing different voices to be heard is not a solution, since it leads only to an unrealistic illusion of a harmonious pluralism. (Cannella and Viruro, 2004, pp 146-7)

MacNaughton (2003) expresses concern that too much emphasis on the 'voice of the child' in early childhood services may put children with the least power at a disadvantage, "privileging the voices and meanings of the powerful" (p 179). She points to examples, including how "in mixed gender groups girls may feel inhibited ... [while] children who have experienced racism may have poor self esteem and believe their contribution will be ignored or dismissed by the group" (MacNaughton, 2003, p 179). In Chapter Four of this book, Warming also shows how listening can empower some children and marginalise others.

The question of whether the effects of power relations can be eliminated to achieve equal participation has been one of the controversies surrounding Habermas's concept of communicative ethics, involving the public negotiation of difference and the formation of consensus. This is premised on the possibility of rules that enable all to participate equally in discussion. But this premise, the possibility of creating a genuinely level playing field, has been questioned as being implausible, as has the desirability of consensus. Mouffe, for example, argues that Habermas, by envisaging a well-ordered democratic society without exclusions or antagonisms, cannot grasp the crucial role of conflict and its integrative function in a pluralist democracy: "taking pluralism seriously requires that we give up on the dream of a rational consensus which entails the fantasy that we could escape from our human form of life" (Mouffe, 2000, p 98).

A second area of risk concerns how *the process of listening itself may become a means of supporting, rather than subverting or resisting, power.* Listening may, for example, be used as a political or managerial tactic for currying favour or for gaining support for some unpopular move or for hiding the realities of power. In such cases, the language of participation, empowerment and listening becomes a ploy for "masking a real concern for managerial effectiveness" (Cooke and Kothari, 2001, p 14). Listening ('I hear what you say') may, thus, be a substitute for contestation and conflict (which, as Mouffe argues above, can be seen as signs of a healthy democracy), a means of reducing pressure by 'letting off steam', 'getting things off your chest'.

Listening can also be a tool of management through focusing attention on some issues and diverting it away from others, helping to define what can and cannot be spoken about. The question here is what bounds listening is kept within, and what is *not* spoken about and *not* listened to. Thus, as Kjørholt illustrates in Chapter Nine, participation in Danish early childhood centres has often been limited to individual choices within a group setting: children are not able "to choose to participate in an intergenerational relationship and interact with age groups other than preschool children … [or] participate in working activities, or decide to engage in activities together with their parents or older siblings" (see page 165, this book).

A third area of risk develops this theme of management. Listening can be *a means to govern the child more effectively*, albeit behind a mask of child-centredness and children's rights, as part of a process of bringing the child ever more constantly under the adult gaze. Listening becomes a surveillance and confessional technique for knowing and grasping otherness and managing conduct more effectively through governing the soul. Fendler (2001) describes how Foucault uses "the term 'soul' to refer to aspects of humanity that were previously sacrosanct but that have recently been constructed as objects of psychological and regulatory apparatuses … the innermost qualities of being human … [such as] desire, fear and pleasure" (p 123). Listening can provide a window into the soul, rendering "the innermost qualities of being human" more manageable or governable by making them visible and audible.

A fourth area of risk is again the subject of Chapter Nine: how listening and participation may become means by which *the child is created as a particular sort of subject*. This is the normative subject of advanced liberalism and neoliberalism, whom we have already introduced: the autonomous, calculating individual for whom self-realisation is the highest value. Listening is not the only technique that contributes to creating the ideal liberal subject. Fendler (2001) has argued that other pedagogical methods widespread today, such as 'whole child education' and 'developmentally appropriate practice', contribute to creating a subject who is not only autonomous but flexible and problem solving. This risk seems to us to be very great when listening is too closely bound to a rather narrow, rights-based participation discourse, where the emphasis is on the individual asserting their rights, their autonomy, their self-realisation.

A fifth risk, raised in Chapter Four, concerns *the authenticity of voice*, the claim that there is a decontextualised reality that can be transmitted without mediation from one individual to another: the essentially technical challenge is to capture this objective reality ('I hear what you say'). The problem with this claim is its denial of the interpretive element in any communication, the listener claiming to have heard and grasped the authentic voice of the person listened to, thus giving authority to the listener; power relations are ignored. But the problem with authenticity claims runs deeper, in the failure to recognise how the experience of the person listened to is constituted within particular contexts and discourses, and as such is a work both complex and in progress.

Such reasons lead Hanne Warming in Chapter Four to argue that "there is no essential or authentic children's perspective; rather children's perspectives must be approached as multiple and changing, as well as being contextualised socially, culturally, historically and biographically. This theoretical approach denies the authentic child voice" (see page 53, this book). This is not an argument for dismissing voice and listening, but for acknowledging the provisionality of voice and the complexity of listening in which the listener is an active participant, co-

constructing meanings in a reciprocal and contextualised relationship, rather than a passive and objective receptor to whom a clear and incontestable message is transmitted.

Overall, we can see that most of these risks are related to one tendency in late modernity: to control the future through children and that listening can become part of a technology intended to achieve this end. So as Prout (2000) has pointed out, we are living in a period that emphasises children's participation and voice within a discourse of choice, autonomy and citizenship; while at the same time we govern children more strongly then ever before through increasingly powerful technologies of normalisation and subjectification. In this confused situation, 'listening' can never be neutral but can figure both in projects for regulation and projects for emancipation.

To say that listening is dangerous does not mean abandoning listening, throwing the baby out with the bath water. Rather it means being prepared to recognise the risks we run when listening, and the impossibility of being free of power and of escaping power relations by somehow being able to stand outside of them. It means being aware of power through thinking critically about the meaning, process and consequences of listening. Thinking critically has been described by Rose (1999) as:

> ... partly a matter of introducing a critical attitude towards those things that are given to our present experience as if they were timeless, natural, unquestionable: to stand against the maxims of one's time, against the spirit of one's age, against the current of received wisdom. It is a matter of introducing a kind of awkwardness into the fabric of one's experience, of interrupting the fluency of the narratives that encode that experience and making them stutter. (p 20)

Ethical practice, how we conduct listening, also has an important part to play, a theme in several of the chapters in this book including Chapters Five and Six.

Why 'beyond listening'?

In choosing this title for the book, we want to indicate a certain ambivalence towards the term 'listening' and a certain ambition. On the one hand, we feel that 'listening' is in danger of becoming an empty concept, a sort of cliché much used without sufficient consideration given to meaning, process, possibilities and risks – another of those 'motherhood and apple pie' terms to which no one can object largely because no one really knows what it signifies. On the other hand, we find it a term that can and has attracted rich meanings and inspired amazing work, and a term that has the potential to contribute to making early childhood services loci of ethical and political practice (Dahlberg and Moss, 2005).

Our ambition is to contribute to a developing discourse on listening that, as we have already said, goes beyond a narrow and simplified idea of listening as hearing one form of language, the spoken word, or as a means to improve customer satisfaction or management performance. Getting beyond this idea can take us to a more complex and more hopeful place, where listening is understood as a pedagogy and a way of researching life, a culture and an ethic, a continuous process and relationship. This opens up the question of what listening is for. Is it just hearing and, perhaps, interpreting – or does it go beyond that? If we treat listening as an important part of a democratic and respectful relationship with children, does it have the possibility to lead to truly radical change – in learning (Chapter Two), in policy making (Chapter Seven), in assessment (Chapter Eight), through provoking adults to question, to risk uncertainty and to think (Chapters Four, Five and Eight)?

The rest of the book

The chapters that follow start with a contribution from Carlina Rinaldi, formerly the pedagogical director of the Municipal Infant-Toddler Centres and Preschools in the northern Italian city of Reggio Emilia, whose theories and practice have achieved world-wide attention and admiration. Central to this work has been the theory and practice of a 'pedagogy of listening and relationships', and this chapter explores this pedagogy and how it relates to a particular understanding of listening. We put this chapter first because it provides a theoretical and conceptual framework that relates to subsequent chapters, and it also emphasises the importance we attach to opening up discussion of the meaning of listening.

The next three chapters give accounts from researchers – Alison Clark from England, Hanne Warming from Denmark and Brit Johanne Eide and Nina Winger from Norway – of how they have approached listening to young children and some of the issues, including ethical reflections, that have arisen for them in conducting their research. It introduces a number of different methods that have been adopted for listening to young children in research, methods, however, that can also contribute to work by practitioners.

The following three chapters – by Valerie Driscoll and Caron Rudge from England, Linda Kinney from Scotland, and Margaret Carr, Carolyn Jones and Wendy Lee from New Zealand – present the experience of listening to young children in practice, respectively in an early childhood centre, in a local authority and in the development of assessment at a national level. As in the earlier group of 'research' chapters, these chapters fuse discussion of methods with experience of their application. By this stage of the book, the reader may well decide that distinctions between 'research' and 'practice' are blurry if not entirely redundant, with a lot of actual or possible border crossing.

The penultimate chapter, by Anne Trine Kjørholt from Norway, uses textual analysis of two texts produced from a Danish project of the 1990s ('Children as Fellow Citizens') to provide a critique of participation and listening, in particular exploring how discourses on these subjects emerge from particular ideological and moral contexts and are inscribed with particular values. It demonstrates some of the elements of risk that we have discussed above, in particular the way in which participation and listening may contribute, if not subject to critique, to the construction of the child as a particular subject, in this case the autonomous, self-determining subject of late modern societies. Following this, we end the book with some reflections, in particular on two rationales for listening: rights discourses and relational ethics.

We want to make two other points before the reader moves on to the book's main chapters, concerning collaborative writing and language. Edited volumes are treated with reservation by some publishers and in some academic circles. While there may be some grounds for such reservations, we think there is also a substantial and unique value in such publications if they represent real collaboration and dialogue and if they result from listening to others and being open to them. While preparing this volume, most of the authors were able to meet for two days to discuss contributions while still in draft form. This proved a stimulating and convivial occasion, an opportunity for dialogue and listening; at least one more meeting, with all authors, would have been ideal.

This book is in English, but English is not the first language of half of our contributors. Even though the English of these contributors is very good and has been edited, it is important that readers for whom English is a first language do not take matters for granted. Writing in another language is not only difficult, but it risks important meanings embedded in the original language getting lost in translation. In the process of translation, the English language grasps the other language and tries to make it into the same: diversity and otherness wither in the process. As the English language becomes increasingly hegemonic, it is important to recognise the risks entailed through this emerging power relationship and how real and important cultural differences can be rendered invisible. For this reason, we have not translated certain terms, encouraging authors to use their own language rather than struggle to translate words that lose meaning in translation. We hope, too, that the appearance of non-English words will act as a constant reminder to the reader that the voice of some contributors is more mediated than that of others.

Language can be seen as part of a wider dimension of diversity: culture. Policy, provision and practice is embedded in national and, sometimes, more localised, cultures, with their own histories, traditions, values, ways of thinking and relating and forms of language (not only verbal). Each author is viewing the subject of listening not only from a personal perspective but also from a particular cultural perspective, which gives, for example, terms like 'listening' or 'participation' or 'rights' particular meanings and forms of expression. While we hope and expect that the book will 'speak' to people from many countries and backgrounds, we recognise that readers will 'listen' to our authors through a process of interpretation and that those being listened to, the authors, are speaking from different positions within different contexts.

References

Bloch, M. (1992) 'Critical perspectives on the historical relationship between child development and early childhood education research', in S. Kessler and B. Swadener (eds) *Reconceptualising the early childhood curriculum*, New York, NY: Teachers College Press, pp 3-20.

Cannella, G. and Viruro, R. (2004) *Childhood and (post) colonization: Power, education and contemporary practice*, London: Routledge.

Christensen, P. and James, A. (eds) (2000) *Research with children*, London: Falmer Press.

Cohen, B., Moss, P., Petrie, P. and Wallace, J. (2004). *A New Deal for children? Reforming education and care in England, Scotland and Sweden*, Bristol: The Policy Press.

Cooke, B. and Kothari, U. (eds) (2001) *Participation: The new tyranny?*, London: Zed Books.

Critchley, S. (2001) *Continental philosophy: A very short introduction*, Oxford: Oxford University Press.

CYPU (Children and Young Persons Unit) (2001) 'Core principles of participation for children and young people' (available at www.cypu.gov.uk/corporate/participation/coreprinciples.cfm).

Dahlberg, G. (2003) 'Pedagogy as a loci of an ethics of an encounter', in M. Bloch, K. Holmlund, I. Moqvist and T. Popkewitz (eds) *Governing children, families and education: Restructuring the welfare state*, New York, NY: Palgrave Macmillan, pp 261-86.

Dahlberg, G. and Moss, P. (2005) *Ethics and politics in early childhood education*, London: Routledge.

Daycare Trust (1998) *Listening to children: Young children's views on childcare, A guide for parents*, London: Daycare Trust.

Dupree, E., Bertram, T. and Pascal, C. (2001) 'Listening to children's perspectives on their early childhood settings', Paper presented at the 11th European Early Childhood Education Research Association Conference, Alkmaar (Netherlands), 29 August-1 September.

Fendler, L. (2001) 'Educating flexible souls', in K. Hultqvist and G. Dahlberg (eds) *Governing the child in the new millennium*, London: Routledge, pp 119-42.

Foley, P., Roche, J., Parton, N. and Tucker, S. (2003) 'Contradictory and convergent trends in law and policy affecting children in England', in C. Hallett and A. Prout (eds) *Hearing the voices of children: Social policy for a new century*, London: RoutledgeFalmer, pp 106-20.

Foucault, M. (1987) 'The ethic of care for the self as a practice of freedom', in J. Bernauer and D. Rasmussen (eds) *The final Foucault*, Cambridge, MA: MIT Press, pp 1-20.

Halpérin, D. (2004) 'Focus on Janusz Korczak: educator, poet and humanist', *Children in Europe*, no 7, pp 26-7.

James, A. and Prout, A. (1997) *Constructing and reconstructing childhood* (2nd edn), London: Falmer.

Kirby, P., Lanyon, C., Cronin, K. and Sinclair, R. (2003) *Building a culture of participation*, London: National Children's Bureau.

Kjørholt, A.T. (2001) '"The participating child": a vital pillar in this century?', *Nordisk Pedagogik*, vol 21, pp 65-81.

Kjørholt, A.T. (2002) 'Small is powerful: discourses on "children and participation" in Norway', *Childhood*, vol 9, no 1, pp 63-82.

Langsted, O. (1994) 'Looking at quality from the child's perspective', in P. Moss and A. Pence (eds) *Valuing quality in early childhood services: New approaches to defining quality*, London: Paul Chapman Publishing, pp 28-42.

Lansdowne, G. (2004) 'Participation and young children', *Early Childhood Matters*, November, No 103, pp 4-14.

Lewis, A. and Lindsay, G. (eds) (2000) *Researching children's perspectives*, Buckingham: Open University Press.

MacNaughton, G. (2003) *Shaping early childhood: Learners, curriculum and contexts*, Maidenhead: Open University Press.

Miller, J. (1997) *Never too young*, London: National Early Years Network.

Mouffe, C. (2000) *The democratic paradox*, London: Verso.

Nasman, E. (1994) 'Individualisation and institutionalisation of children', in J. Qvortrup, M. Bardy, S. Sgritta and H. Wintersberger (eds) *Childhood matters: Social theory, practice and politics*, Aldershot: Avebury, pp 165-88.

Norwegian Ministry for Children and Family Affairs (1996) *Framework plan for day care institutions: A brief presentation*, Oslo: Norwegian Ministry for Children and Family Affairs.

O'Neill, J. (1994) *The missing child in liberal theory*, Toronto, Canada: University of Toronto Press.

Prout, A. (2000) 'Children's participation: control and self-realisation in British late modernity', *Children & Society*, vol 14, pp 304-31.

Prout, A. (2003) 'Participation, policy and the changing conditions of childhood', in C. Hallett and A. Prout (eds) *Hearing the voices of children: Social policy for a new century*, London: RoutledgeFalmer, pp 11-25.

Readings, B. (1996) *The university in ruins*, Cambridge, MA: Harvard University Press.

Rinaldi, C. (2005) *In dialogue with Reggio Emilia*, London: Routledge.

Roberts, H. (2003) 'Children's participation in policy matters', in C. Hallett and A. Prout (eds) *Hearing the voices of children: Social policy for a new century*, London: RoutledgeFalmer, pp 26-37.

Rose, N. (1999) *Powers of freedom: Reframing political thought*, Cambridge: Cambridge University Press.

Tolfree, D. and Woodhead, M. (1999) 'Tapping a key resource', *Early Childhood Matters*, no 91, pp 19-23.

Warming, H. (2003) 'Danish literature review on listening to young children', in A. Clark, S. McQuail and P. Moss (eds) *Exploring the field of listening to and consulting with young children*, Research Report 445, London: DfES, pp 62-80.

TWO

Documentation and assessment: what is the relationship?

Carlina Rinaldi[1]

Reggio Emilia is a city of about 150,000 people in the Emilia Romagna region of northern Italy, one of the wealthiest parts of Europe. It is an old and comfortably sized city, whose population has been growing in recent years with an influx of immigrants from around the world. When people in the early childhood field talk about Reggio, they refer in the first place to a network of centres for young children, some for children from a few months old up to three years (*asili nido*), others for three-'to six-year-olds (*scuole dell'infanzia*). In Reggio they speak of these as 'municipal schools', for this network has been built up and supported by the municipality – it is the child of a strong and democratic local government. This network of services has been growing, innovating and changing for more than 40 years, since the first municipal school opened in 1963.

But most important, Reggio is a body of pedagogical thought and practice, permeated by cultural values, making the early childhood centres into social and political spaces. Great importance is attached to the image of the child and Reggio's choice to take the image of the rich child, an active subject with rights and extraordinary potential and born with a hundred languages. Reggio has also chosen a very particular understanding of knowledge and learning: knowledge as the construction of meaning; and learning as the process of construction, based on relationships (so really co-construction) and listening – 'a pedagogy of listening and relationships' – and made visible and supported through the process of pedagogical documentation. It is through pedagogical documentation that learning processes can be shared, discussed, reflected upon and interpreted – not only by educators, but also by children, parents and anyone else wishing to gain deeper understanding.

This chapter, written by a former pedagogical director of Reggio's municipal schools, explores Reggio's understanding of and work with the concept of listening, and its relationship to the process of pedagogical documentation.

The concept of documentation as a collection of documents used for demonstrating the truth of a fact or confirming a thesis is historically correlated to the birth and evolution of scientific thought and to a conceptualisation of knowledge as an objective and demonstrable entity. It is thus tied to a certain historical period and to profound reasons of a cultural, social and political nature that I will not examine here. Rather, I find it interesting to underscore how the concept of documentation, which has only recently moved into the school environment, and more specifically into the pedagogical-didactic sphere, has undergone substantial modifications that partially alter its definition. In this context, documentation is interpreted and used for its value as a tool for recalling; that is, as a possibility for reflection. From this perspective, the educational path becomes concretely visible through in-depth documentation of data related to educational activities, making use of verbal, graphic and documentary instruments as well as the audiovisual technologies most commonly found in schools.

I want to emphasise one aspect in particular regarding the way documentation is used in this way; that is, the materials are collected *during* the experience, but they are read and interpreted *at the end*. The reading and recalling of memory therefore takes place after the fact. The documents (video and audio recordings, written notes) are collected, sometimes catalogued, and brought back for rereading, revisiting, and reconstruction of the experience. That which took place is reconstructed, interpreted and reinterpreted by means of the documents that testify to the salient moments of a path that was predefined by the teacher: the path that made it possible for the objectives of the experience to be achieved. In short, according to this conceptual approach and didactic practice, the documents (the documented traces) are used after and not during the process. These documents (and the reflections and interpretations they elicit from teachers and children) do not intervene during the learning path and within the learning process in a way that would give meaning and direction to the process. Herein lies the substantial difference with the approach to documentation in Reggio Emilia.

In Reggio Emilia, where we have explored this methodology for many years, we place the emphasis on documentation as an integral part of the procedures aimed at fostering learning and for modifying the learning–teaching relationship. To clarify further what I mean, a number of assumptions should be stated that may initially seem far from the issue at hand but that – or so I hope – will aid in understanding that our choice and practice are neither random nor indifferent. In fact, I believe that documentation is a substantial part of the goal that has always characterised our experience: the search for meaning – to find the meaning of school, or rather, to construct the meaning of school, as a place that plays an active role in the children's search for meaning and our own search for meaning (and shared meanings).

In this sense, among the first questions we should ask ourselves as teachers and educators are these: How can we help children find the meaning of what they do, what they encounter, what they experience? And how can we do this for ourselves? These are questions of meaning and the search for meaning (why? how? what?). I think these are the key questions that children constantly ask themselves, both at school and outside of school.

It is a very difficult search and a difficult task, especially for children who nowadays have so many spheres of reference in their daily lives: their family experience, television, the social places they frequent in addition to the family and school. It is a task that involves making connections, giving meaning to these events, to these fragments that are gathered over the course of many and varied experiences. Children carry out this search with tenacity and effort, sometimes making mistakes, but they do the searching on their own. We cannot live without meaning; that would preclude any sense of identity, any hope, any future. Children know this and initiate the search right from the beginning of their lives. They know it as young members of the human species, as individuals, as people. The search for the meaning of life and of the self in life is born with the child and is desired by the child. This is why we talk about a child who is competent and strong – a child who has the right to hope and the right to be valued, not a predefined child seen as fragile, needy and incapable. Ours is a different way of thinking and approaching the child, whom we view as an active subject with us to explore, to try day by day to understand something, to find a meaning, a piece of life.

For us, these meanings, these explanatory theories are extremely important and powerful in revealing the ways in which children think, question and interpret reality and their own relationships with reality and with us.

Herein lies the genesis of the 'pedagogy of relationships and listening', one of the metaphors that distinguishes the pedagogy of Reggio Emilia.

For adults and children alike, understanding means being able to develop an interpretive 'theory', a narration that gives meaning to events and objects of the world. Our theories are provisional, offering a satisfactory explanation that can be continuously reworked; but they represent something more than simply an idea or a group of ideas. They must please us and convince us, be useful, and satisfy our intellectual, affective and aesthetic needs (the aesthetics of knowledge). In representing the world, our theories represent us.

Moreover, if possible, our theories must please and be attractive to others. Our theories need to be listened to by others. Expressing our theories to others makes it possible to transform a world not intrinsically ours into something shared. Sharing theories is a response to uncertainty.

Here, then, is the reason why any theorisation, from the simplest to the most refined, needs to be expressed, to be communicated, and thus to be listened to, in order to exist. It is here we recognise the values and foundations of the 'pedagogy of listening'.

The pedagogy of listening

How can we define the term listening?

Listening as sensitivity to the patterns that connect, to that which connects us to others; abandoning ourselves to the conviction that our understanding and our own being are but small parts of a broader, integrated knowledge that holds the universe together.

Listening, then, as a metaphor for having the openness and sensitivity to listen and be listened to – listening not just with our ears, but with all our senses (sight, touch, smell, taste, orientation).

Listening to the hundred, the thousand languages, symbols and codes we use to express ourselves and communicate, and with which life expresses itself and communicates to those who know how to listen.

Listening as time, the time of listening, a time that is outside chronological time – a time full of silences, of long pauses, an interior time. Interior listening, listening to ourselves, as a pause, a suspension, as an element that generates listening to others but, in turn, is generated by the listening that others give us. Behind the act of listening there is often a curiosity, a desire, a doubt, an interest; there is always an emotion.

Listening is emotion; it is generated by emotions and stimulates emotions. The emotions of others influence us by means of processes that are strong, direct, not mediated, and intrinsic to the interactions between communicating subjects.

Listening as welcoming and being open to differences, recognising the value of the other's point of view and interpretation.

Listening as an active verb that involves interpretation, giving meaning to the message and value to those who offer it.

Listening that does not produce answers but formulates questions; listening that is generated by doubt, by uncertainty, which is not insecurity but, on the contrary, the security that every truth is such only if we are aware of its limits and its possible 'falsification'.

Listening is not easy. It requires a deep awareness and at the same time a suspension of our judgements and above all our prejudices; it requires openness to change. It demands that we have clearly in mind the value of the unknown and that we are able to overcome the sense of emptiness and precariousness that we experience whenever our certainties are questioned.

Listening that takes the individual out of anonymity, that legitimates us, gives us visibility enriching both those who listen and those who produce the message (and children cannot bear to be anonymous).

Listening as the premise for any learning relationship – learning that is determined by the 'learning subject' and takes shape in his or her mind through action and reflection, that becomes knowledge and skill through representation and exchange.

Listening, therefore, as 'a listening context', where one learns to listen and narrate, where individuals feel legitimated to represent their theories and offer their own interpretations of a particular question. In representing our theories, we 're-know' or 're-cognise' them, making it possible for our images and intuitions to take shape and evolve through action, emotion, expressiveness, and iconic and symbolic representations (the 'hundred languages').

Understanding and awareness are generated through sharing and dialogue. We represent the world in our minds, and this representation is the fruit of our sensitivity to the way in which the world is interpreted in the minds and in the representations of others. It is here that our sensitivity to listening is highlighted; starting from this sensitivity, we form and communicate our representations of the world based not only on our response to events (self-construction), but also on that which we learn about the world from our communicative exchange with others.

The ability to shift (from one kind of intelligence to another, from one language to another) is not only a potential within the mind of each individual but also involves the tendency to shift across (to interact among) many minds. We enrich our knowledge and our subjectivity thanks to this predisposition to welcoming the representations and theories of others – that is, listening to others and being open to them.

This capacity for listening and reciprocal expectations, which enables communication and dialogue, is a quality of the mind and of the intelligence, particularly in the young child. It is a quality that demands to be understood and supported. In the metaphorical sense, in fact, children are the greatest listeners of all to the reality that surrounds them. They possess the time of listening, which is not only time *for* listening but a time that is rarefied, curious, suspended, generous – a time full of waiting and expectation. Children listen to life in all its shapes and colours, and they listen to others (adults and peers). They quickly perceive how the act of listening (observing, but also touching, smelling, tasting, searching) is essential for communication. Children are biologically predisposed to communicate, to exist in relation, to live in relation.

Listening, then, seems to be an innate predisposition that accompanies children from birth, allowing their process of acculturation to develop. The idea of an innate capacity for listening may seem paradoxical but, in effect, the process of acculturation must involve innate motivations and competencies. The newborn child comes into the world with a self that is joyous, expressive, and ready to experiment and explore, using objects and communicating with other people. Right from the beginning, children show a remarkable exuberance, creativity and inventiveness toward their surroundings, as well as an autonomous and coherent consciousness.

Very early in life, children demonstrate that they have a voice, but above all that they know how to listen and want to be listened to. Sociality is not taught to children: they are social beings. Our task is to support them and live their sociality with them; that is the social quality that our culture has produced. Young children are strongly attracted by the ways, the languages (and thus the codes) that our culture has produced, as well as by other people (children and adults).

It is a difficult path that requires efforts, energies, hard work and sometimes suffering, but it also offers wonder, amazement, joy, enthusiasm and passion. It is a path that takes time, time that children have and adults often do not have or do not want to have. This is what a school should be: first and foremost, a context of multiple listening. This context of multiple listening, involving the teachers but also the group of children and each child, all of whom can listen to others and listen to themselves, overturns the teaching–learning relationship. This overturning shifts the focus to learning; that is, to children's self-learning and the learning achieved by the group of children and adults together.

As children represent their mental images to others, they represent them to themselves, developing a more conscious vision (interior listening). Thus, moving from one language to another, from one field of experience to another, and reflecting on these shifts and those of others, children modify and enrich their theories and conceptual maps. But this is true if, and only if, children have the opportunity to make these shifts in a group context – that is, in and with others – and if they have the possibility to listen and be listened to, to express their differences and be receptive to the differences of others. The task of those who educate is not only to allow the differences to be expressed but to make it possible for them to be negotiated and nurtured through exchange and comparison of ideas. We are talking about differences between individuals but also differences between languages (verbal, graphic, plastic, musical, gestural, for example), because it is the shifting from one language to another, as well as their reciprocal interaction, that enables the creation and consolidation of concepts and conceptual maps.

Not only does the individual child learn how to learn, but the group becomes conscious of itself as a 'teaching place', where the many languages are enriched, multiplied, refined and generated, but also collide, 'contaminate' and hybridise each other, and are renewed.

The concept of 'scaffolding', which has characterised the role of the teacher, also assumes new and different methods and meanings. It is the context, the web of reciprocal expectations (more than the teachers themselves) that sustains the individual and group processes. In addition to offering support and cultural mediation (for example, subject matter, instruments,), teachers who know how to observe, document and interpret the processes that the children undergo autonomously will realise in this context their greatest potential to learn how to teach.

Documentation, therefore, is seen as visible listening, as the construction of traces (through notes, slides, videos, and so on) that not only testify to the children's learning paths and processes, but also make them possible because they are visible. For us this means making visible, and thus possible, the relationships that are the building blocks of knowledge.

Documentation

To ensure listening and being listened to is one of the primary tasks of documentation (producing traces/documents that testify to and make visible the ways of learning of the individuals and the group), as well as to ensure that the group and each individual child have the possibility to observe themselves from an external point of view while they are learning (both during and after the process).

A broad range of documentation (videos, tape recordings, written notes, and so on) produced and used in process (that is, during the experience) offers the following advantages:

- it makes visible (although in a partial way, and thus 'partisan') the nature of the learning processes and strategies used by each child, and makes the subjective and intersubjective processes a common patrimony;
- it enables reading, revisiting and assessment in time and in space, and these actions become an integral part of the knowledge-building process.

Documentation can modify learning from an epistemological point of view (enabling epistemological assessment and self-assessment, which become an integral part of the process in that they guide and orient the process itself). It seems to be essential for metacognitive processes and for the understanding of children and adults. In relation to recent studies that increasingly highlight the role of memory in the learning and identity-forming processes, we could hypothesise that significant reinforcement can be offered to the memory by the images (photographs and video), the voices, and the notations. Likewise the reflexive aspect (fostered by the 're-cognition' that takes place through use of the findings) and the capacity for concentration and interpretation could benefit from this memory-enhancing material. This is only a supposition, but in my view it deserves to be confronted and discussed. In this movement, which I would define as a spiral as it weaves together the observation, the interpretation and the documentation, we can clearly see how none of these actions can actually be separated or removed from the others. Any separation would be artificial and merely for the sake of argument. Rather, I would talk about dominance in the adult's level of awareness and consequently of action. It is impossible, in fact, to document without observing and, obviously, interpreting.

By means of documenting, the thinking – or the interpretation – of the documenter thus becomes material, that is, tangible and capable of being interpreted. The notes, the recordings, the slides and photographs represent fragments of a memory that seems thereby to become 'objective'. While each fragment is imbued with the subjectivity of the documenter, it is offered to the interpretive subjectivity of others in order to be known or reknown, created and recreated, also as a collective knowledge-building event.

The result is knowledge that is bountiful and enriched by the contributions of many. In these fragments (images, words, signs and drawings) there is the past, what took place – but there is also the future (or rather what else can happen if…).

We are looking at a new concept of didactics: participatory didactics, didactics as procedures and processes that can be communicated and shared. Visibility, legibility and shareability become supporting nuclei because they are the basis of communicative effectiveness and didactic effectiveness. Didactics thus becomes more similar to the science of communication than to the traditional pedagogical disciplines.

At this point, a particular aspect emerges that structures the teaching–learning relationship and that in this context is made more visible, more explicit. At the moment of documentation (observation and interpretation), the element of assessment enters the picture immediately, that is, in the context and during the time in which the experience (activity) takes place. It is not sufficient to make an abstract prediction that establishes what is significant – the elements of value necessary for learning to be achieved – before the documentation is actually carried out. It is necessary to interact with the action itself, with that which is revealed, defined and perceived as truly significant, as the experience unfolds. Any gap between the prediction and the event (between the inherent meanings and those which the child/children attribute in their action) should be grasped readily and rapidly. The adult's schema of expectation is not prescriptive but orientative. Doubt and uncertainty permeate the context; they are part of the 'documenter's context'. Herein lies true didactic freedom, of the child as well as the teacher. It lies in this space between the predictable and the unexpected, where the communicative relationship between the children and teachers' learning processes is constructed. It is in this space that the questions, the dialogue, the comparison of ideas with colleagues is situated, where the meeting on 'what to do' takes place and the process of assessment (deciding what to 'give value to') is carried out.

The issue, then, is to consider the child as a context for himself or herself and for the others, and to consider the learning process as a process of construction of interactions between the 'subject being educated' and the 'objects of education' (seen as including knowledge as well as social-affective and axiological models of behaviour). This means that the object of education is seen not as an object but as a 'relational place'. With this term I underscore the way in which the teacher chooses and proposes the knowledge-building approach (assuming all due responsibility). It is a construction of relationships that are born of a reciprocal curiosity between the subject and the object. Curiosity is sparked by a question that stimulates the subject and the object to 'encounter each other', showing what the child knows (understood as theories and desires for knowledge) and the knowledge of the object in terms of its cultural identity. This identity is not limited to the elements that are immediately perceivable, but is also directed toward the cultural elaborations that have been produced around it, and above all those that *can* be produced in this new knowledge-seeking relationship. This re-knowing of the object is not only 'historical', thus reproducing what is culturally known about the object (for example, what we know about a tree in its disciplinary interpretations: biology, architecture, poetry, and so on). It is also a living organism because it comes to life in the vitality, freshness and unpredictability of this encounter, where the children can give new identity to the object, creating a relationship for the object and for themselves that is also metaphorical and poetic.

Documentation is this process, which is dialectic, based on affective bonds and also poetic; it not only accompanies the knowledge-building process but also in a certain sense impregnates it.

Documentation not only lends itself to interpretation but also is itself interpretation. It is a narrative form, both intrapersonal and interpersonal communication, because it offers those who document and those who read the documentation an opportunity for reflection and learning. The reader can be a colleague, a group of colleagues, a child, children, parents, anyone who has participated or wants to participate in this process. The documentation material is open, accessible, usable, and therefore readable. In reality this is not always the case, and above all the process is neither automatic nor easy. Effective documentation requires extensive experience in documentary reading and writing.

Legibility

Documentation is thus a narrative form. Its force of attraction lies in the wealth of questions, doubts and reflections that underlie the collection of data and with which it is offered to others – colleagues and children. These 'writings', where different languages are interwoven (graphic, visual, iconic), need to have their own code, their own convention within the group that constructs and uses them – this in order to guarantee, even though partially, the effectiveness of communication. That is, these writings must be legible, effectively communicative for those who were not present in the context, but should also include the 'emergent elements' perceived by the documenter. They are three-dimensional writings, not aimed at giving the event objectivity but at expressing the meaning-making effort; that is, to give meaning, to render the significance that each author attributes to the documentation and the questions and problems she or he perceives within a certain event. These writings are not detached from the personal biographical characteristics of the author, and we are thus aware of their bias, but this is considered an element of quality.

The documenter looks at the events that have taken place with a personal view aimed at a deep understanding of them and, at the same time, seeks communicative clarity. This is possible (although it could seem paradoxical) by bringing into the documentation the sense of incompleteness and expectation that can arise when you try to offer others not what you know, but the boundaries of your knowledge; that is, your limits, which derive from the fact that the 'object' being narrated is a process and a path of research.

Assessment: a perspective that gives value

What we offer to the children's processes and procedures, and to those which the children and adults together put into action, is a perspective that gives value. Valuing means giving value to this context and implies that certain elements are assumed as values.

Here, I think, is the genesis of assessment, because it allows one to make explicit, visible and shareable the elements of value (indicators) applied by the documenter in producing the documentation. Assessment is an intrinsic part of documentation and therefore of the entire approach of what we call *progettazione*[2]. In fact, this approach becomes something more than a prescribed and predefined procedure; it is a procedure that is nurtured by the elements of value that emerge from the process itself.

This makes the documentation particularly valuable to the children themselves, as they can encounter what they have done in the form of a narration, seeing the meaning that the teacher has drawn from their work. In the eyes of the children, this can demonstrate that what they do has value, has meaning. So they discover that they 'exist' and can emerge from anonymity and invisibility, seeing that what they say and do is important, is listened to, and is appreciated: it has a value.

It is like having an interface with yourself and with whoever enters into this sort of hypertext. Here the text acts as vector, support and pretext of the children's personal mental space.

The teacher's competency

In this context, it is obvious that the role and competency of the teacher are qualified in a different way from how these elements are defined in an educational environment in which the teacher's job is simply to transmit disciplinary knowledge in the traditional way.

The task is not to find (and teach) a specific series of rules, or to present certain propositions organised into formulas that can be easily learned by others, or to teach a method that can be replicated without modifications.

The teacher's competency is defined in terms more of understandings than of pure knowledge. It indicates a familiarity with critical facts, so as to allow those who possess this familiarity to say what is important and to hypothesise what is suitable for each situation – that is, what is helpful for the learner in a particular situation.

So what is the secret? There is no secret, no key, if not that of constantly

---

examining our understandings, knowledge and intuitions, and sharing and comparing them with those of our colleagues. It is not a transferable 'science', but rather an understanding, a sensitivity to knowledge. The action and the results of the action, in a situation where only the surface is visible, will be successful in part thanks to the success of the actors – children and teachers – all of whom are responsible, though at different levels, for the learning processes.

Proceeding by trial and error does not debase the didactic paths; indeed, it enriches them on the process level (that is, the process and our awareness of it), as well as on the ethical level.

There is also an element of improvisation, a sort of 'playing by ear', an ability to take stock of a situation, to know when to move and when to stay still, that no formula, no general recipe, can replace.

Certainly there are also risks, quite a few in fact: vagueness and superficiality can lead to mistaking a series of images or written notes for documentation, which, without the awareness of what one is observing, only creates disorientation and a loss of meaning.

The issue that emerges clearly at this point is the education of the teachers. The teacher's general education must be broad-based and range over many areas of knowledge, not just psychology and pedagogy. A cultured teacher not only has a multidisciplinary background, but possesses the culture of research, of curiosity, of working in a group: the culture of project-based thinking. Above all, we need teachers who feel that they truly belong to and participate in this process, as teachers but most of all as people.

Loris Malaguzzi[3], architect of the pedagogical and philosophical thinking that permeates the Reggio experience, once said that we need a teacher who is sometimes the director, sometimes the set designer, sometimes the curtain and the backdrop, and sometimes the prompter. A teacher who is both sweet and stern, who is the electrician, who dispenses the paints, and who is even the audience – the audience who watches, sometimes claps, sometimes remains silent, full of emotion, who sometimes judges with scepticism, and at other times applauds with enthusiasm.

Notes

[1] This chapter originally appeared in Giudici, C. and Krechevsky, M. (eds) (2001) *Making learning visible: Children as individual and group learners*, Cambridge, MA: Project Zero and Reggio Emilia: Reggio Children. The first two pages have been edited slightly.

[2] In Italian, the verb *progettare* has a number of meanings: to design, to plan, to devise, to project (in a technical-engineering sense). The use of the noun form *progettazione* by Reggio educators, however, has its own special meaning. It is used in Reggio in opposition to *programmazione*, which implies predefined curricula, programmes, stages, and so on. The concept of *progettazione* thus implies a more global and flexible approach in which initial hypotheses are made about classroom work (as well as about staff

development and relationships with parents), but are subject to modifications and changes of direction as the actual work progresses.

[3] Loris Malaguzzi, who died in 1994, was the first pedagogical director of the Reggio municipal schools and one of the greatest pedagogical thinkers and practitioners of the 20th century.

Further reading

Dahlberg, G. and Moss, P. (2005) *Ethics and politics in early childhood education*, London: Routledge.

Edwards, C., Gandini, L. and Forman, G. (eds) (1998) *The hundred languages of children: The Reggio Emilia approach, advanced reflections* (2nd edn), Norwood, NJ: Ablex.

Rinaldi, C. (2005) *In dialogue with Reggio Emilia*, London: Routledge.

THREE

Ways of seeing: using the Mosaic approach to listen to young children's perspectives

Alison Clark

The Mosaic approach, developed and used in England since 1999, is a strength-based framework for viewing young children as competent, active, meaning makers and explorers of their environment. Starting from this viewpoint, the Mosaic approach brings together a range of methods for listening to young children's perspectives about their lives. Observation sits alongside participatory tools. It adopts an interpretivist approach that acknowledges the need to seek to understand how children 'see' the world in order to understand their actions. Children's perspectives become the focus for an exchange of meanings between children, practitioners, parents and researchers.

This chapter, written by the originator of the Mosaic approach, examines the approach as a framework for listening to young children and explores the links between this approach and the pedagogy of listening discussed by Rinaldi in the previous chapter.

The Mosaic approach was developed during a research study to include the 'voice of the child' in an evaluation of a multiagency network of services for children and families. The process is explained in detail elsewhere (Clark and Moss, 2001; Clark, 2003). A second study, *Spaces to play*, adapted the Mosaic approach to listen to young children about their outdoor environment (Clark and Moss, 2005). This chapter will refer to case studies from this second study in order to illustrate the complex, multifaceted and sometimes surprising process of listening to young children.

The Mosaic approach was developed in the context of research. But subsequent discussions with practitioners through conferences and workshops have led to its use by early years practitioners. This illustrates how the distinctions between research and teaching can blur. The distinction is also questioned in Reggio Emilia[1]. Discussing the roles of the municipal schools of Reggio Emilia and a team of American researchers, one of the researchers comments that "the actions of instruction, assessment, documentation and research come to contain each other. They cannot be pulled apart in any practical sense; they are a piece. No dichotomy between teaching and research remains" (Seidel, 2001, p 333). While within the Reggio schools, they emphasise the teacher as researcher, engaged in a constant process of constructing knowledge about children and learning: "That is why [Rinaldi says] I have written so often about the teacher as a researcher.... [I]t's not that we don't recognise your [academic] research, but we want our research, as teachers, to be recognised. And to recognise research as a way of thinking, of approaching life, of negotiating, of documenting" (Rinaldi, 2005, p 192).

Starting points

Concepts of competence are a key feature of the theoretical perspectives that have influenced the development of the Mosaic approach (Clark, 2003). One source has been the active view of the child promoted through the sociology of (or for) childhood (Mayall, 2002). Children are seen not as passive objects in the research process or in society in general but as social actors who are "beings not becomings" (Qvortrup et al, 1994, p 2). This places an emphasis on exploring children's perceptions of their lives, their interests, priorities and concerns (for example, Christensen and James, 2000).

A second influence has been theoretical perspectives about 'voice' as explored in the field of international development, and through Participatory Appraisal techniques in particular (for example, Hart, 1997; Johnson et al, 1998). These methodologies have been devised in order to make visible the voices of the least powerful adult members of communities, as a catalyst for change. This begins with an expectation of competency: local people are presumed to have a unique body of knowledge about living in their community. The techniques developed include visual and verbal tools. Despite some criticism about the genuine benefits to communities of these approaches (Cooke and Kothari, 2001), the ideas remain of interest to debates about listening.

Third, and most importantly, the theoretical perspectives explored in the municipal preschools[2] of Reggio Emilia have inspired the Mosaic approach. These have hinged around the notion of the competent child and of the pedagogy of listening and the pedagogy of relationships. Malaguzzi, the first pedagogical director of the preschools, focused his work around the view of a rich active child (Edwards et al, 1998) in contrast to viewing children as passive and in need. This change in expectation seems key to understanding the critical thinking and creativity the children attending the schools have consistently demonstrated (for example, through 'The Hundred Languages of Children' touring exhibition).

These perspectives informed the framework for listening that led to the development of the Mosaic approach. The elements of this approach are:

- *multi-method:* recognises the different 'voices' or languages of children;
- *participatory:* treats children as experts and agents in their own lives;
- *reflexive:* includes children, practitioners and parents in reflecting on meanings, and addresses the question of interpretation;
- *adaptable:* can be applied in a variety of early childhood institutions;

- *focused on children's lived experiences:* can be used for a variety of purposes including looking at lives lived rather than knowledge gained or care received;
- *embedded into practice:* a framework for listening that has the potential to be both used as an evaluative tool and to become embedded into early years practice.

Developing the Mosaic approach

The development of the Mosaic approach has taken place through two studies and an international review. The aim of the original study was to develop methodologies for including the voices of young children in the evaluation of early childhood services. The name, the Mosaic approach, was chosen to represent the bringing together of different pieces or perspectives in order to create an image of children's worlds, both individual and collective. The Mosaic approach combines the traditional methodology of observation and interviewing with the introduction of participatory tools. Children use cameras to document 'what is important here'; they take the researcher on a tour and are in charge of how this is recorded, and make maps using their photographs and drawings. Each tool forms one piece of the mosaic. There were two stages in the original study. Stage One focused on gathering material using these varied methods. In Stage Two, these pieces of documentation were brought together with parents' and practitioners' comments to form the basis of dialogue, reflection and interpretation, a process involving children and adults.

An international review of listening to and consulting with young children (Clark et al, 2003), provided a wider perspective on current practice, policy and research developments. The review focused on young children's views and experiences of education and childcare. Young children's participation in the planning, designing and developing of indoor and outdoor spaces was one area identified for future research. The review ends with this remark: "Young children will best be served by changes to policy and practice which remain alert to their differing perspectives and interests as well as their needs" (Clark et al, 2003, p 48).

The review led to the outdoor environment being chosen as the focus for the second study, *Spaces to play* (see Clark and Moss, 2005 for a full account of this research). This set out to make young children's perspectives the starting point for change to the physical environment. The study was a collaboration with Learning through Landscapes, a charity based in England that works to promote the use, development and maintenance of school playgrounds. This was part of a wider initiative by Learning through Landscapes to work with a local authority and 15 early years settings to develop accessible, replicable, 'low tech' and affordable solutions to developing their outdoor environment.

The study was based in a preschool for three- to four-year-olds. Twenty-eight children were involved, together with parents and practitioners. The preschool included a number of children with special physical or behavioural needs,

Photograph 3.1: Showing part of the outdoor play space

including several with speech and language difficulties. It served a mixed locality including an area of social disadvantage.

The manager, practitioners and a group of parents wanted to take more advantage of the small outdoor space available to the preschool. This included a soft play surface, a small area of decking, a muddy bank and 'boggy' ground where there was an underground spring. The space was surrounded by a high-security fence, which separated the preschool from a park.

Table 3.1 shows the range of methods used when working with the Mosaic approach in this study. Starting with observation, the researcher worked with groups of children to find out their views and experiences of this existing play space in order to form the basis for any changes to the provision. Children took photographs of the space and made these into individual books. Others took the researcher on a tour of the site, recording the event with a camera and by making an audiotape. Working in pairs or small groups, the children made maps of the outdoors using their photographs and drawings.

The researcher interviewed children individually or in groups outside or on the move. Four practitioners and four parents were also interviewed for their perspectives on how the children used the outdoor space.

A new tool was added to the Mosaic approach for this study: the magic carpet. This was designed to open up new conversations with the children about their wider environment. What local spaces were the children aware of, what were their experiences of these places and what additional insights could these give to

Table 3.1: Methodological 'pieces' of the Mosaic approach

Method	Comments
Observation	Qualitative observation accounts
Child interviewing	A short structured interview conducted one to one or in a group
Photography and book making	Children's photographs of 'important things' and books
Tours	Tours of the site directed and recorded by the children
Map making	2D representations of the site using children's own photographs and drawings
Interviews	Informal interviews with practitioners and parents
Magic carpet	Slide show of familiar and different places

the current and future uses of their outdoor space? A slide show was made using images of the local town centre, local landmarks and the park (all taken from a child's height). The researcher added images of her local park as well as images taken during the study of the preschool's outdoor space. The home corner was converted into a darkened tent and children sat on a 'magic carpet' to watch the slides in groups. Christine Parker (2001) had tried this idea after her trip to Reggio Emilia as a way of talking to young children about different places.

There were two stages in the original study: first gathering material, then reflection and interpretation. The practical focus of the *Spaces to play* study led to the articulation of a third stage to the Mosaic approach, in order to emphasise the decision-making element of the listening:

- Stage One: gathering children's and adults' perspectives;
- Stage Two: discussing (reviewing) the material;
- Stage Three: deciding on areas of continuity and change.

Although this describes the gathering and reviewing as two distinct phases, in reality these stages become to some extinct blurred. For example, practitioners began to review the children's use of the outdoor space when the researcher placed photographs from the observation in the cloakroom area during the first weeks of the study. Reflecting on meanings and reassessing understandings is implicit throughout the whole approach, but this second stage allows a concentrated period of reflection.

Reviews were held with children, practitioners and with Learning through Landscapes. The aim was to make the review as focused as possible on the children's perspectives. The researcher made a book of the children's comments and photographs to centre the review on the children. This was designed in story form with Barney the dog as the main character together with a cartoon caterpillar. Barney, a toy dog, had been introduced by the researcher and was used as an intermediary in many of the conversations with the children. Children discussed the book with the researcher and this piece of documentation became the focus of two sessions to review the material with practitioners during staff meetings.

The researcher and Learning through Landscapes' Development Officer reviewed the visual and verbal material. Each of the tools was discussed in turn in order to reveal emerging themes. Discussions centred around two main questions:

• Which places do children see as important in this outdoor space?
• How do the children use these places?

The results of these discussions were mapped out on a large plan. Similar ideas were linked and conflicting meanings noted. This led to Stage Three: deciding areas of continuity and change.

Four categories of place in the outdoor space were identified through the review process.

Places to keep: the caterpillar

A large plastic caterpillar tunnel was regularly placed outside. It had been apparent from the first visit that the children enjoyed this strange shape. However, the use of the different research tools had emphasised just how important this piece of equipment was for the children. This was a play space not to try to change.

Places to expand: the house

Observing the children revealed the house to be a key resource for them. The children confirmed this through their photographs, the tour and their interviews. Parents also mentioned the house as an important space in the preschool. However, the interviews with practitioners showed that the house was a source of tension. They felt it was too small. The review with children, practitioners and Learning through Landscapes recognised these opposing views and raised some possible solutions. The preschool has now turfed a new area for children to use to build their own temporary structures.

Places to change: the fence

The children's photographs and maps emphasised how the security fence dominated the outdoor space. Close observation revealed another dimension. The gaps in the security fence were wide enough for the children to see through. Solutions needed to bear in mind the importance of leaving these gaps, so the people spotting and dog watching could continue. The parents have designed and made paint and chalking boards in the shapes of caterpillars and butterflies to attach to the fence. This distracts from the steel but still gives room for children to spy through.

Places to add: new seating and digging areas

The research process identified places that could be added to the outdoor space to enhance the children's enjoyment. The first was more places for adults and children to sit together. Parents have added seating so children and adults can now sit together by a fountain or on a brightly painted bench.

The second was places to dig. Observation had shown the popularity of the inside sandpit: one child included a photograph of the inside sand tray in his book of important outdoor spaces! The preschool has now added an outdoor sandpit.

The pedagogy of listening and the Mosaic approach

In Chapter Two of this book, Rinaldi describes the multifaceted nature of the pedagogy of listening, which has been one of the cornerstones of practice in Reggio Emilia. The elements include:

- internal listening or self-reflection;
- multiple listening or openness to other 'voices';
- visible listening, which includes documentation and interpretation.

Each of these features relate to the listening processes, which have emerged from working with the Mosaic approach. The following section will examine these elements in turn with the help of case studies taken from the *Spaces to play* study.

Internal listening

Internal listening acknowledges the importance of listening as a strategy for children to make sense of their world. Listening is, therefore, not just an avenue for other people receiving information but a reflective process for children to consider meanings, make discoveries and new connections and express understandings. In the previous chapter, Rinaldi describes one of the first questions the educators in Reggio ask themselves: 'How can we help children find the meaning of what they do, what they encounter, what they experience?'.

The question at the centre of the Mosaic approach has been: 'What does it mean to be in this place?'. The question can be interpreted in many ways but at one level it is asking children: 'What does it mean *to be you* in this place now in this present moment, in the past and in the future?'. There is a physical dimension to this question. It has directed children to reflect on the specific environment of their early childhood institution, whether inside or outside. However, the place could be a city, a park or a bedroom. This links to the early learning goal 'a sense of place' in the Foundation Stage[3] curriculum guidance for England, which encourages children to explore their local environment. The important ingredient here is that children are given the opportunity to reflect on their lived experiences rather than an abstract concept. This is in keeping with constructivist models of learning in which the environment is a key factor in children's search for meanings (MacNaughton, 2003).

It is a question with no 'wrong' answer. Children can explore their understandings without the fear that they have to second-guess the intended response. This helps to make the internal listening a creative process in which there is the freedom to express an idea for the first time or in a new way. This dimension of listening is in contrast to the understanding of listening as 'extracting the truth', a viewpoint encountered during the development phase of the Mosaic approach when discussions with some children's rights officers implied that children should be enabled to say what they thought, without the interference of adult interpretation. The Mosaic approach is more in keeping with the view that "it's not so much a matter of eliciting children's preformed ideas and opinions, it's much more a question of enabling them to explore the ways in which they perceive the world and communicate their ideas in a way that is meaningful to them" (Tolfree and Woodhead, 1999, p 21).

Developing a multimethod framework has helped the Mosaic approach to promote internal listening. This was one of the reasons for including more than one research tool. The greater the diversity of methods with different learning styles used then the more opportunity children will have to find new ways of thinking, of looking at the same question in a variety of ways. Taking photographs, leading a tour or watching slides provide different mirrors for reflecting on the central question: 'What does it mean to be in this place?'.

Some young children would be barred from answering this question if they were only offered one traditional research tool, such as interviewing. This might include children with limited verbal skills. The multimethod approach is necessary if as many children as possible are to be allowed opportunities for internal listening.

So using different methods is designed to be beneficial to the children who participate. It has another advantage for adults by enabling different understandings to be compared and for common themes and areas of disagreement to emerge. This theme of multiple listening will be examined later.

The following case study will illustrate different dimensions of internal listening through the use of the Mosaic approach in the *Spaces to play* study.

Case study: Internal listening and inclusive practice

Rees was four years old, and about to start school. He was an affectionate child who appeared to be thoroughly enjoying preschool.

However, his verbal language skills seemed limited, in the context of the preschool. He was, however, fascinated with cameras. He took great interest in the researcher's camera and was keen to volunteer to take his own photographs. He was delighted with the results and concentrated for an extended period on making a book of his images (see Table 3.2). Rees insisted on 'writing' his own

Table 3.2: Description of the photograph book compiled by Rees

Rees's photographs	Captions	Researcher's description
Cover	The house	Close-up of girl by the side of the climbing frame (house to the side)
Page One	The pram	Close-up of pram with pebbles
Page Two		Small barrier with cartoon figures
Page Three	[name of staff member]	Two members of staff on the edge of the play surface
Page Four		Close-up of girl, fence in background
Page Five		Close-up of inside of the house, boy in the corner

captions. The practitioners were surprised when they saw his book as he had shown little interest in experimenting with writing in the preschool.

Rees's photographs were taken in a great hurry. They covered a range of subjects including other children and members of staff, but there was only one shot of just one other child. Rees did not appear to have a particular friend at the preschool.

He chose a photograph of the playhouse for the cover. The house was not the obvious focus of the photograph but Rees's naming of the photograph clarified its subject. This prioritising of the house tallied with the responses of many of the children who indicated the significance of this play space.

His choice of the pram was interesting. He filled the pram with pebbles from the edge of the play space before taking his photograph. This indicated his awareness of detail and interest in natural objects. Observation had revealed that Rees was one of the boys who enjoyed playing with the pram and pushchairs.

Rees was invited to take part in the child interview. This was designed to be as flexible as possible with some children choosing to answer the questions on the

Figure 3.1: Diagram to show Rees's participation in the study

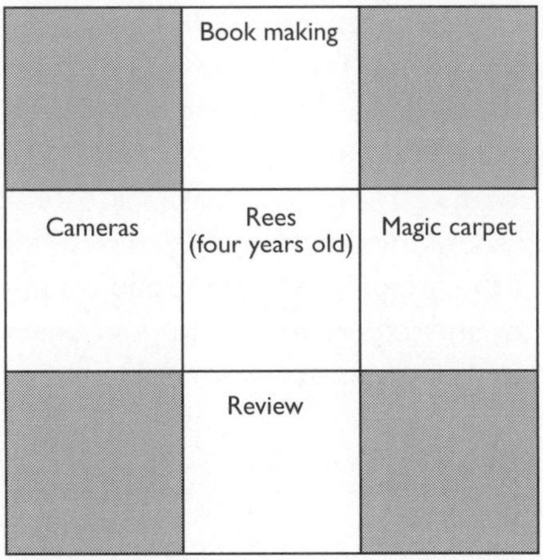

move. However, when the researcher started the interview Rees copied the questions but made no other response.

Rees enjoyed taking part in the magic carpet slide show. He was captivated by the mechanics of the slide projector and expressed his delight at learning how to operate the buttons to produce a new image: "I've got that one", he explained. When a slide appeared showing Barney he picked up the toy dog and matched him to the image on the screen.

Rees chose to hold Barney as he took part in the review of the study and listened attentively as the researcher read the book of the children's words.

Rees had been able to convey important features of his experience at the preschool. These included the pleasure of being with other children but with no particular friend, his liking for the playhouse and the pram and an interest in mechanical objects. Rees had conveyed these 'ways of seeing' through the Mosaic approach, using a range of languages and learning styles (see Figure 3.1). This in turn led to Rees displaying an interest in communicating through developing graphic skills as well as entering into more conversations with the researcher.

However, had the study relied solely on the interview he would have been another invisible child and Rees would not have had the opportunity to engage with the question 'what does it mean to be in this place?' and perhaps more importantly 'what does it mean *to be me* here?'. One concern is that Rees will not be offered the same range of languages and learning styles in order for him to make sense of the transition to school.

This section has focused on the links between the Mosaic approach and internal listening. The emphasis will now move to examine the role of multiple listening in the Mosaic approach.

Multiple listening

In Chapter Two, Rinaldi describes multiple listening as the opportunities for practitioners, groups of children and individual children to listen to each other and to themselves. This conveys the multifaceted nature of listening: it is not limited to one exchange between two individuals but is a complex web of interactions, continually moving from the micro to the macro level. This is in keeping with an interpretivist model of learning (Carr, 2000; MacNaughton, 2003), which acknowledges the importance of multiple perspectives.

Multiple listening recognises the need to make space for the 'other', emphasising listening as an ethical issue. Researchers and practitioners who promote multiple listening acknowledge the importance of time and resources to enable children to reflect on their ideas and experiences with their peers and with adults. The Mosaic approach creates opportunities for multiple listening:

- with practitioners and parents;
- with the researcher and other professionals;
- through individual, paired, small and large group interaction.

The Mosaic approach acknowledges the importance of a framework for listening, which does not exclude the perspectives of practitioners and parents; a culture of listening should extend to all involved with an early childhood institution (Clark et al, 2003). There are opportunities in the Mosaic approach for listening to practitioners and parents through interviews and through the second-stage review process. Listening to practitioners' perspectives in the *Spaces to play* study focused on their general perceptions of children's interests and priorities outdoors, rather than focusing on individual children. It was important to interview the manager as well as a range of new and more experienced practitioners. This acknowledged that there was not a hierarchy of listening that privileged senior practitioners at the expense of the views of younger members of the team. The review process provided other opportunities for multiple listening with practitioners. The staff meetings led by the researcher to review the children's material provided a formal opportunity for reflecting on different perspectives (see the case study below).

Many parents have an in-depth understanding about the details of their children's lives that represent their current concerns, passions and interests (see, for example, Chapter Six, this book). Interviewing parents, in the Mosaic approach, is a formal way of acknowledging the different 'ways of seeing' parents can offer. One of the disadvantages of working within the confines of a research study is the limited time available for such listening. While the numbers of opportunities to listen to parents' perspectives have been small, the insights have added an important element to the overall picture of 'what does it mean to be in this place?'. Several parents, for example, mentioned that their children enjoyed having opportunities at home to dig and this reinforced the practitioners' desire to expand the outside digging spaces at the preschool.

What is the researcher's role in the Mosaic approach in relation to multiple listening? The researcher is at times 'architect': a creator of spaces and opportunities where multiple listening can take place and at other times more of an intermediary relaying different perspectives between different groups and individuals. An example of the 'architect's' role is the book-making activity. The children in the *Spaces to play* study worked on their books of their own photographs. This opened up discussions with other children who gathered round the table, watched with interest and discussed the images. Practitioners were interested in what was happening and talked to the children about the images they had taken.

The intermediary role relates to the researcher facilitating listening between the children and other professionals with an interest in children's perspectives. This is a way of extending the process of listening beyond the bounds of adults who are in daily contact with young children. This may involve professionals working in a range of disciplines, for example social workers (see Clark and Statham, 2005). However, in the *Spaces to play* study these conversations have been with professionals concerned with redesigning play spaces. The researcher led the review with the Development Officer from Learning through Landscapes, which focused on the documentation of the children's perspectives. Reflection on the role of documentation or visible listening will be discussed later.

The following case study will illustrate the opportunities for multiple listening for adults and children by focusing on the playhouse in the *Spaces to play* study.

Case study: Multiple listening – the playhouse

The playhouse was a small wooden shed given to the preschool by a local business. It had a door, which opened out onto decking, and two windows, which had clear views of the play surface, the decking and muddy ground. There was a plastic barbeque set, table and chair in the house. Four children or more could squeeze inside. Observation showed that the house was in use most of the time. It was regularly used for group role play and at different times of day for a 'time out' space.

Interviewing children about the playhouse revealed more details about the imaginative play that took place in this space, but also the noise level. The following are excerpts from child interviews:

Researcher: "Tell Barney about the house."

Henry: "This is where we play and talk and cook."

Bob: "… and sit on the chair. Henry and I can whistle."

Milly, Alice and Bill: "He can play doctors.…There is a seat to sit on, and a table to sit on but you're not all allowed to sit on the tables."

Julie: "Play. We play doctors, we play vets. See this you put the chair there and you lay down on it [then Jessica stops to play vets with the 'dogs']."

Jim: "When it's night-time it gets dark. Bats are hanging on the windowsills. I love staying there, all there."

Robert: "I don't like playing doggies in here – it's too noisy too many in here some of the teachers gets one of them out."

Children's photographs emphasised the importance of the house by the number of images, which showed close-ups of the inside of the house or games happening outside. Children took the researcher to the house on their tours and chose photographs and drawings of the house for the maps.

Listening to practitioners' views highlighted some differences of opinion between the children and the adults. The practitioners were aware of how popular the house was but they each had reservations about its current use:

Heather: "Children use the house; they tend to use it as a buffer. Some think it's a wonderful activity in there ... then it can become a fight, [they] lob things out of the window or shout. But I don't think it's used successfully, even if three [children are there]. They like taking toys in but ... the main problem is it's too small."

Louise [the manager]: "The house originally faced the shed. It was absolutely hopeless. They belted from one side to the other so we moved it round so it is part of the quiet area. It's all right for two children but it isn't big enough to put things in. We are trying to make use of it.... I wish it was twice as large."

While practitioners were aware of the popularity of the house, they were concerned that it had become overcrowded, encouraged aggressive play and as a result needed constant supervision.

Parents indicated the importance of role play in the house and how one child had his own playhouse at home, which acted as a retreat: "He loves his little house. He puts pictures up in his house of trains" (Jim's mother).

As noted earlier, the multiple listening made the differences of opinion about the house visible (as summarised in Table 3.3). These different ways of seeing

Table 3.3: Multiple listening using the Mosaic approach to focus on the playhouse

Research tool	Playhouse
Observation	Children used the house as a social place. It is a space for being noisy, talking together and for imaginative play.
Cameras and book making	The house was in 12 of the 60 photographs taken by the children and chosen for inclusion in their books. These included inside and outside shots. This was a place in which to hide, talk to friends and watch what was happening outside.
Tours and map making	Children took inside and out photographs on their tours and included these photographs on their maps.
Practitioners' interviews	Practitioners recognised the children used the house for multiple purposes. Three out of the four practitioners interviewed named the house as the item they would like to give away.
Parents' interviews	One parent identified the house as some where she thought her child enjoyed doing outside at the preschool:"Role play is a key thing here". Another parent described how her child had a playhouse at home.
Child interviews	The children gave detailed descriptions of what happens in the house. Several identified the house as their favourite place while others recognised that it could get too noisy.

formed the basis for discussions, which led to the creation of a newly turfed outdoor space for the children to build temporary structures where they can 'sit, talk and cook'.

Visible listening

Moving on from examining the links between internal listening and multiple listening and the Mosaic approach, this next section will examine the role of documentation or visible listening. Rinaldi, in Chapter Two of this book, describes the process of documentation as visible listening through the construction of traces. She describes how these traces, through note taking, photographs, slides and other means, not only record the learning process but make the learning possible by bringing it into being – making it visible. There is a connection here with multiple listening because documentation allows listening to take place at different levels and with a range of individuals and groups. Others in this volume (for example, in Chapters Six and Seven) have described the pivotal role of documentation for listening in an early childhood institution. This section will focus on the role of documentation within the Mosaic approach, led by a researcher.

The Mosaic approach creates opportunities for visible listening by promoting platforms for communication at an individual, group, organisational and wider community level. Children's book making is one example of visible listening at an individual level. The process of map making is visible listening at a group level, which opens out into listening at an organisational level by displaying the maps for practitioners, parents, other children and visitors to engage with.

Further opportunities for promoting visible listening were added in the *Spaces to play* study during the review and evaluation phase. The review focused on a book made by the researcher, which was a collective record of the children's responses and photographs (in contrast to the children's own individual book making). This *Spaces to play* book provided a platform for communication at an organisational level with practitioners and children. These discussions led to the subsequent changes to the outdoor environment.

Documentation was a key part of the discussions with Learning through Landscapes. The chart assembled by the researcher provided the focus for discussions about the children's use of the play space, drawing on the researcher's notes, the children's photographs and maps and the interviews. This illustrates how the Mosaic approach provided a platform for communication with the wider community, in this instance with an external organisation interested in working with the preschool but not engaged with the children on a daily basis.

Traces of the study were drawn together for the evaluation. This collection of photographs acted as a platform for children to discuss together what they remembered and had enjoyed about participating in the study.

One question arises from this process: who is the documenter? The Mosaic approach enables both researcher and children to be co-documenters. The participatory methods have emphasised the children's role as documenters of their experiences of 'being in this place'. The researcher has in turn documented her observations and reflections on the process, which include both a visual and verbal contribution to the process. One possibility would be to extend the documenting role to the practitioners thus strengthening the platform for communication and encouraging future visible listening.

The following case study illustrates how one of the tools, map making, provided several opportunities for visible listening at a number of levels, from the individual to the community.

Case study: Visible listening – map making

Ruth and Jim (both three-year-olds) met with the researcher to make a map of the outdoor space. This was based on the photographs they had taken on a tour of the site and copies of photographs chosen for their books. The children added their own drawings to these images. The map became both an individual and a joint record.

Both children were keen to see themselves depicted on the map and Ruth added her name. Jim ensured that there were traces of his love of trains on the map, with close-ups of his mobilo train and of the shed "where the toys sleep". Ruth chose the photograph she had asked Jim to take of the close-up of the pebbles, and Jim and Ruth added drawings of the trees, which surround the play space, beyond the fence.

During the map-making session, Gina, a visitor from Learning through Landscapes, came to see the study in action. The map provided the basis for 'visible listening' and one in which the children played a central role.

Ruth: "This is a very pretty map."

Researcher: "It's a very pretty map. You know, it tells me such a lot about outside. Shall we see what Gina can see on our map? Gina, what do you think about our outside…."

Gina: "I can see that Ruth and Jim have very special things outside. I can see that you chose the prams and the buggies, and I can even see you in the picture so I know you like playing with those things, maybe. And, Jim, your favourite thing…. I think your favourite thing outside might be the train. Yes? And can we have a picture of you outside with the train?"

Ruth: "What do I like?"

Gina: "You tell me what you like. Do you like Heather [member of staff] with the climbing frame?"

Child: "No, I like going on."

Gina: "Oh, you like going on the climbing frame."

This extract illustrates how the map making enabled Ruth to take control of the meaning making. Ruth asked the visitor to interpret her priorities and then enjoyed contradicting this interpretation.

Photograph 3.2: Heather and Jim discussing Jim's map

Practitioners, parents and other children became part of this meaning making and exchange through the display of the maps in the cloakroom area. Display space was at a premium in the crowded building but the cloakroom provided one space where parents and children visited daily. Visitors to the preschool were another group to interpret meanings.

This section has illustrated different aspects of listening facilitated through using the Mosaic approach. However, there is a considerable time commitment involved in such a way of working. While efforts were made to include every child in the sample in more than one of the tools, this was not always possible. A detailed impression was gained of some of the children's understandings of being 'in this place', but for others their part-time attendance or the limits imposed by the preschool's or the researcher's timetable meant that a more cursory impression was gained.

Discussion

This final section will raise three questions emerging from the development of the Mosaic approach in relation to listening to young children. These questions have arisen after many discussions with practitioners, researchers and policy makers arising from training days and conference talks:

• the question of power
• the question of 'the hundred languages'
• the question of visibility.

A question of power

Communicating with young children involves questions of power: whether this is adults imparting 'knowledge' to children or children communicating their ideas to adults. Whichever way round the exchanges happen, there are differences in status, which are difficult to address. These differences are, perhaps, most noticeable when adults are working with young children. Many factors contribute to this imbalance, but expectations are one element. Adults' expectations of young children influence how they communicate with children and how they enable children to communicate with them. Viewing young children as weak, powerless and vulnerable may lead to high expectations of the adults' role in terms of protection and nurture but low expectations of children in terms of how they can express their perspectives, priorities and interests.

Viewing young children as competent communicators requires researchers and practitioners to readdress their relationship with young children and therefore their roles. The Mosaic approach includes an element of *role reversal* for the adults involved. Children participate as documenters, photographers, initiators and commentators. Children play an active role, taking the lead in which ideas, people, places and objects are given significance.

An early years trainer who had been using the Mosaic approach in a research study discussed the following example of these shifting relationships. The trainer was talking to a practitioner about a child. The practitioner commented: "She listens if she thinks she is getting what she wants. She would like to reverse roles". The trainer remarked that this was exactly what the Mosaic approach allowed this child to do. The roles were reversed and she was able to lead the process. She particularly enjoyed giving her commentary to the visiting adult on the tour.

This example perhaps highlights the contrast between the role that children are enabled to play in using the Mosaic approach and the day-to-day position that many young children experience where adults expect to take the lead, whether in delivering a curriculum or creating an appropriate environment. One of the challenges in allowing a shift in relationships is accepting the place of the unexpected. In research terms this may mean being relaxed about the focus of the study and not worrying if children lead the study into unplanned areas. This occurred in the *Spaces to play* study where children sensibly blurred the distinction between indoor and outdoor play. One child, for example, took photographs of the toilets and the indoor sandpit and included them in his book about the outdoor space. The advantages of accepting a shifting in power are a release from the need for adults to 'know all the answers'. Listening in the ways discussed in this chapter releases adults from this burden.

A question of 'the hundred languages'

Language has an important part to play in debates about power. If exchanges between adults and young children are focused on the written and spoken word, then it is difficult for young children to have the 'upper hand'. The case studies have illustrated how children of different abilities can be supported in sharing their perspectives if they are given a range of multisensory means to communicate. These visual, spatial and physical tools should not been seen as a 'creative extra' but offer a challenge to the dominant learning styles that value verbal/linguistic skills at the expense of other means of communication. It is interesting to note that the verbal/linguistic skills are often the languages adults feel most secure in using. The Mosaic approach requires adults to relearn other languages they may be unfamiliar with using in an educational context or to acquire new skills.

Digital technology offers many possibilities for developing new shared languages between adults and children. Future studies using the Mosaic approach will incorporate young children's use of digital cameras. There was an initial reluctance on the part of the researcher to include digital cameras partly due to the cost, but also due to a lack of personal competency with the technology. It is a good example of how adults may need to take the leap to be co-learners with children in order to listen more effectively.

A question of visibility

Documentation is a powerful advocate for the competencies of young children. This was illustrated in 'The Hundred Languages of Children' exhibition, which was on tour in England in 2004. One of the opening panels showed photographs of two sculptures made from ready-made objects. One was by a two-year-old and one was by Picasso. This was not a glib gesture but a serious contribution to debates about the artistic process. The sculpture could have remained a personal delight for the child but not reached a wider audience. The documentation enabled this individual child's achievement to help a wider audience possibly rethink their views and expectations of young children.

The *Spaces to play* study has raised the possibility of using the Mosaic approach to create a platform for communication between young children, early years practitioners, architects and designers. The focus in this study has been on outdoor spaces but this same approach could facilitate exchanges between adults and children concerning the built environment. A three-year study beginning in July 2004, called Living Space[4], uses the Mosaic approach in the planning, designing and changing of indoor and outdoor provision. Starting with a case study of a project to build a new early childhood centre, the researcher will work with three- and four-year-olds to document their experiences of their existing space in order to inform future spaces. The young children's photographs and maps will form a visible hub for conversations involving the whole school community about 'what we want it to mean to be in this place'. This platform for communication will then extend to architects who will feed these insights into the final building.

This is one example where visible listening could have wide applications not only within a learning environment but also in altering the expectations and the role that young children can play in the wider community.

Conclusion

This chapter has examined a particular framework for listening to young children, which plays to children's strengths rather than to adults. Listening using the Mosaic approach has been shown to encourage listening at different levels and in different contexts, whether this is children 'listening' to their own reflections, enabling multiple listening to take place between children, their peers and adults or creating possibilities for visible listening. This is an important endeavour to continue because "unless adults are alert to children's own ways of seeing and understanding and representing the world to themselves, it is unlikely that the child will ever manage to identify with the school's and teacher's ways of seeing" (Brooker, 2002, p 171).

Notes

[1] Since 1981, the Reggio exhibition – 'The Hundred Languages of Children' – has travelled the world, accompanied by speakers from Reggio: in this time, it has had well over a hundred showings in more than 20 countries.

[2] 'Preschools' (previously called 'playgroups') are a widespread form of early childhood service in the UK, mostly attended by three- and four-year-olds on a part-time basis (that is, most children attend three to five morning or afternoon sessions per week during term time). Community groups or other non-profit organisations mostly run them, and many today are funded by government, to deliver early education, following the Foundation Stage curriculum (see end note 3 below).

[3] Foundation Stage curriculum guidance in England applies to children from three to six years old (that is, in the first year of compulsory schooling and the two preceding years). The Foundation Stage relates, in turn, to over 60 early learning goals specified by the government.

[4] Funded by the Bernard van Leer Foundation.

Further reading

Carr, M. (2000) 'Seeking children's perspectives about their learning', in A. Smith, N.J. Taylor and M. Gollop (eds) *Children's voices: Research, policy and practice*, Auckland, New Zealand: Pearson Education, pp 37-55.
Langsted, O. (1994) 'Looking at quality from the child's perspective', in P. Moss and A. Pence (eds) *Valuing quality in early childhood services: New approaches to defining quality*, London: Paul Chapman Publishing, pp 28-42.
Tolfree, D. and Woodhead, M. (1999) 'Tapping a key resource', *Early Childhood Matters*, no 91, pp 19-23.

References

Brooker, L. (2002) *Starting school: Young children's learning cultures*, Buckingham: Open University Press, p 171.
Carr, M. (2000) 'Seeking children's perspectives about their learning', in A. Smith, N.J. Taylor and M. Gollop (eds) *Children's voices: Research, policy and practice*, Auckland, New Zealand: Pearson Education, pp 37-55.
Christensen, P. and James, A. (eds) (2000) *Research with children*, London: Falmer Press.
Clark, A. (2003) 'The Mosaic approach and research with young children', in V. Lewis. M. Kellett, C. Robinson, S. Fraser and S. Ding (eds) *The reality of research with children and young people*, London: Sage Publications, pp 157-61.

Clark, A. and Moss, P. (2001) *Listening to young children: The Mosaic approach*, London: National Children's Bureau for the Joseph Rowntree Foundation.

Clark, A. and Moss, P. (2005) *Spaces to play: More listening to young children using the Mosaic approach*, London: National Children's Bureau.

Clark, A. and Statham, J. (2005) 'Listening to young children: experts in their own lives', *Adoption and Fostering*, vol 29, no 1, pp 45-56.

Clark, A., McQuail, S. and Moss, P. (2003) *Exploring the field of listening to and consulting with young children*, Research Report 445, London: DfES.

Cooke, B. and Kothari, U. (eds) (2001) *Participation: The new tyranny?*, London: Zed Books.

Edwards, C., Gandini, L. and Foreman, G. (eds) (1998) *The hundred languages of children: The Reggio Emilia approach to early childhood education* (2nd edn), New Jersey, NJ: Ablex Publishing Corporation.

Hart, R. (1997) *Children's participation*, London: Earthscan/UNICEF.

James, A. and Prout, A. (1997) *Constructing and reconstructing childhood* (2nd edn), London: Falmer.

Johnson, V., Gordon, G., Pridmore, P. and Scott, P. (eds) (1998) *Stepping forward: Children and young people's participation in the development process*, London: Intermediate Technology.

MacNaughton, G. (2003) *Shaping early childhood: Learners, curriculum and contexts*, Maidenhead: Open University Press.

Mayall, B. (2002) *Towards a sociology for childhood: Thinking from children's lives*, Buckingham: Open University Press.

Parker, C. (2001) 'When is she coming back?', in L. Abbott and C. Nutbrown (eds) *Experiencing Reggio Emilia: Implications for pre-school provision*, Buckingham: Open University Press, pp 80-92.

Qvortrup, J., Bardy, M., Sgritta, G. and Wintersberger, H. (eds) (1994) *Childhood matters*, Vienna: European Centre.

Rinaldi, C. (2005) *In dialogue with Reggio Emilia*, London: Routledge.

Seidel, S. (2001) 'Perspectives on research in education', in C. Giudici, C. Rinaldi and M. Krechevsky (eds) *Making learning visible: Children as individual and group learners*, Reggio Emilia: Reggio Children, pp 330-5.

Tolfree, D. and Woodhead, M. (1999) 'Tapping a key resource', *Early Childhood Matters*, no 91, pp 19-23.

FOUR

Participant observation: a way to learn about children's perspectives

Hanne Warming

Children in Denmark today spend much of their early childhood in services, either family day care or centres. In 2003, 56 per cent of children under three years of age and 94 per cent of children from three to six years of age were in these services (Danmarks Statistik, 2004), most of the cost of which is publicly funded as part of the Danish welfare state. Indeed it has become culturally normative that children from nine months of age attend an early childhood service, with a universal entitlement to a place introduced in 2005 following legislation (Lov om Social Service, 2004). By the end of 2004, 149 out of 171 municipalities already fulfilled this commitment (Danmarks Statistik, 2005).

In Denmark, as in Norway, early childhood services distinguish themselves from schools, with different professional workers (pedagogues rather than teachers) and a more 'child-centred' approach emphasising free play. A framework curriculum has only been introduced into these services in 2005, after much debate.

This institutionalisation of early childhood in Denmark has been matched by an interest in listening to young children, in research, policy (see, for example, Chapter Nine) and practice. In this field, Denmark can be said to be a world leader. This chapter is about the potential of a particular method for listening to young children, participant observation, but also shows how the development of work in this field has led to critical reflection on the meaning, purpose and ethics of listening to young children.

Although the term 'participant observation' covers a variety of methodological practices (Adler and Adler, 1987; Atkinson and Hammersley, 1998), it refers to an ethnographically inspired methodological approach, the aim of which is to learn about 'the other'[1] by participating in their everyday life. I hope to inspire further studies in participant observation, as from my perspective this method has great potential for listening to children. But the chapter will not promote participant observation as *the* method, nor will it present a guide about how best to employ it. Rather the purpose of the chapter is to present a critical examination of methodological and ethical issues, based on experiences and reflections from a research project that adopted the participant observation approach for listening to young children.

At the beginning of the chapter, I distinguish between listening as a tool and listening as a democratic ethos of giving voice. I argue that listening as a democratic ethos involves particular methodological and ethical challenges. Next, on the basis of a relational constructionist perception of identity, I approach children's perspectives and their possibilities of expressing them as multiple, changing and contextualised, and thus reject the idea of an essential – 'authentic' – children's voice. However, the generational order as well as children's participation in the broader culture make it possible to identify some common features in children's perspectives at a more abstract level. Further, I emphasise that experience and knowledge are positioned and produced in (power) relations: there is no privileged position from which the researcher or practitioner can neutrally observe and listen. Thus, the focus of the chapter is on dilemmas and reflections about how the participant observer can listen and give voice to children taking into account both that there can be no authentic children's voice and the positioned or perspectival (rather than objective) character of experience and knowledge.

Stylistically, the chapter emphasises 'I', and by so doing deviates from the norm of most academic writing. This is a deliberate choice, intended to recognise the positioned character of experience and knowledge. By contrast, the more 'impersonal' form of academic writing risks making the positioned character of experience and knowledge invisible and inaccessible.

Listening as a tool or an ethos

One can listen to children in different ways and for different purposes. For instance, the method and purpose can be conversation analysis to learn about children's culture as in the case of Sacks (1991) or, in contrast Opie and Opie (1982, 1991), who used fieldwork to learn about children's specific culture. Or the purpose could be to enable more effective interventions in children's interactions as in the study by Sutton et al (2004) of social cognition and bullying. These are just three examples of studies working with different methods for different purposes, but common to them all is that listening to children is used as a tool – none intends to give voice.

By contrast, giving voice through listening is part of the basic ethos of the new childhood research paradigm (James et al, 1998; Christensen and James, 2000) as well as in some pedagogical practices (see, for instance, Chapters Two, Six and Seven in this volume). Listening as a democratic ethos of giving voice is today a powerful ideology in social and pedagogical work with children in Denmark (Warming, 2003; Kampmann and Nielsen, 2004). However, in practice, the picture is more blurred, as the workers involved – social workers and *pædagoger* (pedagogues)[2] – often do not make the distinction. This can be regarded as quite problematic, though elaborating on this is beyond the scope of this chapter (for a critical discussion of this issue, see Warming, 2003; Bo and Warming, 2004; Kampmann and Nielsen, 2004; Warming and Kampmann, 2005).

However, the point that I want to emphasise here is the distinction: that listening as a tool and listening as constituting a basic ethos of giving voice are not necessarily the same, and may even be in conflict with each other. Giving voice involves listening, whereas listening does not necessarily involve giving voice. Listening as a tool requires hearing and interpreting what you hear, whereas giving voice further requires 'loyal' facilitation and representation, making a common cause with the children.

In my study, the aim of listening was to give voice to the children regarding their perception of everyday life in an early childhood institution, and on the basis of that to identify *det gode børneliv* (the ideal child life) from a child's perspective as well as the mechanisms that either promote or discourage this ideal child life. Later in the chapter, I will return to a discussion of whether I actually fulfilled this demand of loyal facilitation and representation; however, asking about children's perceptions of *det gode børneliv* and the conditions that either promote or discourage it can be regarded as my first and decisive step towards making a common cause with the children.

Choosing participant observation as my method

How can one examine young children's perception of *det gode børneliv*, and how can one examine the conditions that either promote or discourage this ideal life? The answers to these questions are closely connected with the ontological and epistemological position of the researcher. However, in practice such methodological choices often seem to be guided more by preferences, skills and previous practice than by strictly scientific considerations (Atkinson and Coffey, 2000).

I was used to and very comfortable working with qualitative in-depth interviews with both adults and children. Nevertheless, or maybe rather because of these experiences, I did not pick qualitative in-depth interviews as my method. This decision was reinforced because of my relational understanding of children's identity, the ideal life and the conditions that either promote or discourage realising this ideal life; or put another way, because I do not accept an essentialist and individualistic understanding, for example that there is a 'real' child, untouched by context, that can be discovered and known through scientific method and knowledge. Drawing on thinkers such as Bourdieu (1990, 1992, 1998; Bourdieu, 1999), Foucault (1979, 1986, 1988, 1997) and Goffman (1971a, 1971b, 1986, 1990), I approached children's perceptions of the ideal life and the conditions that promote or discourage its realisation as shaped (or constructed) in concrete contextualised interactions, which are neither completely determined nor independent of social, cultural, historical and biographical influences. From this perspective, there is no essential or authentic children's perspective; rather children's perspectives must be approached as multiple and changing, as well as being contextualised socially, culturally, historically and biographically. This theoretical approach denies the authentic child voice but at the same time assumes the existence of some common contextually based features that shape children's perceptions.

Participant observation would allow me to study children's interactions with each other, with pedagogues and with the physical surroundings, whereas interviews would only allow me to study narratives about these interactions, producing a construction of children's cognitive perception of *det gode børneliv* contextualised by the interview process itself. Thus participant observation from this perspective seemed more appropriate, as what I wanted to study was not the construction of the ideal child life in an interview setting, but on the contrary in the everyday life in the early childhood centre.

Furthermore, interviewers primarily rely on the spoken word, whereas experience, knowledge and communication about *det gode børneliv* are also expressed in other ways, through the body for example. It is also my experience that the spoken word is not every child's preferred or most informative way of expressing themselves. Participant observation would allow me to get to know the children as they act and react both in verbal and body language in the specific context of the *børnehave*[3] (kindergarten), and it would allow me to learn about this specific context[4].

What to look for

All these considerations made me choose participant observation as my method; however, they did not inform me more precisely about how to approach my study of the *det gode børneliv*. How can one operationalise images of the ideal life, as they are expressed in words and body language, for a participant observation study? To do this, I drew on Danish everyday life theory. This theory suggests that everyone has an idea or sense of the ideal life as part of the 'meaning universes' that guide their everyday practices and experiences (Bech-Jørgensen, 1990, 1994)[5]. This should not be interpreted as people always acting rationally in terms of achieving the ideal life, but rather that striving for the ideal life, together with the conscious and unconscious evaluation of the degree to which we achieve the ideal life, is part of our everyday life – our hopes, our acts, our reactions to what happens to us, our way of experiencing, our feelings and so on. Furthermore, I drew on Bourdieu's concept of *habitus*, which emphasises that everyday practices are, to a great extent, also guided by a sense of what is possible, and that our endeavours are very much restricted by this sense of the possible.

Thus to understand children's perception of *det gode børneliv*, I looked at their actions and reactions: what they did and how they looked emotionally, and how this changed with the possibilities of the social spaces. For instance, I looked for what they were engaged in, what they fought for and against, what they tried to escape from and what they tried to gain. And I looked for what kind of emotions different situations and reactions evoked: what made the children laugh, get angry, get sad, what made them silent, engaged, comfortable, irritated, confused and so on.

——

Snapshot One is an example of how I observed actions and reactions, and how I tried to make sense of the observations in relation to reflections about the context. Furthermore, it is also an example of how I not only observed or listened with my eyes and ears, but with all my senses.

Listening with all the senses

Snapshot One

I am in the playground of the *børnehave* making observations, when a girl, Tine, falls and gets hurt. She cries. I go to her with the purpose of comforting her. Tine nestles against me, and very soon she just snuffles a bit. "What has happened?", a pedagogue asks in a loud voice. She is standing in a place from where it is possible to look over almost the entire playground, and she continues: "Come up here. I can't hear what you are saying!". Tine crawls down under a climbing frame from where she is hidden from the pedagogue's gaze. And, what afterwards puzzles me a bit, I instinctively do the same, motivated by a feeling of having done something wrong but – at that moment – without being able to pinpoint what it may be. It is just a feeling. I don't feel comfortable either in the pedagogue's gaze.

Interpretation

At first, neither Tine's nor my way of acting seems reasonable. However, when reflecting on my feeling about having done something wrong, I come to an interpretation where both Tine's and my own way of acting seem meaningful.

In this *børnehave*, it was an unspoken ideal that the children should come to the pedagogues to get comfort if they were sad or had got hurt. Acting in another way, for example crying and waiting for a pedagogue to come to you or just going around sadly on your own, was regarded as immature and inappropriate. I guess Tine knew this ideal, and that she – probably without being able to put it into words – knew that she had not lived up to the ideal. So she might very well have experienced the command of the pedagogue – "Come up here, I can't hear what you are saying!" – as a reproach rather than an invitation to comfort. If that is the case, it is not surprising that she prefers to hide from the pedagogue's gaze.

Also my reaction can be interpreted in terms of the power of this ideal. There is an unspoken assumption that appropriate adult behaviour should support the children's adjustment to this ideal. I did the opposite when I went to Tine instead of asking her to come to me or to go to one of the pedagogues. My instinctive knowledge about this, acquired through participation in the everyday practice in the kindergarten, can explain my feeling of having done something wrong, which otherwise, at least viewed from my personal norms, was absolutely groundless. Thus this snapshot from my days in the kindergarten can be interpreted as a narrative about 'tacit knowledge', what is taken for granted, and how to learn about this knowledge.

I would emphasise that this is just one interpretation among many that are possible. I have suggested this interpretation because of an analysis of the context, and in accordance with approaching the concrete interaction as contextualised in a specific as well as a broader historical, social and cultural context (for further discussion, see Nielsen, 2001).

Observation or participation

As mentioned in the introduction to this chapter, the term 'participant observation' refers to a variety of methodological practices. One distinction between the different practices is the degree to which the researcher emphasises observation or participation. Those who emphasise observation primarily register and analyse the verbal and non-verbal interactions of the others. Those who emphasise participation try to learn about 'the other' by participating, such as I did. The researcher then uses her unfamiliarity with the culture being studied, as this unfamiliarity makes her capable of becoming amazed by what is taken for granted by 'the natives' – what is familiar to them may seem strange to her. Therefore, the researcher in her notes includes not only her observations of 'the other' but also her own experiences, feelings and reactions to her way of participating. Furthermore, she also includes notes on changes in her experiences arising from, for example, changes in the participation role or position and to progressive familiarisation (Hastrup, 1995). This way of working takes into account how what you observe and how you interpret (make sense out of) observations depends on your relation to the studied phenomenon, a consideration that may qualify your reflections on the research.

Emphasis on either observation or participation can be said to differ in terms of how many senses you use. In the first approach, the researcher uses her eyes and ears, whereas in the participant approach the researcher uses all her senses to listen to (as Rinaldi describes in Chapter Two) "the hundred, the thousand languages, symbols and codes we use to express ourselves and communicate, and with which life expresses itself and communicates to those who know how to listen" (see page 20, this book). Listening with all the senses, besides using your ears, eyes, nose and taste includes feeling with your body, as when you try to comfort a crying child by holding him in you arms and feeling his body tremble, or when you feel ashamed, puzzled or amazed. In the first case, you listen to and may get a sense of the child's experience; in the latter you listen to and may get a sense of the culture. Listening with all senses is basically about empathy and reflections on the limits of empathy.

Clifford Geertz has made some critical reflections on the possibility of 'deep empathy'. On the basis of this, he questions the value of the researcher's empathic listening with all senses as a source for knowledge about 'the other'. I am not sure myself whether empathy to such a degree that you feel and think in the

---

same way as 'the other' is possible, and I certainly agree with Geertz that one has to be very wary of presuming that this is the case (Geertz, 1984). The point is, however, that the benefit of 'listening with all senses' does not mainly depend on either the researcher's personal ability to empathise or the possibility of empathy as such: rather it depends on the researcher's reflections on her experiences of trying to familiarise herself with the other. Her experiences should not be taken as a *direct* source for knowing how 'the other' feels and thinks, as the experience is produced in the relationship between, on the one hand, the culture and personality of the researcher (which she can not just take off like a coat) and, on the other hand, the culture which is studied. Thus I would argue that 'listening with all senses' is a source for knowing about 'the other', but an indirect or mediated one.

If we return to Snapshot One, I cannot presume that Tine experienced the happening in the same way as I did; but I can use my experiences, the feeling of having done something wrong, as the basis for producing a meaningful interpretation of both Tine's and my way of acting. I interpret Tine's nestling against me as her liking to get comfort, so that getting comfort when hurt is part of the ideal life for Tine. This is not, I believe, a very revolutionary suggestion. Further I interpret her crawling down under a climbing frame as meaning that 'something' prevents her getting comfort from the pedagogue and thus hinders her realisation of the ideal life. I suggest that this 'something' is the ideal of how children should act in such situations, which in many different situations seems to be at work in this kindergarten.

So, I will not claim to have found the essential ideal child life regarded from a child's perspective. I do not even believe in the existence of such a thing as an authentic child perspective. However, I will argue that I did learn about the ideal child life and the conditions for this as viewed from a child perspective. In this respect I agree with Allison James when she argues that "to claim to write from 'the child's' perspective, is not to make claims to reveal the authentic child but, more humbly, to provide a rendering of what childhood might be like" (James, 1996, p 315).

From the theoretical approach of this chapter, 'lived' childhood might be understood as a specific case of contextualised childhood[4]. In the analysis of Snapshot One, I have further suggested that listening to the child and the context is an interrelated process in participant observation. In the following section, I will discuss whether the specific context of an early childhood institution like a *børnehave* is a single context or multiple contexts.

The specific context of the day care institution: single or multiple contexts?

From an institutional perspective, the history, rules, norms, physical surroundings, and so on of the *børnehave* formed the specific context of my study. However, one can question whether the *børnehave* constitutes one single context, or rather multiple contexts. Corsaro has analysed how children in their interactions reproduce the culture of their adult carers, but do this in a creative, interpretive way (Corsaro, 1992, 1993, 1997). Taking this creative, interpretive dimension of children's reproduction into consideration, one must assume that the *børnehave* constitutes multiple contexts that are under constant change: "From this perspective we argue that the whole time children are developing individually, the collective processes that they are a part of are also changing. These processes are collectively produced by children and adults in the many interwoven local cultures making up children's lives" (Corsaro and Molinari, 2000, p 180).

Moreover, the norm in many Danish kindergartens is to avoid too many rules and strict norms, as these are regarded as limiting the possibilities of listening to children, including supporting their development in an individually tailored way. Instead, a flexible practice based on considering specific situations is valued. In practice, this means that the culture of the kindergarten, such as, for example, spoken and un-spoken rules, norms and values, will change with the different pedagogues who are present.

The cultures of the kindergarten as a context for childhood must, therefore, be conceptualised as characterised by multiplicity, change and breaks. Participant observation only allows you to get glimpses of these cultures by capturing moments of interactions between the children and between children and pedagogues. These glimpses, however, are an important source for an honest rendering of what childhood might be – an honest rendering that might not be possible if we rely on a more unitary and simple conceptualisation of the kindergarten as a context for childhood.

Access to the social worlds of children

A fundamental condition for getting these glimpses of multiple cultures as a basis for providing an honest rendering of what childhood might be is to get access to the social worlds of children. Adopting as my method participant observation with an emphasis on participation, getting this access was not only a matter of being allowed to be present in the kindergarten, but rather about being allowed to *participate*, and thus about the children's trust and willingness to engage with me and involve me in their social worlds. This is what the next part of this chapter is about.

Snapshot Two

Gritt (a girl) and two friends have invited me together with some children to their theatre performance. We are sitting waiting for the performance to begin; however, the beginning makes slow progress. First, they negotiate about where the scene is, what should be in the scene, and who should be allowed to act. Afterwards they have trouble with the tape recorder. Until now, the audience (children) has acted in an impressively disciplined manner, but they start to get a bit restless. Gritt turns to me and says: "You must make the audience quiet". "No, I'm a member of the audience myself", I protest. She is not willing to give up. She continues: "You are an adult, so you have to!". "Well, then I don't want to be an adult", I try to evade. For a moment she gives up, however, soon turning to me again, she, with an accusing voice, says: "There you see: They yell and fool about". As I do not react to her accusation, she finally takes on the responsibility of the audience. However, I have a sense that she feels that I have let her down.

Choosing the 'least adult role'

I act as I do in Snapshot Two, because I try to adopt what has been called the 'least adult role' (Corsaro, 1985; Mandell, 1991; Eder, 1991; Thorne, 1993; Mayall, 2000). This participant role means that the researcher makes an effort to participate in the children's everyday life in the kindergarten, and as far as possible in a way like the children do: play with the children, submit to the authority of the adult carers, abdicating from one's own adult authority as well as from one's own adult privileges. My motivation for this role was recognition of the power relation between adults and children in general as well as in the specific case of the kindergarten, which in some situations might be a barrier for getting access to part of children's social worlds (Mandell, 1991).

This does not mean that my choice of this role was motivated by an illusion about the possibility of dissolving the power relation as such in the research process, but rather from a post-structural recognition of how differences in the meaning and consequences of this power relation are related to different adult and child attitudes towards each other. On the basis of this recognition, I suggest that my relationship with the children, once I chose not to pick a 'natural adult role', was an issue for negotiation. Snapshot Two can be seen as one example of numerous such negotiations, an example that does not seem to succeed, as Gritt seemingly feels that I let her down. Later, however, I reap the benefits of my effort to escape a 'normal adult attitude', as some of the other children, including, after some time, Gritt, ask me to play with them, and tell me secrets they tell me not to tell to "*de voksne*" (the adults: in Denmark children call the staff in early childhood centres 'adults').

Thus adopting a 'least adult role' is not something that you do once and for all. It is a continuous endeavour that sometimes and with some children seems to progress successfully, while at other times and with other children it seems quite hard and not very successful. In the next snapshot, adopting the 'least adult role' comes easier with no resistance from the children.

Snapshot Three

Everybody is out on the playground, when we hear one of the pedagogues, MARTIN (I use capital letters to indicate Martin is an adult) shout: "Everybody must wash their hands. We will meet indoors in a minute". "Urrgh!", I heard from different directions in the playground. I myself, too, feel a bit annoyed, as the sun is shining, and I'm busy making observations of some children's interactions.

When everybody had come indoors, MARTIN said: "Sit down. Today, you must sort Lego bricks by colours, the red ones in this box, the white ones in this, the blue ones in this and the yellow ones in this. I will bring you another box for stuff, which is not Lego. Be careful to put the right colours in the right boxes. It might be a bit difficult."

I am amazed. Has MARTIN ordered us to go indoors on a day with such fine weather just to sort Lego bricks by colours? Why do the Lego bricks have to be sorted by colour at all? In my notebook I write the word SENSELESSNESS!!!!!!!!!!!!!!

We (the children and I) are placed around a long oval table. The boxes for the Lego bricks are placed in the middle of the table. Several children are not able to reach them without leaving their chairs. Some of these children do nothing. Others call attention to the problem, but nothing happens. And again others start to play with the Lego bricks instead. One child starts to look in a book, but is told that she has to sort Lego bricks. Eventually most of the children are clearly bored. They turn around on their chairs, fool about and fight – then try to sneak away, play 'fart play' (who can make the noisiest or longest fart) and make songs about who has farted. I am bored too.

Suddenly – without having planned it – I play a 'magic play' with some of the children. Using an imagined magic wand we, in turn, fulfil each other's gradually more and more bizarre wishes. Much of the fun is about coming up with as bizarre a wish as possible. It feels nice to do something, to fight the senselessness and boredom – however, a little dangerous too. What will happen if MARTIN realises that I take part in sabotaging his Lego-sorting project?

Positioned participation: access and experience

My participation in the children's sabotage of MARTIN's agenda was not planned. It just arose, because I participated in a position similar to the children. In the situation I felt subordinated to demands and rules I neither understood nor wanted to fulfil. Instead I reacted with what might be classified as childish resistance. I played 'magic play', which by the force of amusement and magic enriched the situation with meaning and counter-power.

For the children who participated in the magic play, and maybe for MARTIN as well, this abandonment to the child inside me, to the positioned experience of the moment, became an important sign of my otherness in relation to a normal adult role. In terms of access, this can be seen as beneficial or counterproductive, depending on whether one regards the children or the adult workers as the most important or critical gatekeepers to the social worlds of children. In this case, it proved beneficial, as MARTIN did not punish me for the sabotage, and as my playmates afterwards treated my presence and participation with increasing confidence. The narrative illustrates how the participant role and access to the social worlds of children is an issue not only of verbal and conscious negotiation, but also for silent more intuitive negotiations or construction processes.

Furthermore, it made me reflect upon how what you experience depends on the position from which you experience it. If I had acted like a 'normal adult', if I had not taken part in the magic play and instead helped MARTIN maintain order, I would undoubtedly have experienced the situation differently. I probably would not have experienced the senselessness, and for sure I would neither have felt the liberation of the magic play nor the fear that MARTIN would realise my sabotage of his Lego-sorting project and punish me.

My point is that the experiences as a participant positioning myself in a child-like position is different to that of adopting a position more akin to a normal adult. This is not to claim that my experience is the same as the children's as I even doubt that all the children experienced the situation in the same way. However, I do suggest that the experiences gained from a child-like position offer a better starting point than a traditional adult role for trying to interpret the children's reactions and for asking meaningful questions, for providing "a rendering of what childhood might be like" (James, 1996, p 315).

Making a common cause with the children

Research with children

From the very beginning of this chapter I stated that my aim when listening was to give voice to the children about their perception of everyday life in an early childhood institution, and on the basis of that to identify *det gode børneliv*, the ideal life as seen from a child's perspective as well as the conditions that either promote or discourage this ideal child life. With this aim, I situate my research within the new child research paradigm, which emphasises the generational order, and on this basis distinguish between research *on* children and research *with* children. The concept of generational order relates to a social construction of children as incompetent, unreliable and developmentally incomplete compared to adults, and which thus situates children unfavourably in a child–adult power relationship. Research *on* children takes this social construction for granted; research *with* children challenges it (Mayall, 2000; Alanen, 2001). Thus the motivation for doing research *with* children, of listening to children, is both democratic – giving voice to the children – and epistemological – "good information about childhood must start from children's experience" (Mayall, 2000, p 121).

Motivated in this way, Alderson has argued that children should be involved in all stages of the research process from idea and design, through data production[6], all the way to further analysis and dissemination of research findings (Alderson, 2000). The role of the researcher is then changed to being a kind of facilitator or research partner for the children. Although I have never seen the ideal of involving children in all stages of the research practice fully realised in practice, I find it an inspiring and challenging idea to reflect on.

Involvement of the children

In my research project, I did not involve the children when deciding the purpose of the research. I – and not the children – decided that the main research question was the ideal child life and the conditions that either promoted or discouraged this life. I did not even tell all of the children about the purpose or that I was a researcher. This was not because I didn't want the children to know, or so I could do a 'fly on the wall' study. On the contrary, I actually wanted the children to know who I was and what I was doing. In principle, I find this the most ethical practice. I was just not sure whether giving this information would be more for my benefit than the children's. Maybe by giving them this information that might not be important viewed from their position, I would just disturb them in what they were doing, which might be important for them: then what might seem, in principle, the most ethical practice might turn out to be unethical. This was quite a dilemma for me. The choice became to inform the children, when and if they asked. Some did, others were not interested in my presence at all.

Saying that I did not involve the children in deciding the purpose of the research is not to say that the children would not agree on the choice. On the contrary, as I suggested earlier in this chapter, researching children's perception of the ideal child life and the conditions that either promote or discourage it can be regarded as a first and decisive step towards making a common cause with the children. One five-year-old boy supported this suggestion by commenting on my research focus as follows: "That's good. Most adults don't know much about children and what makes them happy". I felt – and still feel – really good and satisfied with this comment.

In the next stage, the design stage, one can argue that I actually did involve the children, at least to some degree, as I did not work with a predefined concept of the ideal child life. On the contrary, step by step, I built up, dissolved and changed the concept on the basis of my participation in the everyday life of the children, and my experiences, observations and conversations with them. In this way I involved the children in the design, as I listened to them.

In the data production stage I also involved the children, although to a quite limited degree – and not without reservation. I invited them to help me to understand what I saw, heard and experienced. For example: "I see that you cry, are you sad?" or "You seem happy, tell me about it!". I did not just observe, but talked to the children about what I saw. For a period I also took photographs and recorded episodes of the children's everyday life on video, and afterwards I asked the children to tell me about the photographs and video clips. This was one more way to invite them to tell me about their lives and perspectives, but it was me who chose the photographs. If a child asked me to take a photograph or record something, I did, of course. But children choosing were the exception rather than the rule, and when some of the children asked if they could borrow the video camera, I dared not let it out of my sight.

I did something else, however, something I had not thought out in advance, but which worked quite well as a strategy for involving at least some of the children. What I did was very simple. I sat down and made notes in my notebook while I observed the children. This provoked some children's curiosity. They asked me what I was doing, and I answered: "I am writing down what the children are doing and saying to learn about children's life in a kindergarten. I want to learn about what makes children happy, what makes them sad or angry, what is important for them, and about their views". The first time this happened the boy who had asked me just replied: "hmm..." and then he disappeared. I thought: "Oh God, I am not very pedagogical. That was too wordy for him. He didn't understand a thing". I was afraid that he had lost all desire to talk with me ever again, but I was wrong. Later he came again and again telling me what he had experienced as well as about his views on different issues, and he invited me to participate with him and his friends. Sometimes he told me: "Write this or that". What is more, he also told his friends about what I was doing.

The evasive children

The above narrative about the boy tells how easy it actually was to gain the confidence of the children, and by doing so to learn about the children's views. I was so delighted by this that it took me a while to realise that this did not apply to my relations with all of the children. Realising this, I decided to make special endeavours to get in contact with those children who did not contact me on their own. But with some of the children this was not that easy, as they only answered with a few words when I asked them about something. Observing their interactions, I realised that they did not talk that much with each other either; they talked as necessary in games they were playing, but they just did not talk for the sake of talking.

In other words, they were 'acting people' rather than 'talking people'. They accepted my presence if I participated without too much talking. But if I started asking questions that were not part of the game, they turned away from me. Just observing was not a possibility either as they then moved away. If I wanted to learn about them and their views, I had to learn by participating. Participating with these children, I learned a lot, for instance how to keep out of the pedagogue's sight literally and figuratively. Thus adopting (and fighting for) a 'least adult role' can be said to be even more important in gaining access to the social worlds of these children, as in many situations they proved to have a well-developed skill in making themselves invisible for adults.

Although I learned a lot about these children's perspectives through participation, I was not sure how to represent these perspectives in a valid way. I did not have many words from these children, and I dared not tell stories from my participation in their (invisible) social worlds, as I felt that it would be unethical, breaking my unspoken contract with those children. What I did instead was to report my interpretations of their perspectives on a quite abstract level; however, I would have preferred 'something more concrete'. I thought of asking them to make drawings, but many of these children were not very fond of drawing either[7].

Making common cause with the children in the analysis and dissemination of research findings

In the final analysis phase I wanted to get some distance from the everyday experiences of meaning, intention, free choice, individuality and multiplicity, in order to make an analysis of some general features of sameness within the group of children as well as some general features of difference between the children, and further to relate those features of sameness and difference to the specific and broader context. In other words, I wanted to objectify – and by that politicise – the conditions, possibilities and barriers for children obtaining what they perceive as 'the ideal life' in the *børnehave*. I suggest this as a way of 'making a common cause with the children' beyond just listening[8].

In the dissemination of my research findings my way of 'making common cause with the children' was to (try to) tell good stories that encourage the audience to identify with the child I am talking about, and at the same time make the specific and broader context very visible as promoting or/and discouraging the child's endeavours to achieve the good life.

The (im-)possibility of representing children?

The story above about the evading children highlights a more general critical question, which has been more or less in focus during the whole chapter and which is a pressing critical question in the new child research as such: namely whether and how it is possible to represent children's experiences and views.

If representation means a neutral, objective and essential mirroring, I doubt that it is possible. My doubts are both ontological and epistemological. Ontologically, I doubt the existence of an essence in children's experiences and views. Children are different from each other: what might be important for one child might be less important for another. Furthermore, children's experiences and views (exactly as adults') change over time and with the specific and broader context. What might be possible to construct, however, is how different contexts in interaction with different biographical, social and cultural influences make certain experiences more probable than others. Epistemologically, I doubt the possibility of neutral and objective knowledge. We cannot escape the presenter's perspective on the presented in the presentation. In other words, knowledge cannot escape being perspectival, although this is not to say that knowledge is irrelevant or that all kinds of knowledge are equally important and valid.

The question then is how we can make important and valid studies that give voice to children's hundreds and thousands of languages. In this chapter, I have told about my endeavours and reflections adopting participant observation with an emphasis on participation as my method of listening to the many languages of children. Participating in children's everyday lives may not only allow one to listen closely to what the children say in words and through body language, it might further one's learning about children's cultures and one's familiarisation with children's life worlds, allow one to ask better questions, as well as to interpret what the children say and do. In that way, participant observation is a method that, with improvements, can be adopted by practitioners as well as researchers.

However, an important critical point in my reflections has been that experience and knowledge are positioned and produced in relations. Our participant roles are negotiated continually, not only verbally and explicitly, but also in silent, intuitive and often unacknowledged ways that are shaped by institutionalised roles. It might be even more important to be aware of this if participant observation is adopted as a method of listening by a person who already has a role in the field, as for instance a pedagogue.

I do believe that it is possible to hear children's different voices and perspectives listening not only with one's ears, but also with all senses. However, it is important to recognise that both hearing and representing are constructed processes. Thus my suggestion, inspired by (Chia, 1996), is to substitute an illusionary ambition of representation with endeavours of 'reflexive re-presentations' based on listening with all senses to children's different and contextualised voices.

In this chapter I have discussed participant observation, emphasising participation and bodily experience as one way to 'listen with all senses'. I believe that this kind of participant observation could be usefully supplemented by other methods, such as, for instance, using disposable cameras[7], so being integrated with advantage in a multi-approach strategy, which I agree with Clark (2004; see also Chapter Three, this volume) is appropriate for taking into account children's differences. Further, I have argued that 'making common cause with the children' beyond just listening might involve an objectifying analysis of the specific and broader context, as children's childhoods are subject to – as well as part of – the construction processes of those contexts.

With my reference to Chia's term 'reflexive re-presentations' above, I sought for presentations that acknowledge the perspectival and constructed character of the presented. Further I sought for re-presentations that allow children's own representations, for example narratives, drawings, theatre performances and photographs – together with an objectifying analysis – to be part of what Richardson (2000) has called a 'crystallic re-presentation'. A crystallic representation does not claim to tell the whole and only truth. Rather it tries to present different, not necessary congruent, perspectives on the same object. Such representations would have a potential for giving voice to the multiple and changing, as well as socially, culturally and historically contextualised, traces of the perspectives of children, and thus for challenging our often quite simplistic and taken-for-granted images of childhood. By so doing, they could inspire the reflections of those who work with children and children's life experiences.

Notes

[1] The term 'the other', as used here, has a relational and anti-essentialistic meaning, 'otherness' being regarded as a product of processes of social construction.

[2] Pedagogues are professional workers, with an initial education at degree level, who work with the theory and practice of pedagogy, a strong tradition in Continental Europe with its origins in 19th-century Germany. The approach is relational and holistic: "the pedagogue sets out to address the whole child, the child with body, mind, emotions, creativity, history and social identity" (Moss and Petrie, 2002). Pedagogues are found in many Continental European countries, although there are significant variations in education and the range of work they do. In Denmark, pedagogues constitute half or more of the workforce in a wide range of services for children, young people and adults, including early childhood centres (Jensen and Hansen, 2003; Korintus and Moss, 2004).

[3] *Børnehave* (kindergarten) is one of the main types of early childhood institution in Denmark, providing for children from three to six years of age and open, usually, all day and all year round. Other types of Danish institution include *vuggestuer*, for children under three years, and *aldersintegrerede institutioner* (age-integrated institutions) for children under and over three years.

[4] I use the term 'the specific context of the early childhood institution', as, with inspiration from Bourdieu's concept of field (Bourdieu, 1990, 1998, 1999), I approach this institution as a specific case of the broader child and early childhood institution field. Thus the specific context of the early childhood institution is neither determined nor independent of broader social, cultural and historical influences, and it contributes to reproduction and change of the social and cultural order.

[5] In Bech-Jørgensen's theory, these 'meaning universes' seem quite cognitive. However, inspired by Bourdieu (1990, 1992, 1998), I emphasise that 'meaning universes' are also bodily.

[6] I prefer the term 'data production' to 'data collection', as the latter indicates a positivist or realist epistemology assuming that the data is out there, just waiting to be picked by the researcher. With the term 'data production' I intend, in contrast, to emphasise the constructive aspect: data are – whether the researcher accepts it or not – produced in the interaction between the researcher and the researched. Furthermore, in this production stage interpretation is involved, and thus it is quite difficult – not to say impossible – to distinguish strictly between collection and (first) analysis of data (Burr, 1995; Kvale, 1995; Chia, 1996; Gubrium and Holstein, 1997; Czarniawska, 1998).

[7] In retrospect I think that cameras or other kinds of technology would have been a possibility. I regret that I did not take the chance with the video camera, and I wish that

I had bought some disposable cameras so that, with peace of mind, I could have let the children take photographs themselves, especially as I know that other researchers have found disposable cameras very useful (see Chapter Three, this volume and Clark et al, 2003).

[8] In another research project, about children in foster care, I involve children in this analytical objectifying phase. In this project I combine individual in-depth interviews, focus group interviews and an Internet-based forum for debate and comparison of experiences. The children participating are eight years and above. There is a publication in Danish (Warming, 2005), with a paper in English in preparation.

Further reading

Christensen, P. and James, A. (eds) (2000) *Research with children*, London: RoutledgeFalmer.

Denzin, N.K. and Lincoln, Y.S. (eds) (2000) *Handbook of qualitative research* (2nd edn), London: Sage Publications.

Hastrup, K. (1995) *A passage to anthropology: Between experience and theory*, London: Routledge.

References

Adler, P. and Adler, P. (1987) *Membership roles in field research: Qualitative research methods series (Volume Six)*, Thousand Oaks, CA: Sage Publications.

Alderson, P. (2000) 'Children as researchers', in P. Christensen and A. James (eds) *Research with children: Perspectives and practices*, London: RoutledgeFalmer, pp 241-57.

Alanen, L. (2001) 'Explorations in generational analysis', in L. Alenen and B. Mayall (eds) *Conceptualising child–adult relations*, London: RoutledgeFalmer, pp 11-22.

Atkinson, P. and Coffey, A. (2000) 'Revisiting the relationship between participant observation and interviewing', in J.F. Gubrium and J.A. Holstein (eds) *Handbook of interview research: Context and method*, Thousand Oaks, CA: Sage Publications, pp 801-14.

Atkinson, P. and Hammersley, M. (1998) 'Ethnography and participant observation', in N.K. Denzin and Y.S. Lincoln (eds) *Strategies of qualitative inquiry*, Thousand Oaks, CA: Sage Publications, pp 110-13.

Bech-Jørgensen, B. (1990) 'What are they doing, when they seem to do nothing?', in J. Ehrnrooth and L. Siurala (eds) *Construction youth*, Helsinki: WAPK-Publishing.

Bech-Jørgensen, B. (1994) *Når hver dag bliver hverdag (When every day becomes everyday)*, Copenhagen: Akademisk Forlag.

Bo, I.G. and Warming, H. (2004) 'Recognizing the power of recognition – different practices in social work with children and youth', Revised edition of paper presented at ISA's RC26 Conference 'Social Capital and Social Trasformation in the Age of Globalization', Lesvos, 11-14 June.

Bourdieu, P. (1990) *The logic of practice*, Cambridge: Polity Press.

Bourdieu, P. (1992) *An invitation to reflexive sociology*, Cambridge, Oxford: Polity Press.

Bourdieu, P. (1998) *Practical reason: On the theory of action*, Cambridge: Polity Press.

Bourdieu, P. (1999) *The weight of the world: Social suffering and impoverishment*, Cambridge: Polity Press.

Burr, V. (1995) *An introduction to social constructionism*, London: Routledge.

Chia, R. (1996) 'The problem of reflexivity in organizational research: towards a post-modern science of organization', *Organization*, vol 3, pp 31-59.

Christensen, P. and James, A. (eds) (2000) *Research with children*, London: RoutledgeFalmer.

Clark, A. (2004) 'The Mosaic approach and research with young children', in V. Lewis, M. Kellett, C. Robinson, S. Fraser and S. Ding (eds) *The reality of research with children and young people*, London: Sage Publications, pp 142-61.

Clark, A., McQuail, S. and Moss, P. (2003) *Exploring the field of listening to and consulting with young children*, Research Report 445, London: DfES.

Corsaro, W. (1985) *Friendship and peer culture in the early years*, Norwood, NJ: Ablex.

Corsaro, W. (1992) 'Interpretive reproduction in children's peer cultures', *Social Psychology Quarterly*, no 55, pp 160-77.

Corsaro, W. (1993) 'Interpretive reproduction in children's role play', *Childhood*, vol 1, no 1, pp 64-74.

Corsaro, W. (1997) *The sociology of childhood*, Thousand Oaks, CA: Pine Forge Press.

Corsaro, W. and Molinari, L. (2000) 'Entering and observing in children's worlds', in P. Christensen and A. James (eds) *Research with children*, London: RoutledgeFalmer, pp 179-200.

Czarniawska, B. (1998) *A narrative approach to organization studies*, Qualitative Research Methods Series 43, Thousand Oaks, London, New Delhi: Sage Publications.

Danmarks Statistik (2004) *Danmark i tal* (*Denmark in numbers*), Copenhagen: Danmarks Statistik.

Danmarks Statistik (2005) 'Pasningsgaranti' ('Day care guarantee') (www.dst.dk/pasningsgaranti).

Eder, D. (1991) 'The role of teasing in adolescent peer grooup culture', *Sociological Studies of Child Development, vol 4: Perspectives on and of children*, pp 181-97.

Foucault, M. (1979) *The history of sexuality: An introduction*, London: Allen Lane.

Foucault, M. (1986) *The history of sexuality: The use of pleasure*, London: Viking.

Foucault, M. (1988) *The history of sexuality: The care of self*, London: Vintage Books.

Foucault, M. (1997) *Madness and civilization: A history of insanity in the age of reason*, London: Routledge.

Geertz, C. (1984) 'From the native's point of view', in A. Shweder and R.A. LeVine (eds) *Culture theory: Essays on mind, self and emotion*, Cambridge: Cambridge University Press, pp 123-36.

Goffman, E. (1971a) *Asylums: Essay on the social situation of mental patients and other inmates*, Harmondsworth: Penguin.

Goffman, E. (1971b) *Relations in public: Micro studies of the public order*, London: Allen Lane.

Goffman, E. (1986) *Frame analysis: An essay on the organization of experience*, Boston, MA: Northeastern University Press.

Goffman, E. (1990) *The presentation of self in everyday life*, Harmondsworth: Penguin.

Gubrium, J.F. and Holstein, J.A. (1997) *The new language of qualitative method*, New York, NY: Oxford University Press.

Hastrup, K. (1995) *A passage to anthropology: Between experience and theory*, London: Routledge.

James, A. (1996) 'Learning to be friends. Methodological lessons from participant observation among English schoolchildren', *Childhood*, vol 3, pp 313-30.

James, A., Jenks, C. and Prout, A. (1998) *Theorizing childhood*, Cambridge: Polity Press.

Jensen, A.M., Ben-Arieh, A., Conti, C., Kutsar, D., Nic Ehiolla Prádraig, M. and Nielsen, H.W. (eds) (2004) *Children's welfare in ageing Europe, Vol I & II*, Tartu: Tartu University Press.

Jensen, J.J. and Hansen, H.K. (2003) 'The Danish pedagogues – a worker for all ages', *Children in Europe*, no 5, pp 6-9.

Kampmann, J. and Nielsen, H.W. (2004) 'Socialized childhood: children's childhoods in Denmark', in A.M. Jensen, A. Ben-Arieh, C. Conti, D. Kutsar, M. Nic Ehiolla Prádraig and H.W. Nielsen (eds) *Children's welfare in ageing Europe, Vol I & II*, Tartu: Tartu University Press.

Korintus, M. and Moss, P. (2004) 'Work with young children: a case study of Denmark, Hungary and Spain' (available at www.ioe.ac.uk/teru/carework.htm).

Kvale, S. (1995) 'The social constructoin of validity', *Qualitative Inquiry*, vol 1, no 1, pp 19-40.

Lov om Social Service (Law about Social Service), revised December 2004 (www.minft.dk/1/lovservice/2004-134-175-1120-1121/1).

Mandell, N. (1991) 'The least-adult role in studying children', in F.C. Waksler (ed) *Studying the social worlds of children: Sociological readings*, London: Falmer Press, pp 38-59.

Mayall, B. (2000) 'Conversations with children: working with generational issues', in P. Christensen and A. James (eds) *Research with children*, London: RoutledgeFalmer, pp 120-35.

Moss, P. and Petrie, P. (2002) *From children's services to children's spaces: Public policy, children and childhood*, London: RoutledgeFalmer.

Nielsen, H.W. (2001) 'Børn i medvind og modvind: en relational analyse af børns livtag med livet i det refleksivt moderne' ('Children facing support and opposition: a relational analysis of children's struggles in their everyday life in the reflexive modern society'), PhD thesis nr 27/2001, PhD series 'Comparative welfare systems', Roskilde University [the thesis is in Danish, but there is an abstract in English].

Opie, I. and Opie, P. (1982) 'The lore and language of schoolchildren', in C. Jenks (ed) *The sociology of childhood – Essential readings*, London: Batsford, pp 173-80.

Opie, I. and Opie, P. (1991) 'The culture of children 1: Introduction' and 'The culture of children 2: Half-belief', in F.C. Waksler (ed) *Studying the social worlds of children: Sociological readings*, London: Falmer Press, pp 123-44.

Richardson, L. (2000) 'Writing: a method of inquiry', in N.K. Denzin and Y.S. Lincoln (eds) *Handbook of qualitative research* (2nd edn), London: Sage Publications, pp 923-43.

Sacks, H. (1991) 'On the analysability of stories by children', in F.C. Waksler (ed) *Studying the social worlds of children: Sociological readings*, London: Falmer Press, pp 195-215.

Sutton, J., Smith, P. and Swettenham, J. (2004) 'Social cognition and bullying: social inadequacy or skilled manipulation?', in V. Lewis, M. Kellett, C. Robinson, S. Fraser and S. Ding (eds) *The reality of research with children and young people*, London: Sage Publications, pp 44-60.

Thorne, B. (1993) *Gender plan: Girls and boys in school*, New Brunswick, NJ: Rutgers University Press.

Warming, H. (2003) 'The quality of life from a child's perspective', *International Journal of Public Administration*, vol 26, no 7, pp 815-29.

Warming, H. (2005) *Har andre plejebørn det som mig? (Do other children in foster care feel the same way as I do?)*, Copenhagen: Frydenlund.

Warming, H. and Kampmann, J. (2005) 'Children in command of time and space?', in H. Zeiher, H. Strandell, D. Devine and A.T. Kjørholt (eds) *Children's times and space: Changes in welfare in an intergenerational perspective*, Odense: Syddansk Univeritetsforlag.

FIVE

From the children's point of view: methodological and ethical challenges

Brit Johanne Eide and Nina Winger

The development of early childhood services in Norway has been rather slower than in neighbouring Denmark and Sweden, reflecting a society that has been more rural and less industrialised. But in recent years there has been a rapid growth of these services, and by 2003 two thirds (69 per cent) of children between one and six years of age were in publicly funded services, mostly spending from six to nine hours a day there.

Like the other Scandinavian countries, Norway has had a strong discourse of children's rights. It was one of the first countries to have a Children's Commissioner (or ombudsman), established in 1981 with a worldwide reputation today. There is now a strong emphasis on listening to children, both in school and early childhood services. This chapter considers various methods of talking with children, to gain insight into their perspectives, and considers what conditions are needed, including the competences required of adults, and what ethical issues need to be considered – not least, what gives adults the right to seek children's views and perspectives.

> First I stayed in a playground, then in a childcare institution, now I am in kindergarten and then I will go to school and then to work, and then I will stop working and I will be free all day because I am growing old – Hans, 6 years old. (Eide and Winger, 1995, p 25)

We met Hans some years ago, when we visited some Norwegian *førskoleklasser*[1] and primary schools and interviewed children about their experiences and thoughts about participation, belonging and care (Eide and Winger, 1994, 1995, 1996, 1999). Hans's ideas about his former, present and future life are one of many examples of how children can give us well-qualified reflections and descriptions. We consider his perspectives on his position within institutional life most interesting and thought provoking.

A small girl in an urban *barnehage*[2] made some observations about the quality of care. She had recognised that there were several categories of grown-ups in her centre:"'there was not that kind of grown-up there who takes care of children, just that kind of grown-up who looks after children' (Monica, four years old)"

(Eide and Winger, 2003, p 135). In other words, she had an idea that some workers cared about children, but that others were only present because it was their job to look after children. Monica's thoughtful reflections represent a perspective that might not have been available to us as adults if we had not specifically asked about the child's thoughts about care. Other children we have met during our projects have similarly informed us about matters and viewpoints that we, as researchers, had not appreciated.

Fortunately, there has been a major change in recent years in how we recognise children, both in research and practice. To an increasing extent, children are seen as participants and actors. This is in line with the United Nations Convention on the Rights of the Child (1989) and the current scientific discourse on childhood (for example, Qvortrup, 2000; Cannella, 1997; Dahlberg et al, 1999; Alderson, 2000; Jenks, 2000; Nilsen, 2000; Christensen and James, 2000; James et al, 1998; Kjørholt, 2001; Halldèn, 2003). This 'new paradigm', with its emphasis on children's right to participate, challenges us to reflect on our former perspectives and to question established theories, practices and research methodologies within early childhood education. It calls for new perspectives and approaches. This process of de- and reconstruction can be demanding, because it implies that we may have to change our basic understanding.

In our research we have been concerned for a long time about 'the participating child', and have most recently been especially interested in methodological issues related to this new discourse within child research. We have, through our research, learned a great deal about everyday life, as it is experienced and interpreted from children's own perspectives (Eide and Winger, 1995, 1996, 2003). We have experienced that children are able to give us very competent information about their everyday life within early childhood institutions. Talking to children has opened our eyes and has often made us reconsider our ideas about pedagogical practice and knowledge. If we give children an opportunity to talk and tell their stories, we feel confident that we will be enlightened and sometimes astonished. However, giving children 'a voice', listening to them and being genuinely interested in their stories, raises many crucial questions.

In this chapter we will concentrate on some challenges and dilemmas in searching for knowledge from children's point of view in early childhood settings and child research. As mentioned above, our position is within child research and, as such, we meet children from an 'outside' position. We do not know our informants personally and they do not know us. As we will discuss in this chapter, we therefore have to be extremely sensitive and careful in our approach to children and their institutional context. Johansson (2003) mentions that a pedagogue's position is somewhat different from the researchers in the search for a child's perspectives (see end note 2 in Chapter Four for a discussion of the profession of pedagogue; trained workers in Norwegian kindergartens are called *pedagogisk leder*). Whereas a pedagogue tends to be 'normative' and educative in her approach, the agenda of the researcher is descriptive and analytic.

Even so, in the process of listening some fundamental relational qualities have to be developed, whether you meet the child as a pedagogue or a researcher. Formalities, settings and the time available may differ, but the main goal in both cases is that the adult should be informed and enlightened by getting a more competent and qualified view on how life is from children's point of view. Only the child knows what it is like to be a child in his or her specific context, whether it is an early childhood institution or school. And we think that the same basic sensibility and respect is demanded from pedagogues, teachers or researchers. In this chapter, therefore, although our frame of reference is primarily from within child research, we will not distinguish very much between everyday talk and interviews with children.

What does it mean to search for children's perspectives?

Due to the ongoing ideological and theoretical reconstruction of childhood, there has recently been an increased focus on how we determine what is 'best' for children and who is in the right position to determine this. Giving children rights to participate has given us an obligation to search for their own perspectives and experiences.

One could perhaps say that this new approach is after all not very new. Within Nordic early childhood services, we have long supported a pedagogical idea where children's well being and development has been the main aim. Many professionals will claim that they have been searching for children's perspectives, that they have been spokespersons for children in various ways, and that they have tried to develop pedagogical settings with high quality in the interests of children. This may very well be the case. But what is considered 'best' is not necessarily the same from different positions (Katz, 1993). What we, adults, consider as a 'child's perspective' is not necessarily the same as a child's own point of view or perspective. Yet "traditionally, childhood and children's lives have solely been explored through the views and understandings of their adult caretakers" (Christensen and James, 2000, p 2). Today, perspectives of the child should always imply that the child has made his or her own contribution (Halldèn, 2003). Their story has to be heard. We have to ask children themselves to get knowledge about what the world is like from a 'bottom-up' position (Katz, 1993).

This, of course, does not mean that the child's voice should always be considered the most important or qualified opinion, or that knowledge from children's point of view should always be preponderant in a debate about quality or a process of innovation. But what children can tell should be taken into account together with other opinions on everyday life and learning processes in pedagogical settings. An important issue here is also that there is not one authentic child perspective (see also Chapter Four). Children in different social and cultural positions and contexts represent multiple childhoods and perspectives. We must, therefore, be sensitive about both contextual and relational aspects when we talk about children's perspectives, especially if we are not familiar with the child's culture or language.

For some children, for example, it may not seem at all natural to expose their own opinions verbally (Viruru, 2001).

The main question is then *how* children can be given the opportunity to become constructive participants and competent informants on issues concerning their everyday life experiences. In other words, we need more knowledge on how to seek knowledge from children's point of view in a respectful and serious way.

Talking to children within child research really commits us and challenges us. There is therefore an increased focus on methodological questions, on how to do this in a competent and respectful way (for example Tiller, 1991; Skoglund, 1998; Christensen and James, 2000; Jørgensen, 2000; Coady, 2001; Eide and Winger, 2003; Halldèn, 2003; Johansson, 2003; Grover, 2004). There is also a discussion on how to relate to information from children's point of view since listening to children is a complex matter: "listening to children, hearing children and acting on what children say are three very different activities, although they are frequently elided as if they were not" (Roberts, 2000, p 238).

Searching for children's perspectives, therefore, relates to a basic understanding of children's position and role in society in general and within early childhood (and other) institutions in particular.

Ideological and formal legitimation of the search for children's perspectives

Both the *Framework plan for day care institutions* (Norwegian Ministry for Children and Family Affairs, 1995) and the *Curriculum for the 10-year compulsory school* (Norwegian Ministry of Education, Research and Church Affairs, 1996), which regulate early childhood services and schools in Norway, oblige pedagogues and teachers to consider the children's points of view both in planning and in evaluating their work. The *Framework plan*, for example, states that "a children's perspective must be present throughout in all planning in day care institutions … [and that] children should be enabled to participate in evaluating their own play and learning environment and should see that their opinions are taken seriously" (pp 10, 74), while the *Curriculum* says that the 'pupils' are to be active in their own learning and in planning learning activities, and that teachers cannot neglect the pupil's point of view. Cooperation between pupils, teachers and the school administration is essential to the development of the school as a learning environment and workplace. If the pupils are to be included in a social, academic and cultural community and exposed to challenges in keeping with their abilities and interests, the staff must cooperate: "good confidence-building co-operative routines must be established between pupils and adults at the school" (p 62). Every person involved must participate, learn from each other, and coordinate their efforts.

In school, one of the consequences of focusing on the pupil's perspectives has resulted in a special kind of conversation or talk between pupil and teacher called *elevsamtale* (pupil conversation). This kind of conversation is mostly used in the secondary school, and can have several functions; for example, the aim can be to evaluate the teaching or the pupil's learning, or to make the pupil active in planning her or his own learning environment (Fuglestad, 1998). But such conversations between teacher and pupil have become more and more common in primary school as well. Sjøbakken (2004) writes about using *plansamtal* (planning conversation) where teacher and pupil talk about what the pupil will be working on during the coming weeks in relation to overall learning aims. Sjøbakken uses this sort of conversation from the first grade when the pupils are about six years old.

Some *barnehager* practise *barnesamtale* (child conversation) with their children. But in general it is up to the pedagogues in each institution to decide how in fact they will consider the point of view of children.

With what right?

The relationship between adult and child is always asymmetrical. As Johansson (2003) says, there is a power dimension involved when researchers invite children to an interview or when a pedagogue or teacher searches for a child's opinion on a subject. As a researcher, pedagogue or teacher we have to be aware of our responsibility and keep asking ourselves: what gives us the right as grown-ups to search for children's point of view? And is it really possible for us to look at reality from their point of view?

We have already concluded that as pedagogues and teachers in *barnehager* and in schools we have to try to find the children's point of view. As researchers we also increasingly search for children's perspectives. If adults never ask children what they are thinking, feeling or what their opinions are, how can they then get that information? We are, therefore, quite sure that we need this information. The main question is *how*. How can we get the information from children without doing harm to them in any way, but rather putting them at ease and letting them know that they are very important to us?

In our work both as practitioners and as researchers we have experienced that most children like to be asked and like to tell about themselves and what is important to them. But it depends on how we do it and what relationship we manage to establish.

We also find it important for children in the postmodern world to be given serious attention from grown-ups. We will look a little closer now on why we find it important to listen to children in pedagogical and educational institutions.

"Listen to me"

Many children in Western society spend most of their days in public care and educational systems. This 'institutionalisation' of childhood constitutes specific contexts for identity constructions. Small children are participants within formal frames of negotiations, representing themselves as subjects in a public field. They have to define themselves in relation to standards and communication patterns that may or may not correspond with what they experience within their own families and domestic environments.

One of the main challenges for children in a postmodern world is the search for meaning, a sense of belonging, and constructions of identity. Modern man and woman in contemporary Western societies live in complex and rapidly changing contexts. Every day children are confronted with diversity and complexity in many aspects of life. Common standards are not necessarily available and tradition may not always be a functional frame of reference. There is more emphasis today on making our own standards and exploring different ways of living (Giddens, 1991). We seem to experience a loss of the taken-for-granted: "Modern pluralism undermines the common-sense 'knowledge'. The world, society, life and personal identity are called even more into question. They may be subject to multiple interpretations and each interpretation defines its own perspectives of possible action" (Berger and Luckman, 1995, p 40).

We have to search for, explore and make our own identity. Constructing our identity is therefore a continuing, vulnerable and possibly troubling process (Giddens, 1991). Identity constructions are partly defining yourself as an *individual*, stating your uniqueness, and partly negotiating to become *a member of a social community* – or rather, today, multiple social communities or cultures. Identity, although it may have stable elements over the lifecourse, is always changeable and redefinable: "In this sense, identity is always a state of becoming rather than being. It is something which can be reformulated" (Hockey and James, 2003, p 20). The important point here is that when children, to a greater extent today, are recognised as participants and qualified informants in their 'being', they also become more empowered in the process of defining their own future identities – their 'becoming'. This is a complex challenge for children, carers and society.

Children's constructions of meaning and identity are to some extent dependent on the child's ability to sort out and identify which standards and role interpretations are relevant and expected in different settings. This calls for sensibility and flexibility in the definition of situations and relations and an ability to act in a way that other participants identify as relevant. This may seem confusing to many children, and makes identity construction demanding and sometimes troublesome.

In such uncertain contexts, we agree with Landager (1999) that it is very important that children are allowed to *explore* different situations and interpretations, to *express* themselves and to *exchange* viewpoints and feelings. Telling who you are – presenting yourself and your views and being heard – is one of the most important issues in identity construction. This, in turn, requires making time and space for children to express themselves and to be listened to, a good example of how "in order to honour children's participation rights we must establish the conditions in which they can be honoured" (Mayall, 2000, p 132).

———

But at the same time, there needs to be awareness of the 'limits of listening'. Children must also be allowed *not* to speak, *not* to inform, *not* to express themselves, *not* to participate. Listening to children is a balance between inviting the child to openness, but at the same time protecting the child from being manipulated.

We have been talking to children who have wanted to protect themselves from the attentions of curious adults. Although we had informed her very thoroughly in advance, a five-year-old girl being interviewed needed more confirmation of her participation in a research project (Eide and Winger, 1996, p 102): "'What are you going to do with this afterwards?'". At this point she was not at all convinced that her interests were taken care of. We interpreted her to be saying that she did not want everybody to know what she was telling. We had to repeat our intentions with the interview, as well as reassure her once more about how we would use this information and that we would not tell the grown-ups in the *barnehage* what she had told us. After this she was satisfied and ready to proceed with our talk.

Another child, an eight-year-old boy, who had been interviewed twice, was anxious about his role in a longitudinal project: "'Now you have been interviewing me twice, is this the last time? You can't keep on interviewing me until I am in the army'" (Eide and Winger, 1996, p 134). He might just have been tired of it all, or perhaps he was really interested in the longitudinal nature of the project.

Another girl, six years of age, was not very comfortable with the subject we were talking about, her experiences of 'play and inclusion'. So, she changed the subject quickly to another that was less threatening. Hairstyles seemed more to her liking to talk about at that moment: "'Look at me, I have been curling my hair. Just like Madonna'" (Eide and Winger, 1999, p 111), and we had a pleasant talk about hairstyles and pop stars.

In situations like these, it is important to respect children's rights not to talk or to express themselves on unpleasant subjects or to be challenged. As researchers, we very much agree with Fog (1992) that our search for interesting data should never be more important than the informant's integrity.

A setting for constructions of meaning and new knowledge

To improve and develop our knowledge about educational and other institutions and children's positions in them, it is important that the voices of participants at all levels are heard, and children are not to be forgotten. By making a space for serious and interactive meaning making, we construct a setting where the adult gives the child full attention and lets the child know that statements from children matter. To be heard and listened to may be important for children's self-reflective processes and identity constructions both at a personal and collective level (Eide and Winger, 2003).

It has been our experience that children who have been interviewed in specific institutional settings have been very aware of their *collective* identity. We have, for instance, interviewed children about their interpretations of their role and position in their particular kindergarten. We learned that these children were very explicit about their collective identity, their 'we' identity: we the six-year-olds, we the oldest children, we the preschoolers (Eide and Winger, 1996, 2003). Their sense of belonging seemed very strong and important for their collective identity within that specific setting. In reconstructing childhood it is very important, therefore, to search for children's interpretations of their social identity.

At an individual level, being interviewed can serve many functions, dependent on the child's position, experiences and self-reflecting ability. Children today have to participate and be active in their own learning process. They have to negotiate with others in complex, rapidly changing contexts, where an important issue is to present their own identity and uniqueness. In this process, it is important for children to meet pedagogues, teachers and other adults who work closely with them, and make them feel that they are interesting and important. To experience that someone genuinely listens to your 'self-presentations' and your opinions may, again, be central for children's personal identity constructions.

As adults it is a privilege to get the opportunity to be invited into a child's world, and sometimes it may be necessary to reassess one's own constructions of meaning. Thus a child interview can be an enriching experience both for the adult and child. As Tiller (1991) observes: "Child research may also be a voyage of discovery together with children" (p 13; our translation). From our experience, talking with young children is meaningful, exciting and sometimes surprising. Stories and reflections from children's point of view constantly make us wonder and reflect on our own perspectives. As practitioners and researchers we need this corrective to understand children and their situation.

Methodological reflections

If we want to search for children's points of view both as practitioners and researchers, we have to make serious methodological reflections and choose methods that are both suitable and ethical. Within a narrative approach children are allowed to tell what is important to them at the moment. In such situations it is the children who decide the subject or what they want to tell about.

Everyday conversation between children and adults

One approach for practitioners to use can be a kind of 'everyday conversation' between children and adults. Pedagogues in *barnehager* and teachers in schools will have the opportunity to use these methodological approaches in their work, and to do so is of great importance. The information they get through these conversations is necessary both for the teachers and for the children, but it is also important how the adults use this information.

Things that children tell in an intimate talk with the pedagogue or teacher cannot be used in any kind of situation. The adult has to reflect on the responsibility she has to make children's thoughts anonymous if she wants to tell somebody else about them. Moreover, she cannot use them just as she wants without asking the children involved. But if she asks the children for their permission, how can they understand the question? This is a problem for the pedagogues or teachers who know the children, but it may be an even greater problem for a researcher who does not know the children very well.

This is an ethical matter. Is it ethically acceptable for a practitioner to tell anybody what a child has told her in an intimate situation? If the child feels it is okay, it can in special cases be a part of the child's construction of identity: in this case, if the practitioner, with the child's agreement, confirms in her discussion with others that something the child has told her is valuable to know, then she can make positive use of the child's expertise. The child can be regarded as an expert and identify himself or herself as one.

But if the child feels sorry and unhappy or just wants to be like all the other children in the group, she may feel unhappy if the pedagogue tells the rest of the group otherwise. For example, the child may have told the pedagogue that at home they do not celebrate Christmas and that she feels sorry about not receiving any Christmas gifts like the other children. In this case, she may have identified herself as an outsider in the group and the pedagogue will confirm this by telling the rest of the group. From this perspective, a practitioner might confirm both positive and negative constructions of a child's identity. On some occasions, it is impossible to be sure without asking the child concerned.

"Stories from practice"

In addition to the 'everyday conversation' between pedagogue or teacher and child, there is a method called *praksisfortelling* (this might be translated into English as 'stories from practice') that is used in *barnehager:* "The story is different from observation and conversation because the output is occasional, but decided by the storyteller's priority and perspective" (Birkeland, 1998, p 49; our translation).

It is obvious that, if the child is the storyteller, it is possible to focus on the perspective of the child with this method. But we have the same dilemma as mentioned with the 'everyday conversation'. How can we use this information in an ethical way? And how can we interpret a story told by a young child in a way that takes account of the storyteller's intention? And does a child always have an intention when she or he tells a story? But if we use the story as information about a child's point of view, we have to interpret it. Another question is whether it is possible for children to understand that adults in other settings will use their stories and for other purposes? And if it is not possible, is it then ethically correct to use it? This is a real dilemma.

Much more could have been said about this method. But we turn now to concentrate on the method with which we have mostly worked and about which we have most knowledge.

Qualitative interviews with children

We have found a qualitative research interview particularly good for focusing on the perspective of the child. From our experience, inviting children to a formal interview is one of several methods that can make a constructive contribution to the search for new knowledge. We think that children from approximately three years can be interviewed, but it all depends on the skills of the interviewer. Our definition of this method is:

> A semi-structured interview, or a conversation with a special purpose: where the questions are planned according to children's way of thinking. The questions are open and guiding. The interview guide and interpreting the answers are based on a certain theoretical frame of reference and understanding that the interviewer has to be conscious of.

In spite of some dilemmas arising from the use of this method, we believe it is possible to use it without compromising the child's integrity. But it depends on the interviewer's competence. We will try to expand on what competence is required and what dilemmas may arise when using this method.

In the interview setting, the role of the participants must be clear; for example, one of them is the interviewer and the other is the informant or respondent. If a child has a role as informant, it is important to clarify the interview setting: to tell the child where the interview is taking place and to explain what we expect the child to do in that setting and in that role. This information may help the child to enter the role.

Traditionally the informant role is a subservient role, and the relationship between an adult and a child is asymmetrical. This is a big dilemma in using interviews with children. But is it possible to change this? "The researcher is not the only person making decisions about position and role. Participants also make and remake these decisions as they come to know more about the situation and realise benefits and difficulties that were not initially apparent" (Graue and Walsh, 1998, p 76).

In spite of the asymmetrical relationship between interviewer and child, it might be possible to shape a relationship built on equal status and acceptance. But how? Perhaps the researcher's attitude and point of view is the most important element? "Understanding comes out of ways of seeing, knowing, and relating. What we can know is inherently linked to how and why we look, as well as how we interact with those around us" (Graue and Walsh, 1998, p 72).

In an interview setting there are at least two persons who must interact with each other and have an influence on each other. How they perceive each other is important. To make a good and mutually acceptable relationship, the interviewer has to prepare the child for the interview. Good preparations can include telling the child or showing her where the interview will take place and what the interviewer wants her to talk about. She has to be told that she is the expert and that she is the only person who knows the answers. There are no wrong answers in these kinds of interview. If the interviewer is going to use pictures, dolls or other objects in the interview setting, she also ought to tell the child in advance. The interviewer has to assure the child that her participation in the interview is voluntary. All information that can help the child to understand what her role might be is important, and on the basis of this information the child has to decide whether she wants to take part or not.

But we can still ask if it is possible for a young child to understand a new setting before she is placed in it. And being in it, is she then able to realise what is going on and in what she is participating? This is a demanding process for an adult, and even more so for a young child. The child will always carry her early experiences with her, which will influence her experiences of the interview situation. If she has bad feelings stemming from relating and talking with adults in other settings, the interviewer has to work harder to form a good relationship with the child, if one is possible at all. In such cases the interview may not be a good method.

Developing interviewer competence

As we have mentioned, interviewing children demands a special competence (Eide and Winger, 2003). This implies having a firm foundation in reflection about theory and practice and being open to changes and surprises. There is no recipe for a good interview. It always depends on the situation. Nevertheless, we can point to some factors that have emerged during our work that we have realised are important to consider before starting to interview children. Being aware of these factors can be useful for the interviewer, whether as a practitioner or researcher.

Ethical reflections

Interviewing children challenges us to ethical awareness, reflection and constant assessment. Before interviewing children we have to check the requirements for asking formal permission. If we as pedagogues or teachers use interviewing as part of our work in *barnehage* or school, we already have the parents' permission to ask their children about matters that concern everyday life in the institution. But if the interview is part of a research project, we must ask for special permission from the parents.

But we also have to ask permission from the children themselves. As we have mentioned, it is important to try to give children an understanding of what an interview is all about, and what their role is. And this is a dilemma. Is it possible for a young child to understand this? We have to tell her that she has the right to say whether or not she wants to take part in the interview, and that she is allowed to change her mind during the interview. In other words, she has the right to say 'stop' both before the interview has started and during the interview.

Brooker (2001, p 165) presents some ethical guidelines for treating children respectfully in interview situations:

- plan the questioning to be appropriate and acceptable for the respondents, bearing in mind their emotional and social maturity, and their family and cultural background;
- terminate any session that the researcher senses is causing distress of any kind to the respondent;
- conclude the session with debriefing, reassurance, thanks, praise or whatever is appropriate to sustain the self-esteem of the individual child.

The child has the right to know how the interviewer intends to use the information data. The interviewer has to try to tell this in a way that is possible for the child to understand. If the interviewer uses a tape recorder, she should also explain who will listen to the tape. Guaranteeing anonymity of the data is an ethical matter.

Interpreting the data in an ethical way is a challenge. What has the child really told the interviewer and how can the interviewer understand this? Is it possible for the adult interviewer to understand the child's world? How can we know that we have interpreted the data in a correct way? All these are dilemmas, too.

Good relationship with the child

As we have mentioned, any relationship between an adult and a child is asymmetrical and this might be a problem in the interview situation. The interviewer has the power and is responsible for the situation. This might influence the child in different ways such as trying to find out what sort of answers she thinks the interviewer wants, and in other ways trying to please the interviewer.

Children wish to please adults, and they try to do their best in answering our questions. We have found that some children have used fantasy and made up 'nonsense answers' in an effort to please us. When he was asked about rules in his *barnehage*, a six-year-old boy answered, after a quick glance through the window seeing how the wind was blowing in the trees, that "I really think it should be forbidden to shake trees. What if someone passed underneath and the whole tree fell on his head!".

We believe that it is important to try to change this situation in some way, both because we wish to collect 'good' data, but most of all in regard to the child's feelings. The child must be given the opportunity to construct her identity as a person of great value and as a person who can master the interview situation. These concerns focus on forming an 'appreciative' or mutually respectful relationship with the child (Bae, 2004).

We have analysed taped interviews from our research work, and have found some moments that might be characterised as an 'appreciative relationship'. From a pragmatic point of view, these moments can help the interviewer evaluate her own relationship with the child in the interview situation (Eide and Winger, 2003), and include:

- the interviewer and the child have their attention on the same matter
- they have good eye contact with each other
- they communicate the same content through words as well as through non-verbal communication
- they encourage each other to express their thoughts
- they take each other's perspectives.

Insight, interest and creativity

How else can the interviewer create a good and mutual relationship with children in the interview setting in such a way that it is possible for the children to give expression to their thoughts, and for the interviewer to give the children confirmation of their own identity? A good interviewer must show concern for the children and listen to what they have to tell, and at the same time have an understanding of what might interest them and with what they might be preoccupied. The premise is that the interviewer is willing, and able, to take the children's point of view.

Sometimes it will demand intuition and creativity to take the same focus as the child. In planning the interview it is useful to have insight and creativity both in making the interview guide and in deciding whether to use dolls, photos or other objects in the interview situation. It is important to make a good start, both to make the child comfortable and to make her interested. We have to plan how to start the interviews: but in the actual situation, it is necessary to improvise because no two meetings are quite alike. Likewise with the interview guide: you have to make it, but you also have to use it in a different way in each interview. To make good questions is a challenge.

In our experience open questions give the children a chance to tell if something works well. But we believe that children react differently to the same question, and accordingly, it is not easy to tell what a good question really is. The interviewer has to reflect on what is necessary for her to ask the child about, and what will be interesting for the child to tell about. The interviewer should never ask questions to which she already knows the answers. But if the children's thoughts, feelings and meanings are really the focus, it is not possible for the interviewer to know the answer ahead of time.

Purposeful and flexible

A competent interviewer is aware of the purpose of the interview, and manages both to listen carefully to the child and to take her perspective at the same time.

Sometimes this may be rather difficult. The interviewer may be occupied with taking the children's perspective, but then forget the purpose of the interview, or she is so determined to reach her objective that she does not listen carefully. To be sensitive to the child in the interview situation means to try to follow the child's thoughts, having in mind that 'chaining' is a common phenomenon in children's conversation, that is, children tend to make associations to what other people have just said and 'chain' their further comments to those words.

We have realised in most of our work that if the interviewer takes the child's point of view, the child will afterwards take the interviewer's point of view. In one interview a six-year-old boy started to talk about his loose tooth, but suddenly he stopped, looked at the interviewer and said: "but we should not talk about that now". If the child feels that the interviewer is interested in listening, this may also influence the child's competence to express her thoughts since "children's communicative competence improves when they are given control over the content and direction of the conversation" (quoted in Brooker, 2001, p 165).

But this may pose another dilemma. The interviewer is the responsible person in the interview setting, and there is a limit to how far the interviewer can let the child be in control without missing the point of the interview. Yet if the interviewer does not manage to create a mutual relationship, the child may become very silent. To establish a good dialogue is not easy, so when we manage to create one it is a most satisfying experience.

Knowledge about children and their previous experiences

The interviewer should have some knowledge about children and their development. She should know something in general about how a three-year-old is different from a six-year-old, for example with respect to verbal and communication skills, the ability to understand different kinds of questions, and concentration.

In addition to this general knowledge, the interviewer should also have some special knowledge about the particular children she is going to deal with. She ought to know something about the child's cultural background and something about the kindergarten or school she or he attends. In other words, she should know something about the child's everyday life, so as to be more able to understand what the child is telling her and to be able to ask relevant questions in the interview situation. She also should let the child get acquainted with her before they meet in the interview setting. We believe all this will have an influence on the child's behaviour in the interview.

To protect children's integrity, the interviewer must have specialised knowledge of children and be competent in using the method, as well as being aware of its limitations. She must also be a person of integrity herself, and be sensitive to the children's feelings.

Being a humble interpreter reflecting upon the children's statements

To invite children to an interview implies taking a responsible position towards them. The adult must also take care of the information that the children give her in a responsible way and use it in a way that is acceptable. Through our research we have considered the children's point of view as crucial, which demands not only our attentive listening to the children but also using their information in a conscientious and responsible way (Eide and Winger, 2003). But how can the interviewer be certain of having interpreted a child's statements in accordance with the child's intention? We believe the interviewer will never be one hundred per cent sure, but her duty is always to try to be honest and humble in her effort to interpret and to take the whole situation into consideration. Furthermore, how can the interviewer interpret the children's statements, meanings and convictions in such a way that they can recognise them as their own?

Taking into consideration the opinions of the children and being a spokesperson for the children

An interviewer has a duty to bring the information to whom it may concern; to other children, teachers, researchers, parents and perhaps the society at large. If the children therefore have taken their time, and willingly given the information, the interviewer ought to give something back (Tiller, 1991). The question is what information should she pass on to others? She has to use the information in an ethical way that safeguards the informants. If some of the information may be damaging to the children concerned, the interviewer must not pass it on. It may be a dilemma if the information is positive for some children, but may hurt others. In that case, what is the interviewer going to focus on, and in what way? We have no right answers; it depends on the content.

Learning by experiences, reflecting on them and constantly wishing to improve

To become a competent interviewer of children, you have to practise interviewing children and reflect on your own practice. This is an ongoing learning process. No interview is exactly like the previous one. Furthermore, we believe that it is essential to constantly want to improve. In this process, it is useful to collaborate with colleagues to help each other to continue the research process and develop one's own competence in this field. Two or three people who are working together will be able to make a better analysis and reflect more deeply in relation to both theory and practice.

Conclusion

We agree with Mayall (2000, p 32), who claims that how children live their childhood very much depends on "what adults want of childhood". It is paradoxical that the possibility of understanding children's perspectives is really very much about adult perspectives (Johansson, 2003). Our recognition, as adults, of children's position and our acknowledgement of childhood is a main determinant of whether children's point of view will be taken into account in the complex matter of reconstructing early childhood pedagogical theory and practice. For, as one of our five-year-old informants said: "'Grown-ups don't really know what it is like to be a child in day care. We children know. That's why I have to tell you about it'" (Eide and Winger, 2003, p 33).

It is important for us, as adults, to know something about how Hans realises his own situation and how Monica categorises the adults in her *barnehage*. Because as pedagogues, teachers and researchers we are obliged to take account of children's point of view. But moreover because it is our privilege to do so.

Notes

[1] *Førskoleklasser* were kindergarten classes for six-year-olds within the school system. They disappeared in 1997, when school entry age was reduced from seven to six years.

[2] *Barnehage* (kindergarten) is one of the main types of early childhood institution in Norway, providing for children from the first year of life to six years of age and usually open all day and all year round.

Further reading

Eide, B. and Winger, N. (2003) *Fra barns synsvinkel: Intervju med barn – metodiske og etiske refleksjoner (From children's point of view: Interviewing children – methodological and ethical reflections)*, Oslo: Cappelen Akademisk Forlag.

Graue, M.E. and Walsh, D.J. (1998) *Studying children in context*, London: Sage Publications.

MacNaughton, G. (ed) (2001) *Doing early childhood research: International perspectives on theory and practice*, Buckingham: Open University Press.

References

Alderson, P. (2000) 'The rights of young children', in H. Penn (ed) *Early childhood services*, Buckingham: Open University Press, pp 158-69.

Bae, B. (2004) *Dialoger mellom førskolelærer og barn – En beskrivende og fortolkende studie (Dialogues between preschool teachers and children – A descriptive and interpretative study)*, Oslo: Det Utdanningsvitenskapelige Fakultet, Universitetet i Oslo.

Berger, P. and Luckman, T. (1995) *Modernity, pluralism and the crisis of meaning: The orientation of modern man*, Güntersloh: Bertelsman Foundation Publishers.

Birkeland, L. (1998) *Pedagogiske erobringer (Pedagogical conquests)*, Oslo: Pedagogisk Forum.

Brooker, L. (2001) 'Interviewing children', in G. MacNaughton (ed) *Doing early childhood research: International perspectives on theory and practice*, Buckingham: Open University Press, pp 162-77.

Cannella, G. (1997) *Deconstructing early childhood education, social justice and revolution*, New York, NY: Peter Lang Publishing.

Christensen, A. and James, A. (eds) (2000) *Research with children: Perspectives and practices*, London: RoutledgeFalmer.

Coady, M. (2001) 'Ethics in early childhood research', in G. MacNaughton (ed) *Doing early childhood research: International perspectives on theory and practice*, Buckingham: Open University Press, pp 64-72.

Dahlberg, G., Moss, P. and Pence, A. (1999) *Beyond quality in early childhood education and care: Postmodern perspectives*, London: Falmer Press.

Eide, B. and Winger, N. (1994) *"Du gleder deg vel til å begynne på skolen!"* (*"You are looking forward to starting school? Aren't you?"*), Oslo: BVAs Skriftserie.

Eide, B. and Winger, N. (1995) '"Tja – vi får se". Barneperspektiv på pedagogisk tilbud til seksåringer og framtidig skoleliv' ('"Well, we'll see!" Children's perspectives on early schooling'), *Barn*, vol 1, pp 25-53.

Eide, B. and Winger, N. (1996) *Kompetente barn og kvalifiserte pedagoger i den nye småskolen* (*Competent children and qualified teachers in the 'new' primary school*), Oslo: Cappelen Akademisk Forlag.

Eide, B. and Winger, N. (1999) 'Barns deltakelse – en utfordring i den nye småskolen' ('Children's participation – a challenge in the "new" primary school'), in R. Engh (ed) *Skolen i mulighetenes årtusen* (*The school in the millennium of possibilities*), Oslo: Cappelen Akademisk Forlag, pp 98-126.

Eide, B. and Winger, N. (2003) *Fra barns synsvinkel: Intervju med barn – metodiske og etiske refleksjoner* (*From children's point of view: Interviewing children – methodological and ethical reflections*), Oslo: Cappelen Akademisk Forlag, p 135.

Fog, J. (1992) 'Den moralske grund i det kvalitative forskningsinterview' ('Moral issues in the qualitative research interview'), *Nordisk Psykologi*, vol 44, pp 221-9.

Fuglestad, O.G. (1998) 'Elevsamtalen – arbeid med læringsmiljø og skulekultur' ('Pupil conversation – working on learning environments and school culture'), in O.L. Fuglestad (ed) *Reformperspektiv på skole-og elevvurdering* (*Reform perspectives on school and pupil evaluation*), Bergen: Fagbokforlaget, pp 101-29.

Giddens, A. (1991) *Modernity and self-identity*, Cambridge: Polity Press.

Graue, M.E. and Walsh, D.J. (1998) *Studying children in context*, London: Sage Publications.

Grover, S. (2004) 'Why won't they listen to us? On giving power and voice to children participating in a social research', *Childhood*, vol 1, pp 81-93.

Halldèn, G. (2003) 'Barnperspektiv som ideologisk eller metodologiskt begrep' ('Children's perspectives as an ideological and methodological concept'), *Pedagogisk Forskning i Sverige*, vol 8, nos 1-2, pp 12-23.

Hockey, J. and James, A. (2003) *Social identities across the life course*, London: Palgrave Macmillan.

James, A., Jenks, C. and Prout, A. (1998) *Theorizing childhood*, Cambridge: Cambridge University Press.

Jenks, C. (2000) 'Zeitgeist research on childhood', in P. Christensen and A. James (eds) *Research with children: Perspectives and practices*, London: RoutledgeFalmer, pp 62-76.

Johansson, E. (2003) 'Att närma sig barns perspektiv. Forskares och pedagogers möten med barns perspektiv' ('To approach and understand a child's perspective as a teacher and a researcher'), *Pedagogisk Forskning i Sverige*, vol 8, nos 1-2, pp 42-57.

Jørgensen, P.S. (2000) 'Børn er deltagere- i deres eget liv' ('Children are participants – in their own lives'), in P.S. Jørgensen and J. Kampmann (eds) *Børn som informenter* (*Children as informants*), Copenhagen: Børnerådet, pp 9-21.

Katz, L. (1993) 'Multiple perspectives on the quality of early childhood programmes', *European Early Childhood Research Journal*, vol 1, no 1, pp 5-9.

Kjørholt, A.T. (2001) 'The participating child: a vital pillar in this century', *Nordisk Pedagogik*, vol 21, pp 65-81.

Landager, S. (1999) 'Skolen ved en skillevei. Informasjonsteknologiens udfordringer' ('The school at a crossroad. The challenge of information technology'), in R. Engh (ed) *Skolen i mulighetenes årtusen* (*The school in the millennium of possibilities*), Oslo: Cappelen Akademisk Forlag, pp 70-83.

Mayall, B. (2000) 'The sociology of childhood: children's autonomy and participation rights', in A.B. Smith, M. Gollop, K. Marshall and K. Nairn (eds) *Advocating for children: International perspectives on children's rights*, Dunedin: Children's Issues Centre, University of Otago Press, pp 126-40.

Nilsen, R.D. (2000) *Livet i barnehagen. En etnografisk studie av sosialiseringsprosessen* (*Everyday life in day care centre. An ethnographic study of the socialisation process*), Trondheim: NTNU, Dr Polit Avhandling.

Norwegian Ministry for Children and Family Affairs (1995) *Rammeplan for barnehagan* (*Framework plan for day care institutions*).

Norwegian Ministry of Education, Research and Church Affairs (1996) *Læreplanverket for den 10-årige grunnskolen* (*The curriculum for the 10-year compulsory school*).

Qvortrup, J. (2000) 'Macroanalyses on childhood', in P. Christensen and A. James (eds) *Research with children: Perspectives and practices*, London: RoutledgeFalmer, pp 77-95.

Roberts, H. (2000) 'Listening to children and hearing them', in P. Christensen and A. James (eds) *Research with children: Perspectives and practices*, London: RoutledgeFalmer, pp 225-40.

Sjøbakken, O.J. (2004) 'Plansamtalen som anerkjennende dialog' ('Conversation on planing as a appreciative dialogue'), in P. Arneberg, J.H. Kjerre and B. Overland (eds) *Samtalen i skolen* (*Conversation in school*), Oslo: Damm Forlag, pp 136-51.

Skoglund, R.I. (1998) 'Barn som aktive informanter' ('Children as active informants'), *Barn*, vol 3, pp 78-97.

Tiller, P.O. (1991) 'Forskningens gjenstand som objekt. Om etikk, validitet og verdivalg' ('The content of research as an object. About ethics, validity and choice of value'), *Barn*, no 4, pp 7-19.

United Nations Convention on the Rights of the Child (1989) *FN's konvensjon om barns rettigheter av 20 nov*, Oslo: Statens Forvaltningstjeneste ODIN.

Viruru, R. (2001) 'Colonized through language: the case of early childhood education', *Contemporary Issues in Early Childhood*, vol 2, no 1, pp 31-47.

SIX

Channels for listening to young children and parents

Valerie Driscoll and Caron Rudge

Early childhood services have been a priority for public policy in England since 1997, when a new Labour government was elected. A recent development has been Children's Centres. This is a national initiative that brings together education and care, outreach, health and family support: "The purpose of Children's Centres is to provide the most convenient access to a range of services for families" (Sure Start, 2004, p 1). First announced in 2002, the government is now committed to providing 3,500 Children's Centres by 2010.

Fortune Park was granted Children's Centre status in 2003. It meets the needs of young children and their families in Islington, an inner-city area of London. The Centre is attended by 85 children, 60 of whom are over three years of age and six who have complex special needs. The staff team is made up of people with varying experience and qualifications, including qualified teachers with early years specialisms, under-fives education workers (sometimes called nursery nurses or officers in other settings) with two years' formal training and a myriad of experience, and support staff who may be unqualified with varying degrees of experience. Staff at all levels are encouraged and supported by both management and borough-wide initiatives to embark on further training.

Caron Rudge has worked as the Head of Fortune Park since it opened in 1995 and Valerie Driscoll is a teacher there, but the chapter also draws on the ideas and views of a number of other people who are involved with this Children's Centre. This chapter is about 'profile books', an approach to listening that involves children and families and has been used at Fortune Park for a number of years.

At Fortune Park we use the term 'profile book' to mean a blank book that becomes a co-constructed representation of a child: his/her life, interests, learning and development. (For the rest of this chapter when referring to an individual child we will use 'he' and 'his' to mean he/she and his/her respectively; for practitioners we will use 'she' and 'her'.) The participants in this co-construction are the child, the family, the key worker and anyone who shares the profile book with the child.

The term 'profile book' has come to have different meanings in different contexts in the UK. For example, teachers are currently completing a 'Foundation Stage profile' for each child at the end of his first year of compulsory schooling (around the age of six years in the UK), which is a formal assessment document. An 'observation profile' is a term used in many educational establishments to describe a record of assessment, while profile books used in other settings may take forms that differ from ours, for example, they may only include samples of children's work in order to show progression in learning.

At Fortune Park every aspect of a child's life is represented in the profile book. Learning that takes place at home or at nursery is represented, as well as what a child has to say about it. The child's family, special people, pets, and so on will all be included. If the child goes on holiday, or to hospital, these experiences will be illustrated in the profile book. In this way the profile book aims to portray what Alison Clark refers to in Chapter Three as "lives lived rather than knowledge gained or care received" (see page 31, this book).

There are several means of representation used to support and show the child's experience. These include photography, drawing and model making (shown in photographs or children's drawing), as well as written and spoken language. All representations are annotated using the child's words, where possible. All of the children's words and utterances are transcribed exactly. This is an important feature of profile books as over time it will come to show the child's actual language development.

Visual representation such as photography is used a great deal. There are a number of reasons for this. First, it allows us to represent children's learning and experience in a way that does not intrude on the play. Second, the camera acts as an observation tool for the adult, allowing him or her to collect evidence of a child's learning, which in turn aids reflection for the adult. Third, photography allows us to show the learning of a child who may not be accessing activities such as writing, drawing or painting. The child may be very interested in role play, construction or water play, for example, and using photography ensures that we can also demonstrate this learning. Finally, the visual nature of profile books supports the children in gaining ownership in their learning. In the profile book the child has cues for remembering, cues for thinking and cues for discussion.

Profile books have also become a tool for assessing young children's learning. We use them in conjunction with an observation diary to support our reflections on a child's learning. As a team we then ensure that the child's learning needs are discussed in curriculum planning meetings. Profile books are also used to support children as they reflect on their own learning. Providing children with such opportunities for self-reflection is a theme running through this book, for example in Chapters Two, Three and Eight.

Every child at Fortune Park has at least one profile book and some children are on their sixth book! We use profile books to listen to children primarily. However, it has become a system through which others are developing a voice too, for example, the child's family as well as the key worker (explained in the next section). For us at Fortune Park, profile books have become part of the life of the centre as well as part of the child's life. A profile book is a shared resource used by children, parents and staff and it can serve a number of purposes. It can support the settling-in process, for example, and develop knowledge and understanding of the early years curriculum.

There are three strands that are brought together by the profile book at Fortune Park. These are the child, the centre and the family. The profile book provides a means through which all three can to be listened to. For the purposes of this chapter, we will delve more deeply into the three strands separately and explore why and how the profile book supports the needs of all three.

Listening to the child

From the moment a child is offered a place at Fortune Park, a number of systems are put in place to ensure that the transition from home to the centre goes as smoothly as possible. For example, all children are assigned a key worker who will act as a link person for the child and the family. A key worker system affords children the opportunity to develop a close relationship with one and sometimes two particular people within the centre. They will go on to develop relationships with other adults but the key worker remains special for them. All children will also be visited at home before they start at Fortune Park. This is when the profile book is begun. While visiting the family, the key worker will take photographs of the child, members of the family, and the child's favourite objects such as toys. The key worker will gather information about the child as well as share information about the centre.

On the child's first day his key worker greets him; he is shown his profile book with the photos taken at his home. This allows the child and the key worker to revisit the shared experience of the home visit. This is a very important part of the transition from home to centre. Some children, even when they are old enough to move on to school, still like to visit these pages in their profile book and enjoy sharing the pictures of "when you came to my house".

Many children use the profile book as a transitional object between home and centre. The pages that have pictures of their parents and family members are very important to them. Some children will carry their profile book around for a couple of weeks, while they are settling in to the environment. As profile books focus attention onto the child and his life as he lives it, they will also show the child's learning; that is, knowledge, skills, feelings and dispositions. These aspects of a child's learning are inherent in his experience and his profile book. For every child, the profile book comes to represent a meaningful connection between the different strands of his experience.

The pages of the profile book always represent what a child can do, thereby supporting the child's self-esteem and self-confidence. The child is then able to share his achievements with others, an important process as "the young child develops confidence through becoming aware of herself as a separate and worthwhile person, as well as having a realistic view of what she can achieve"

Photograph 6.1: Nathan is absorbed in looking at his profile book

(Dowling, 1999, p 14). In the profile book, the child has a visual, practical point of reference for his development. As he interacts with others, peers, adults and his family, he is reflecting on and consolidating his learning.

The profile books become very special for the children. They often want to share them and even spend time hugging them. Very young children (under two years) have been observed offering a distressed child his profile book for comfort. Through the profile book the children learn that they can have a voice. They also learn that they have another mode of communication, the shared language of the profile book.

In Account One we see the example of Lulu (at age two years, 10 months). Her key worker realised that for a long time the focus of Lulu's attention, as well as her parents', was the imminent birth of her baby brother. Lulu's profile book represented this. There were photos of Lulu's mother at various stages of her pregnancy and photos of Lulu role playing at being pregnant. Lulu was supported in this by her key worker who, through her intimate knowledge of Lulu, was able to trust that for a time this learning had to take precedence.

(In keeping with our ethos of listening, all four accounts in this chapter are quoted exactly from the words or writings of the people involved.)

Account One: key worker Sandy writing about Lulu

When Lulu came into toddlers from babies she was just two. Both mum, Catherine, and Lulu were very anxious and I knew instinctively they would need help, time and support. Catherine began to be able to speak to me about her anxieties and how she wondered if Lulu was too young for nursery, as it was really stressing her out, feeling like she was dragging Lulu somewhere she really didn't want to be. The settling-in process was slow, enabling both Catherine and Lulu to feel secure. This also helped Catherine to see how we work, what activities were happening and how adults are with children. It also helped us to get to know each other and for Catherine to trust that Lulu would be happy when she was not there. I completely understood, listened and the three-way partnership began.

Catherine began to spend time away from Lulu at nursery and Lulu stayed close to me. She brought things from home, which supported her security and confidence. The profile book was crucial in many, many ways. It showed Catherine what Lulu was doing, playing and exploring, during the time she was not with Lulu. Her most precious gift, it showed Lulu being happy, being with her peers, the routine of the day and whom she interacted with. Catherine took the profile book home regularly and Lulu was able to share her day with her mummy. Catherine could have an in-depth conversation about what Lulu was doing, most importantly seeing that she was happy.

Catherine contributed to the profile book and attended a workshop. Lulu's profile book was then filled with what Lulu and her family did together at the weekends etc ... and one of Lulu's favourite interests glitter, and lots more, in fact anything Lulu was interested in. I could then talk to Lulu about her time with her family. Lulu confidently talked about the photos, pictures, writing in her book with Catherine, myself and other trusted adults supporting Lulu's growing confidence, security, happiness and liking of coming to nursery.

Lulu settled and became secure with other key adults, forming relationships and becoming increasingly independent. Catherine began to feel at ease. The profile book and our relationship was the key in Lulu's early journey of learning which I truly feel holds all children at Fortune Park Children's Centre in good stead for the rest of their school life.

When Catherine was pregnant Lulu and I would spend time talking about it, commenting on mummy's tummy getting bigger and obviously the scan pictures of the baby went in the book! We didn't need to pluck ideas out of the air because the visual clues were there in Lulu's profile book; pictures of Catherine and her growing tummy and Lulu with her. When the birth was approaching Catherine put photos of the adults who were going to be looking after Lulu while Catherine was in hospital. Lulu was able to talk about and understand what was going to happen while Catherine was having the baby. Catherine also drew pictures of herself on a bed with Lulu's daddy hugging her for Lulu's profile book. She did this to help Lulu understand that when her mum was in the hospital she would be on a bed and Lulu's daddy would be with her. I was able to share all of this with Lulu before the birth. Between her family, Lulu and me as her key worker, Lulu gained an understanding of what the birth would involve. She is now a big sister and has moved to the over three's environment. She has a new key worker and her profile book continues to support her security. The profile book has helped Catherine to understand what Lulu is doing, her growing friendships and her happiness. And I still get to share in Lulu's profile book with her from time to time!

The nature of profile books invites interaction and participation. They demand to be looked at and shared. The child can initiate an interaction with a peer or an adult through the sharing of his profile book. The child is in charge of making himself heard, when *he* wants to be heard. He is able to stop any time, ask others to join in if he chooses and decide what is of importance today because he is the one controlling the interaction. This is his area of expertise – this is his life. In this way the child is supported in gaining ownership over his experiences and learning. Knowledge is shared through profile books and children are involved in sharing information about their learning.

The fact that each child's home life is represented in the profile book allows others, friends and key workers, into the real lived and living culture of the child's life. The family comes to know that we are genuinely interested in the culture of their home. We want to know because it is intrinsically linked to the child's learning and development. They discover that when we ask them about their religion or home language, for example, we really want to know; the profile book makes this obvious. In this way the child's culture is made accessible for him to share with his friends and others. A child cannot wait to share a significant event such as a family wedding, for example, with his friends. Others are interested in turn because such events are brought alive for them through the representations in the profile book.

In using profile books children also have a point of reference for their developmental history: "that was how I used to draw when I was three"; "when I was small, I couldn't ride a bike properly"; or "that coat doesn't fit me anymore, I'm bigger now". They have meaningful evidence that they are learners involved in a process. It helps them to develop a sense of time through their own personal history.

Developing the use of the profile book for the child is a learning process in itself. It may take time for a child to know that he will be listened to and for some children this may take a long time. His key worker, who is developing a close relationship with him, supports the child. Younger children (that is, from six months to two years) use their profile books in a different way to the older children. For the younger children the profile books are more intrinsically linked to their emotional being. It is a more expressive representation of how they feel. Learning and development in other areas are represented but their books support them as they look out at the world and as the world looks in. Many of these younger children, for example, will carry their profile books around with them. Their profile books assist them to express their emotions; if they want their mothers, they will point to the picture of mummy in the profile book. As Account Two shows, a profile book can also help young children cope with unpleasant experiences.

Account Two: a parent writes about Toby

From a young age my son Toby had to receive medication four times a day. This had always caused great problems, as Toby hated taking this. He would scream and cry and refuse. At the nursery Toby's key worker decided that it would be good to work through this with Toby. He was, at the time, only one-and-a-half years old. Photos were taken of the whole process starting with the medicines, then of the key worker getting them ready, then of Toby crying having his medication. This was then put into his profile book. This was to be a big breakthrough for Toby, as we would talk through this daily with him. The wording of the pictures in the profile book was short and to the point, for example, "Toby does not like having his medicine", "Toby is crying", "He is sad".

I would bring the book home and Toby would share it with his family and friends at home. He then took responsibility for it and it became very important to him and gave him a sense of turning the incident of the medication around and making him feel very proud. He would share this with the rest of his peers at nursery. Soon with great pride we could add the final picture to the medicine incident and that was Toby giving himself the actual medicine, smiling.

The profile book worked because the children take such pride and responsibility in their books. They are always keen and eager to share it with the other children and it allows them to express how they felt or feel. Pictures were taken of the children playing with the syringes in water and these were always included in the profile book.

Toby is now three-and-a-half years old and is very confident in giving himself his medication with no fuss at all. He frequently looks at his old profile books and will talk about how he never liked his medication and how he cried. He then loves the praise we give him when we tell him how brave he is and what a big boy he is now. Toby now has to go into hospital frequently to have regular blood tests so the cycle is about to start again and we are going to use the same process with the photos in the profile book.

> The profile book is so treasured by both the children and parents (and staff). [It] enables communication from such a young age and allows the child to express themselves. It also allows interaction between home and nursery and gives the child the ability to tell others what he has done at home. They will share stories and are very interested in each other's books.

The children in the over-three's section of the centre use their books differently. Their profile books become representations of their thinking. Again, as with children under three, emotions play a large part in this learning. The older child's thought processes, however, as well as the learning taking place, become more explicit as the child develops the ability to express his ideas and reflections on learning.

In order to ensure that *all* children are heard, we often have to be creative about how we listen. For some children, for example, the profile book may become more tactile, as a means to allow the child to interact with it. The profile book also helps a child to have increased status within his peer group. He is able to show his friends what he can do as well as help others to understand the ordinary things about his life. For example, a child who has a standing frame will have photographs demonstrating how he uses it. This will be given as much importance in the profile book as a child who builds a complicated model.

In our interactions with all children it is necessary to listen carefully to what the child is saying and to know how the child communicates. This is all made easier because of the close relationship between the key worker and the child: when you know a child very well, you can be a better listener to his many languages. A mother or main carer, for example, will understand what her baby wants or needs by the baby's cry. A key worker who knows a child very well is able to quickly relate to a child's individual nuances. This is highlighted by Goldschmied and Jackson (1994, p 37), who say that young children, particularly those "who do not have language to express what they are experiencing, need to have special relationships and they need to have them in a very immediate and concrete way". Gerhardt (2004) also highlights the importance of these early interactions, through their actual physiological effects on the brain of a very young child.

Listening at the heart of the centre

We now come to the second strand supported by profile books at Fortune Park. We decided to refer to the centre as a whole here, because the ethos or way of working at Fortune Park is not simply down to the individual practitioner. (While a 'key worker' is usually either a teacher or an education worker, we use the term 'practitioner' to refer to all adults coming into contact with the children.) Many influences, ranging from how the centre's leadership supports practitioners to policies and curriculum, underlie day-to-day interactions with children. That is to say, how well we listen to children is not just a result of personal attributes or intuitions. Listening is greatly influenced by the environment and the many different factors that make up the environment:

> In recent times we have seen the gradual development of a set of ideas about management and leadership that focus on the human side of work....While management is required to keep the centre running efficiently, leadership is concerned with getting the best that is possible. Leadership is an engagement with hearts and minds in the interests of the children and their families. (Whittaker, 2001, pp 20-5)

How we listen, as well as what we have understood from what we have heard, is a question not only of our individual value systems but also of the ethos of the centre in which we work.

At Fortune Park we work hard to maintain a culture of openness and listening. Our ethos – that is, the fundamental values underpinning our work – is one that is caring, expressive, creative and committed to ongoing learning. It also demands trust, trust that is reciprocal between child and adult, adult and management, centre and family. Sometimes in the process of building this trust individuals allow themselves to be vulnerable. This may be a painful process for some but may also become a cathartic experience. This is illustrated by Paley (1986, p 123), who, when reflecting on her early experiences as a teacher, said she came to believe that "real change comes about only through the painful recognition of one's own vulnerability". We embrace all the challenge that this brings to Fortune Park because we know that real development and growth happens when people are allowed to take risks.

Incorporating profile books into our provision has provided evidence of our development as listeners within the centre. When the concept of profile books was first introduced, for example, there were mixed reactions among staff. It had been the experience of many practitioners who were not teachers that, in previous settings where they had worked, their opinions about children were rarely sought. They would write observations but not reports, and would gather information about a child but a colleague who was a teacher would share that information with the parents. Yet they had felt that they were the ones who actually got to know the children really well. It had also been the experience of practitioners who were teachers that they did not get the opportunity to know the children well. This frustrated them and they felt constrained by the curriculum and the need to assess learning in narrow, academic terms.

This difference in experience became particularly evident when *all* practitioners began using profile books with children at Fortune Park. The teachers at first viewed them as 'extra work' on top of their already full timetables. Other staff were very excited about the prospect of having a voice and being able to share their knowledge of children for whom they were key workers. All of the

Photograph 6.2: George dictates what his key worker should write in his profile book

practitioners, however, very quickly realised that listening to the child, as well as feeling listened to themselves, was a great asset.

The management team worked hard to harness this enthusiasm. They had to trust that whatever the stage of development of the individual practitioner, the relationship she had with the child and his family was the important factor. For example, there were some practitioners who were uncomfortable about paperwork. It was important that all adults working with the children felt confident enough to represent their knowledge and feelings about their key children through the profile books. If it had been decided at that point that only certain adults could express themselves in the profile books, using conventional English that is spelled accurately and is grammatically correct, then we might have denied potential role models for our children. We want all adults who are involved in the child's life at Fortune Park to be enabled to express themselves freely, as is their right. We do not want practitioners, children or their parents to feel alienated within our educational setting, as this would be preventing a 'listening' culture.

Practitioners were seeking a means to be heard, a means to share their knowledge and their expertise, while at the same time they had to document the teaching and learning process. Profile books offered a means to do both with the child as the focus, through the child being listened to. Rinaldi says in Chapter Two that "a listening context [is one] … where individuals feel legitimated to represent their theories and offer their own interpretations of a particular question" (see page 21, this book). The children feel this and the practitioner needs to feel it also.

At Fortune Park there are many systems in place that support listening for all, including a counsellor who works with staff and parents. We felt that it was important to acknowledge this in order to place profile books in the context of Fortune Park that is in a "context of listening". The many structures that support listening are complex and take a lot of effort to maintain. They are valued as a very important part of our practice. For example, every key worker will attend three meetings a week: a whole staff meeting, a team meeting, and a key worker meeting. Children are always on the agenda of each of these meetings. The key worker meeting concentrates only on children, and individuals are discussed in detail in relation to their lives, learning and development. Each child is reviewed on a regular basis to ensure a thorough approach.

Profile books are used in all meetings and underpin everything being discussed. In this way the profile book can also support other professionals, enabling them to access a broader picture of the child and to become familiar with the child's strengths and areas for development in a meaningful way. For example, social workers sometimes ask us to help them put the child in the context of his family. Through the profile book we are able to show the child's life story. (Visitors and professionals have access to profile books at the discretion of the key worker and with permission from the child. Parents are made aware that profile books are used for many purposes. They sign a permission slip to support this. If a parent were uncomfortable with this, we would, of course, respect their wishes.)

Profile books also encourage adults to listen in a way that allows the child to direct the discussion. This involves trust on the part of the adult, who will allow the child to take a lead in the interaction and in the sharing of his feelings, experiences and ideas through the profile book. The profile book will allow the child's thoughts and concerns to become explicit, whatever those thoughts or concerns are. It is the job of key workers to listen to and act on what they hear. Developing the ability to do this is a learning process for adults.

A good example of this was when profile books were introduced at Fortune Park. At first the profile books were kept on high shelves out of children's reach, with the key worker deciding when a child could have his book. Because they were listening to the children, the adults came to realise that they needed to get them down to allow the children access to what was essentially *their* profile books. Now not a day goes by without profile books being a central part of the experience, for even our youngest children. Their profile books are dog-eared and torn but they are also loved and respected by all the children.

The importance of young children's emotional well being is another feature of the ethos of Fortune Park. If a child is sad at separation, for example, we will use the profile book to acknowledge that emotional experience. We might put photographs of the parent or a photograph of the parent cuddling the child in the child's profile book. We will show the child that he can access these photographs any time he wants. The child can spend time looking at the photograph if that is what he needs to do. We would not try to bypass that need or ignore it.

We believe that it is inappropriate to expect a child to put away his emotions until a more convenient time. We would not try to distract a child who is sad or

Photograph 6.3: Friends 'being together' looking at their profile books

try to make him laugh. We know from the work of many theorists and researchers, such as Bowlby (1953), Ainsworth et al (1974) and Goldschmied and Jackson (1994), that sadness and genuine feelings of loss at separation from the main carer are natural and appropriate. Feeling sad is as much a part of healthy life as feeling happy. This is not to say that we encourage children to go around crying and pining over photographs of their mothers, but in the same way as we would not try to stop or distract a child who is feeling happy, we will not do this for a child who is feeling sad. The profile book helps us to listen to that sadness and helps a child to deal with it in an appropriate way.

In our centre there is also open acknowledgement of adults' emotional investment in their work with young children, since "it is difficult to sustain close and responsive relationships with young children without an organisational culture that expects and supports a process of reflection on the emotional dimension of practice" (Elfer et al, 2002, p 30). We view it as worthwhile to give over time to dealing with the many issues that often arise in this complex work. We acknowledge that adults involved closely with families often need support in dealing with the emotion this brings. All discussions are welcomed as opportunities to develop. In turn, practitioners are enabled to develop rich, meaningful and rewarding relationships within their work.

Being fully inclusive of children with special educational needs is a significant part of the culture of Fortune Park. Currently we have children on the autistic spectrum, children with physical disabilities, children with language delay and disorder, children with challenging behaviours and children with visual impairment. These children are fully included in the everyday life of the centre. This means that they have a key worker and belong to a key group; they are enabled to develop friendships with peers. They are planned for through their Individual Action Plan, which relates specifically to their needs. As for every child, we also plan activities within our curriculum, taking into account their interests and development. Therapies and specific strategies are part of the daily routine; indeed, a particular exercise may become the focus of a group activity that enhances learning for all. This type of fully inclusive provision is becoming more common across Britain. The English Department for Education and Skills' *Special educational needs code of practice* (DfES, 2001) strongly recommends that, where possible, children with special education needs be included in all educational settings.

We have been using profile books at Fortune Park for nine years. They grew organically from the baby room. The children who came up through the centre brought their books with them. Gradually they spread through the centre. How we use them has been a learning process for everyone involved. Fortune Park works on the principle that everyone is a learner. For this reason we do not feel that how we currently use profile books is the definitive way of using them. They have evolved and continue to evolve through continuous reflection on our practice and structures.

We have also been fortunate to get feedback from teachers at local primary schools. They have told us that a profile book is easier to read and is more meaningful than the written reports we have sent about children in the past. As a result of this feedback, we have developed a system that takes the essential elements of the profile book – photographs, children's words and parents' voices – to create a synopsis of a child's development. The child then has ownership of this practical representation of his knowledge and experience. This format is accessible to children and their new teachers as well as their new friends.

In the future we would like to develop, in conjunction with schools, the continuing use of profile books through the early years of compulsory schooling. We are looking to do this as a result not only of the feedback we have been getting from teachers, but also from children who have moved to school and their parents. They are all indicating that they can see benefits in using profile books in these environments. This is highlighted in Account Three, where Hannah, now at school, says that schoolteachers should know that "you don't just leave them [profile books] so no one can see them, you have to leave them out in a place that you can actually see them".

Account Three: Valerie Driscoll interviews Hannah

Hannah left Fortune Park two years ago (aged four-and-a-half years) to move on to school. She is now just over six-and-a-half and in Year 2. I was Hannah's key worker while she attended Fortune Park. I interviewed Hannah at her home.

What do you think of profile books?

"I love them. Like when I have a really annoying picture of Molly [Hannah's older sister] I love showing them to her like the really embarrassing one of her holding up her pretend rabbit. I'll show you the picture ... I think they're very good fun."

Why?

"I like showing a picture of me when I'm really small to Molly, 'You're so cute!' [says Molly]. I say, 'I look funny'."

When do you read them?

"I would say when I can find them. Daddy reads them to me in the living room."

We then started looking at Hannah's profile book together. Hannah looked at a photo of herself making a model of a dog out of Meccano [a construction toy] at nursery.

"I always liked making that dog. It was always too hard for me but I bet it's going to be really easy for me now if I try to do it again ... I love them [profile books] because they always show what you were doing when you're little. If you're thinking, 'Oh God, what was I doing back then' you can just look in your profile book and see....

I can remember that dress a lot...."

"Did you [Valerie] take all the photos in it?"

Yes I think I did, most of them anyway.

"I know one you didn't do!"

She flicked the profile book open on a page that showed a picture of her and Hannah hugging.

"You definitely didn't take that one! I loved playing with the animals there [at nursery]."

Hannah was able to read all the written text in her profile book and I congratulated her about this.

"I couldn't read a word when I was in nursery only 'it', 'is', 'the', and things like that. Now I think I could read a lot especially more than I could when I was in nursery."

She read what she had said about the climbing frame.

"I called it a 'climbing thing'. I should have called it a climbing frame but I didn't know what it was called then."

What do you think people should know about profile books?

"They're just pictures of you when you were small. If you forget which school you went to, you can look at the pictures and remember. I think they should know about that it's not just you; it can be your friends in it too. If you're sticking in a picture with your mum or your dad, you don't just cut the friends out and the nans [grandmothers] and the people, and leave just you in.... It's nice not to have a hard book but to have a floppy book 'cause if you're reading in bed you don't want a corner stuck in your eye."

I told Hannah that Reception teachers at her primary school have been asking us about profile books. I asked her what she thought I should tell them.

"You should tell them they're really fun to look at in your class. It's not just the children who are in there; it can be all sorts of people. I think you should tell them, 'You don't just leave them so no one can see them. You have to leave them out in a place that you can actually see them'. And when they [the children] are in Year 1 you don't just say, 'Sorry children, I can't find the profile book, so you'll just have to wait for a while'. If you find them when they're in Year 2, when you give them out they [the children] would be just like 'but the year is over now'. It would be pointless because then they'd be in Year 2 and they get last year's one!"

"They should know on the first profile book you have to write the date and whose profile book it is and stuff and then they should know that there can't be just one profile book. As they get into different years they get more and more and more profile books. And even if you're doing a nursery one they don't just have one, they can have six or something like that, they can have ten!"

Listening to the family

At Fortune Park we have learned that listening does not stop at the child in the centre. There are often a great number of people, children and adults, who are involved in each child's life. This is reason enough to try to ensure that we are paying attention to everyone. However, as we discovered, in creating a responsive environment there are a number of benefits to be had for everyone involved.

Children come to Fortune Park with a myriad of experience and expertise that they have developed with their parents. It is our job to show parents that we value this. When a child starts at Fortune Park, his parents are embarking on a journey with us, a journey that will be documented in their child's profile book. Right from the very start, the initial home visit, we have to give parents a very clear message – we trust you, you can trust us and we can both trust your child.

Initially the profile book helps the child and his family to familiarise themselves with the key worker and the environment. As it supports the settling in process, the profile book opens up Fortune Park for the family. Parents are offered the opportunity to attend workshops run by key workers where they will learn more about how we use profile books as well as how we deliver our curriculum. This work has enabled some parents to feel very confident both in their interactions with staff and their interactions with their children, which one parent's account highlights (see Account Four).

Photograph 6.4: Tainan sharing his profile book with his mother

Account Four: Jahziah's mother writes about profile books

By the time our son began nursery, I was already, to my belief, overly involved in his care. Our son has cerebral palsy and so to enable him to eventually lead a somewhat independent life, I 'needed' (this being the operative word), to become a much more involved being than just the natural role of 'mum'. In hindsight this involvement was aimed more at his medical self, than his personal well being which is just as important.

Anyway, as I soon discovered what was normal practice at the nursery, I was soon invited to many parent workshops that were held every week. Still a newcomer and still getting used to the very 'child led' atmosphere, my confidence stayed away as my mind was firm with its allegiance to my previous upbringing of my son. I mean, what could 'they' teach me; I knew what was best for him. Then one day, it all changed and I found myself at a 'profile book' workshop. Again, with hindsight, I was probably more suckered into attending as relations got better.

These were books that were born of the nursery that gave visual evidence about your child and their experiences with the world, while at nursery. Great, I thought. By that time I still had not realised the benefit to my son, and myself, what taking a part in his time at nursery would bring. I did not really believe I had a role to play here. My son had been given a profile book earlier and had been started by his key worker, who had displayed his introduction into this new environment. I did not have any idea what to put inside. It was totally lost on me, as I stared consciously at the blank pages. A staff member took the workshop, so as she talked; my oblivious mind was becoming overtaken with all these ideas being planted by her excited tone. I could do this I began telling myself. My son had plenty of achievements that could illustrate his profile book, his fight for survival for one, so I placed the picture taken when he was in a coma. This was not a bad thing; this was my son's life. Then off I went, like a whirlwind, gathering all his work, taking plenty of pictures and charting his very own development, all in aid of 'the profile book'.

This enabled the partnership to develop and grow between the nursery and myself and we had a common goal in mind – my son. I could now get a sense of what was happening in my son's life when I was not around him and vice versa the nursery. To date we are now on the sixth edition and still going strong with the many different and fabulous ways to make the profile book more appealing. I have another child at another Islington school and have taken to being a parent governor and will now take the profile book to this school. I believe so much in this simple but worthwhile project and feel others should enjoy the beauty that having your own pictorial autobiography can bring to your life.

Gradually, as parents and carers become more comfortable with us, they begin to share insights about their child's learning at home. They learn to use the profile book to do this. Some parents feel self-conscious about writing or drawing. They quickly realise that we are not concerned with 'correct' English and they feel more confident about writing and sharing valuable information with us. They learn that we are not judging them and in turn we have found they do not judge us: in the nine years that we have been using profile books in this way, we have never had a complaint from a parent about a grammatical or a spelling error. Because we are all focusing on something the parents love, their child, this helps to develop the trust and supports the relationship between the family and the centre.

The profile book becomes integral to the relationship between home and school. Parents come to love their child's profile book. We have found that photographs of the child involved in various activities helps to draw the parents in and opens up the life of the nursery to them. They are hungry for knowledge and information about their child and what their child does when he is away from them. In the profile book, the child's family has a window into their child's concerns and experiences at nursery. The visual nature of the profile book allows parents to support their child's learning as they talk with him about his experiences. Annotating photographs of their child involved in activities provides links to curriculum areas. As a result, parents are supported in their understanding of how we deliver our curriculum. It becomes very meaningful for them because they are learning about it through their child's experiences. We get to share what we think is valuable experience for the child, and why, with the child's family.

We have found that the profile book also supports parents who may have concerns about certain aspects of the provision. Because they value the book so much and it helps them to understand what we do, the profile book can explain issues such as children's clothes getting dirty at nursery. Parents come to understand the importance of valuable experiences such as using paint because they see how interested their child is in it. Through the profile book, parents also come to appreciate the complicated process of something like learning to write. They are presented with evidence that their child is involved in a process from his first attempts at mark making to the forming of letters in his name and beyond.

In sharing our provision with families, we try to ensure that we do not underestimate or judge parents. We also do not want to patronise them. As a relationship develops between the family and the centre, the interactions become more meaningful and natural. Dahlberg et al (1999, p 77) support this:

> ... working with parents does not mean pedagogues giving to parents uncontextualised and unproblematised information about what they (the pedagogues) are doing, nor 'educating' parents in 'good' practice by transmitting a simplified version of a technology of child development and child rearing. Rather it means both parents and pedagogues (and others) entering into a reflective and analytic relationship involving deepening understanding and the possibility of making judgments about the pedagogical work, and in which pedagogical documentation plays an important part.

Using profile books to document and support our relationship with parents has helped us to take them with us in our work with the curriculum (in the English context, this means the Birth to Three Matters Framework and the Foundation Stage curriculum for three- to five-year-olds). In turn, parents and carers feel empowered through knowledge and information about what is an appropriate early years curriculum as well as what engages their child in our centre. They take this expertise with them when the child goes on to school.

Conclusion

The accounts we have presented in this chapter are a powerful and moving acknowledgment of how profile books support listening in our centre. This, however, is not the end of the story. We feel at Fortune Park that we are on a learning journey. We know that profile books will develop and change, but we do not know where they will take us. What we do know is that we have to continue to exercise our culture and our ability to listen.

Children will take us wherever they need to go as they continue to be heard. Hannah tells us very clearly that her profile books are very important to her. She demonstrates that she uses them to reflect on her learning and development and that she would like to continue to use them throughout her school career. Parents, too, have shown us that they want to continue to use their voices and feel empowered both in our setting and in future settings.

Using profile books in the way that we do has also helped us to appreciate that all practitioners as well as parents and children can have a voice and that that voice can be powerful. Allowing all the people who use the setting to make a contribution in their own way, whatever form their voice takes, has in turn helped us to listen.

Profile books were conceived within a framework of listening. We know that a profile book does not make a child open or make a practitioner good at listening; rather it supports them as they share and listen. It is not the profile books that make us good at listening any more than it is the key worker system or the use of photography, but all of these support how we listen to children. Profile books offer us channels for listening and make the listening that is going on more visible.

This chapter illustrates how complicated listening is in practice and that it has to be pervasive across a setting. We have shown that how well we listen is directly influenced and dependent on the type of provision that is offered. The thought and effort that goes into creating an environment that listens well cannot be underestimated. The term 'listening' is often not fully appreciated. It can be misunderstood in this context as a very passive interaction. Listening in our setting is anything but passive.

Profile books work in this context because of the relationships and trust between the people involved. At Fortune Park we feel privileged to have developed a meaningful partnership that works in practice. Parents, children and practitioners are listening to each other and a profile book ties the three strands together.

Further reading

Cousins, J. (1999) *Listening to four year olds: How they can help us plan their education and care*, London: National Early Years Network.
Gerhardt, S. (2004) *Why love matters*, Hove: Brunner-Routledge.

Gopnik, A., Meltzoff, A. and Kuhl, P. (1999) *How babies think: The science of childhood*, London: Wiedenfield and Nicholson.

References

Ainsworth, M., Bell, S.M. and Stayton, D.J. (1974) 'Infant-mother attachment and social development', in M. Richards (ed) *The integration of a child into a social world*, Cambridge: Cambridge University Press, pp 99-136.

Bowlby, J. (1953) *Childcare and the growth of love*, London: Penguin.

Dahlberg, G., Moss, P. and Pence, A. (1999) *Beyond quality in early childhood education and care: Post-modern perspectives*, London: Falmer Press.

DfES (Department for Education and Skills) (2001) *Special educational needs code of practice*, DfES 581/2001, London: DfES.

Dowling, M. (1999) *Young children's personal, social and emotional development*, London: Paul Chapman Publishing.

Elfer, P., Goldschmied, E. and Selleck, D. (2002) *Key person relationships in nursery*, London: National Early Years Network.

Gerhardt, S. (2004) *Why love matters*, Hove: Brunner-Routledge.

Goldschmied, E. and Jackson, S. (1994) *People under three*, London: Routledge.

Paley, V. (1986) 'On listening to what the children say', *Harvard Educational Review*, vol 56, no 2, pp 122-31.

Sure Start Unit (2004) *Children's Centres Implementation Update 1*, London: Sure Start Unit, DfES.

Whittaker, P. (2001) 'Management in the early years: challenges and responsibilities module learning guide', unpublished course reader', London: Metropolitan University.

SEVEN

Small voices ... powerful messages

Linda Kinney

Stirling Council is the third smallest local authority in Scotland with a population of 86,150. It is a diverse community, a mixture of urban and rural. A national park and the cultural heritage (including the site of the Battle of Bannockburn) attract tourists and make Stirling a popular place to visit, live and work. But Stirling also has a high degree of social polarisation, with the second greatest spread of wealth and poverty among the former 413 district councils of the UK.

From the time it came into being, in 1996, Stirling Council determined that its focus would be the people using its services and not the mechanics of service delivery. Joint working would take place where it mattered most: in communities, with families, and for children. This approach began with the integration of early years' services for children from birth to five years (previously split between social work and education) into a newly formed Early Childhood Service, and with the establishment of a Children's Committee to develop policy based on a commitment to children's rights, inclusion, achievement and delivering a quality service.

This chapter describes how a local authority, Stirling, has worked with listening to very young children and examines the impact this has had on thinking about children's early learning and on local policy and practice.

> Learning is about being a researcher. The young child is a builder of theories. The young child learns by communicating and expressing their concepts and theories and by listening to those of others. (Rinaldi, 2003)

In 1999, following the earlier establishment of a Children's Committee, Stirling Council took the decision to create a new Children's Service. This would bring together into a single service a wide range of provision for children and families, including early childhood services, schools, social work with children and families, public play areas and play projects. Supporting the move, four principles of working practice were agreed by a wide range of organisations and groups:

- children first
- inclusion
- quality
- partnership.

The need to develop a common understanding of both conduct and practice requirements across the different services and groups working with children within the Children's Service was seen as essential to providing a firm foundation for future developments. A working document was created and a multidisciplinary team teased out their understandings of what these four principles might mean in practice (see below for how these principles were interpreted).

Stirling Children's Service: four principles of working practice

Putting children first means:
- ensuring that children will be at the centre of all policy making and decisions that affect them
- acting in the best interests of children
- listening to children and actively encouraging their participation and expression of views, in all matters that affect them
- supporting children to learn and develop skills and aptitudes that promote confidence, self-esteem and independence so that they can take part in the full range of activities and opportunities that prepare them for their future.

Inclusion means:
- supporting children in the context of the family and wider community
- supporting children to access services
- promoting respect for children's cultural, social and ethnic diversity and values as well as supporting children to respect the values and rights of others
- encouraging agencies and others to be child friendly
- promoting and providing clear information to children, their families and communities on services.

Quality means:
- promoting and supporting an ethos and culture of achievement so that children are encouraged to realise their potential
- supporting children to engage in a wide range of learning opportunities and experiences that promote the development of the whole child
- commitment to raising the expectations and aspirations of children and their families
- adopting approaches that ensure the early identification of children' s needs and intervene at critical stages of children's development
- commitment to continuous improvement

- monitoring and evaluating, to ensure high standards of services
- promoting best practice.

Partnership means:
- actively encouraging and promoting consultation and participation with children and their families
- supporting children in their understanding of the roles and responsibilities of partnership working
- working with children and their families in the planning and development of new services
- promoting multiagency and multidisciplinary working
- a commitment to sharing information and expertise
- sharing responsibility and credit with all partners.

It was also recognised that making whole changes to children's services would require certain conditions to exist, to enable the underpinning principles of service delivery to work in practice. In particular, this required a commitment to making the most of people and their skills, to promoting decision taking at the most practical level, and to encouraging self-evaluation and reflection within a culture of working in partnership and achieving high quality. It is against this backdrop that listening to Stirling's children grew.

The importance of listening to Stirling's children: the early years

There was a commitment to listening to very young children from the outset of the newly formed Early Childhood Service in 1996. The belief that children had the right to be heard and to be listened to was embedded in the early years policy framework and in aspects of early years practice. However, it was my participation in a ministerial study trip to Scandinavia in 1997, led by Children in Scotland (a national agency for organisations and individuals working with children and their families in Scotland) that inspired me to explore further the ways in which we were listening to children in Stirling.

The nurseries, kindergartens and other early years settings that I visited in Denmark and Norway were actively engaged in a range of consultation techniques. These included the use of stories and themes to explore behaviours and feelings, and small group discussions to gather views on a wide range of topics that affected children. For example, in one centre, the story of Punch and Judy using puppets was being used to elicit the children's views on discipline and smacking; one of the key staff members would stop the story and the puppets at various points to ask the children what they thought should happen next and/or to ask what they felt about what they saw. Being able to view some of these techniques first hand was helpful in providing potential ways forward for us in Stirling. However, it was the level of trust and confidence that both adults and children demonstrated, in response to children's views, that stimulated a powerful reaction and belief that we needed to think more about how we were approaching listening to children in Stirling. This led to the beginning of what is turning out to be an exciting and illuminating journey, which starts with how we began to *really hear and make visible* children's voices.

Although many of Stirling's nurseries were actively engaged in consulting with children, two centres in particular were interested in and committed to exploring a range of methods for consulting with children on key issues: Park Drive, a large urban nursery school for three- and four-year-olds in the Bannockburn area of Stirling; and Croftamie, a small centre in rural West Stirling providing extended day and all-year provision for two-, three- and four-year-olds. Terri McCabe, the head of Park Drive nursery school, was asked to take a lead role in developing this area of interest further and she began to explore with her staff and children a range of consultation methods. In taking forward this work, our *belief* was that children not only had the right to be heard but had important things to say and to tell us; our *thinking* was that we needed to understand the messages that children were giving to us and that we would learn more about them as a result of this engagement; and our *aim* was to make the process and the outcomes of consulting with children and the impact of their participation more visible, both to the children themselves and to adults.

Methods of consultation and examples from practice

In the two centres that were exploring consultation with children, two key questions emerged: What do we want to ask children? How can we ask in a way that is meaningful to the children? As a result of seeking answers to these questions, a range of methods and techniques began to evolve. These included the use of:

- small group discussions
- survey sheets
- photograph boards
- concrete figures.

Small group discussions developed as a method of consultation from the experience of staff working within a 'key worker and group system'. This is an arrangement (similar to the one operating in Fortune Park in Chapter Six) in which the early years educator[1] has a key group, usually eight children. This provides the opportunity for the educator to develop a close relationship with the children, both individually and as members of the group. As the group works together and the children and adult get to know and trust each other and share special times together, children become more confident in expressing their views and ideas. The shared knowledge and understandings that develop within the group mean that it can be an important basis for consulting with children. Example One shows how this can work.

Example One: small group discussion. Purchasing new resources – 'the drum'

Small group discussion using pictures and samples of equipment to make decisions on purchasing resources

Children had asked if the centre could have more musical instruments so that everyone in the group could have one each. In small groups children were shown samples of available musical instruments from a catalogue. The instruments were discussed and lots of talking between children and staff and explanations of the different types of instruments and the possible options took place. The children were then invited to choose from a particular range. One instrument in particular caught their eye: they were very excited by the possibility of having a large drum. Faced with a choice of buying several small instruments or one large drum, the majority of children decided that they would choose the drum, although they understood that this meant there would still not be enough musical instruments for everyone in the group.

The impact and outcome of the small group discussions was immediate, both for the children and the staff and led to a great deal of dialogue. Some children had difficulty in accepting that the decision of the majority of children did not match their decision. Some educators also had difficulty in accepting the decision of the majority of the children and were concerned that it might adversely affect the minority who disagreed with choosing the drum. For some, this led to a dilemma. What should they do for the children who 'lost out'? How best should they deal with the children's emotional response? And, should they 'make it okay' for this group by managing other situations to ensure that they got what they wanted?

This led to the staff group reviewing some fundamental principles in relation to their role and responsibilities as early childhood practitioners.

Survey sheets evolved as a method of consultation from listening to children talking about what they liked and did not like. Staff developed an understanding that they could ask children more formally about their likes and dislikes across a range of topics if they could find a way of representing the topic area and record the outcome of the children's views in a meaningful way. The use of pictorial symbols and photographs formed the foundations of the survey sheet, which (as Example Two shows) became a useful tool for consulting children on strategic issues such as development planning, curriculum review and the development and location of new activities and staff.

Example Two: survey sheets. Curriculum planning and review – 'the craft area'

Survey sheets showing pictorial symbols and photographs to review the curriculum

Staff wanted to find out about the children's views on the organisation of the centre and to involve them in the annual self-evaluation process, which is a key element within the 'development planning cycle' (a national framework involving an annual process and system of reflection and reviewing priorities, involving staff and parents). The staff were interested in the children's views on the range of activities in the centre and in gathering their opinions about how they felt when they were engaged in these activities.

A survey sheet was prepared, with diagrams and photographs of the various areas of the centre. In small groups the children discussed the areas. They were then asked to identify what activities they liked best and what they did not like, using happy and sad face stickers. The children were asked to place the stickers beside the diagrams and photographs and their comments were recorded.

Amy, who spent a great deal of time in the craft area, placed a 'sad face' sticker beside this activity and said she did not like it. Amy's keyworker, Diane, was surprised as she spent so much time there. When Diane asked Amy why she went there so often, Amy replied that it was because Chloe, her friend, kept taking her there. Another child, Darren, who placed a 'sad face' sticker beside the block area, said he did not like it because sometimes "people knock my bricks down".

The impact and outcome of this consultation exercise provided important feedback to staff. They had been concentrating on the physical organisation of the various areas and their educational and curricular value, but they had not picked up sufficiently on the impact of friendship and social groups and some behaviour patterns. These insights led to some very detailed discussion within the staff group, which included the effectiveness of their own observation skills and of their interventions in group and individual situations in the nursery. They felt that they needed to provide more opportunities for children to develop negotiation skills to enable them to become more assertive and confident in challenging other children's actions and behaviours, and to be able to ask for adult support.

The use of the happy and sad stickers also led to detailed work with children and educators to identify and understand feelings, through stories, drama, puppets and other activities.

Photograph boards developed as a method of consultation from the response of the children to photographic displays of special activities and events. The staff noticed that when the children looked at the displays of photographs in the centre, they began to recall and reflect on the details of the events, and to offer comments. The use of photograph boards, such as in Example Three, became a useful tool in reviewing events and experiences.

Example Three: reviewing extended day provision – 'James'

Photograph boards showing images of children in the nursery to review the range of provision

The staff in a centre wanted to find out more about the children who attended for extended periods of time, and in particular what the children themselves felt about the amount of time they spent there. Each child in this group was shown a sequence of photographs of themselves, taken throughout the day, beginning with a picture of them arriving at the centre, followed by a sequence of pictures showing how they spent their day and finishing with a photograph of the child leaving to go home. The children were individually asked what they had liked doing, what had made them happy in the centre and whether anything had made them unhappy. The children used the happy and sad face stickers and were invited to put them beside the photographs of the times when they felt this way. The comments that the children made were recorded.

One of the children in this group was James who was in his 'preschool' year. James arrived each morning at 8.30 am, stayed for lunch and was collected by his mother at around 2.30 pm. James was often the first child to arrive in the morning. When he looked at the sequence of photographs, James said that he was happy when he came in because be liked to come to the centre, but he liked it better when his friend arrived. There were two photographs of James with his key group, one in the morning and one after lunch. James put a happy face on the morning group and a sad one on the afternoon group. When asked about this, James said "I like it when I'm in my morning group, but this is afternoon and I want my mummy now".

The outcome of this was that nursery staff felt that they had a valuable insight into James's feeling about his day. He enjoyed coming to nursery in the morning, but preferred it with the companionship of other children. The opportunity to play with his friends was more important to him than the activities that were available. By the time the afternoon session had begun James was aware that it was almost time for him to go home and he was anticipating this. This meant that his key worker was able to plan special activities with some friends that would engage his attention until it was time for him to leave.

Concrete figures such as puppets and other small play figures evolved as a tool for consultation from the positive response of children to the range of other visual and concrete materials that were being used already in the consultation process. Staff noticed that the familiar figures used in the everyday play contexts in the centres provided a means for children to describe people and events and to project or predict what would happen next. Example Four illustrates the use of this tool.

Example Four: nursery staff deployment

Concrete figures using small play figures to describe the role of the adult in the centre

The staff were interested in gaining insights into how the children perceived the role of the adults in the centre. In small groups the children were presented with a survey sheet with the key areas of the centre drawn out and were given small play figures to represent the staff. The children were asked to put these figures onto the plan, according to where they would like the staff to go.

As the children began to do this, they also began spontaneously to give the figures the names of staff and to make comments about why they were putting certain adults in particular areas. These comments came without prompting. The children's comments were extremely insightful. They were able to talk about the strengths, skills and weakness of particular adults. For example, as the children put one of the staff in the 'home corner', they said: "She is good at doing things with you there and talking to you".

The centre's staff had not foreseen that when they began this process it would develop in this way, with children openly making comments about individual people. However, it demonstrated to them how perceptive the children were about the way in which adults worked with them. The children's comments were shared with the staff team and, although at times sensitive, they presented excellent staff development opportunities.

The impact of hearing children's voices

The impact on staff teams

The staff teams in the two pilot early childhood centres believed they had very good understandings and knowledge of the needs and interests of the children. However, when they began to use the techniques described to formalise and make more visible the process and methods of consultation with children, it became clearer to the adults that children had many valuable insights and understandings to offer, particularly in relation to their own needs and what worked for them, which had perhaps not previously been heard properly or not 'heard with understanding'. There was also recognition of the importance and impact of recording what children were *actually* saying rather than only recording the adult summary or interpretation of what children said. For example, when Angela finished painting a picture of herself in the rain, she said to her key worker, "this is me smashing the puddles and I've got on my red boots and hat. This is my pal Joanne and she's only got her shoes on, and she says I should get oot [out] before my ma sees me". This would previously have been summarised with a written note under Angela's drawing as 'Angela playing in the rain'. This major shift in the balance of what was recorded provided greater and more compelling opportunities for educators to enter into dialogue with children and each other. It also led to staff being more interested in sharing their understandings and perceptions about young children's learning and their own learning.

These outcomes were so powerful that it brought about significant changes in the ways in which staff began to *think* about young children's learning and *how* they engaged with the children and each other. The most significant changes related to:

- *Listening to children:* the desire to hear more clearly what children were actually saying and recording this became compulsive. There was also a greater awareness and commitment to increasing and improving adult observation skills and techniques as a means of supporting and understanding children's learning.
- *Dialogue:* the level and intensity of staff discussions and small group discussions increased considerably. Although staff recognised the importance of talking together professionally, they needed support to share their views and thoughts and some were more confident about expressing themselves than others. Time to share and a framework for professional dialogue created more opportunities for group learning among adults in both nurseries.
- *Taking action:* the powerful way in which children's voices were being heard and understood by adults meant that staff both individually and as a group were compelled to respond. The nature and the effectiveness of the responses were the subject of detailed staff and team discussions, and at times some well-established personal and professional theories were challenged.

The impact on children

Staff reported that children were more confident in sharing their views and opinions, and more regularly offered their views on a range of topics. They also reported that children would listen for longer periods of time and would listen to and repeat the views of other children more openly. Some children who previously were reluctant to talk in groups were more confident about doing this and the staff felt that their relationships with children were stronger, as their connections and understandings deepened.

When the group of children who had been involved in the more formal consultation techniques moved from their early childhood centre to primary school, the feedback from some teachers offered interesting insights that were also thought provoking for the early years team. In particular, one teacher complained to the centre about the new children entering her class being "far too assertive". When the centre head asked the teacher what she meant she said: "These children are forever giving their views and opinions and challenging classroom rules and decisions, and they even want to decide which order they do their work in!".

This experience of children entering into primary school gave rise to a great deal of debate within the Children's Service. This included the role and effectiveness of the service in promoting citizenship both in early childhood centres and in schools. We discussed the need for more open debate with some classroom teachers about their role in supporting children to be more active citizens and our responsibility to support the transition process. This led on to how best we could influence the organisation, operation and culture of classrooms in the first year of primary school, to support children's voices. As a result of this, we embarked on a transition initiative that involved early childhood workers, teachers and parents, together with a researcher from Strathclyde University, in order that we could model good practice. This work is ongoing.

The impact on parents

Initially, some parents were cautious. Although they were fully supportive of the consultation approach and recognised the value being given to their children's views and participation, some parents expressed their concerns that what was going on in the early childhood centres was not going to happen, as one parent described it, "out there" in the wider society. Parents' experiences of shopping, visiting cafés and other public places with their young children was that the 'wider society' generally did not value their children or want to listen to them. The culture that prevailed was that children should be 'seen and not heard'.

As the process of consultation developed, and discussion and dialogue with parents continued, some families, who had initially been cautious, became more involved with the work of the centres and in supporting their children in the consultation process. This led to some parents following their children's interests at home. Others began to report that their children were becoming more vocal at home, sharing their ideas, views and understandings with family members. Many parents reported to the staff that they felt really 'proud' of their children, and were amazed at what they knew and what they were capable of doing.

The impact on the Children's Service

The outcome of the consultation initiative had a profound impact on the new Children's Service generally. For some time we had believed in Stirling that young children can give us very powerful messages and that we have a great deal to learn from them. However, the experience of using the techniques described demonstrated clearly two very important constructs. First, what it means to listen to children, in theory and in practice; and second, the richness and the amazing potential of young children.

Hearing children's voices

This experience of consulting with young children led to a great deal of debate, dialogue and discourse on what we thought we were hearing, seeing, feeling and understanding about young children and why we appeared to be so selective about what we had previously been hearing. We began to understand that there were complexities around adult selectivity in hearing children, which arose from both cultural and professional assumptions. For example:

- We are too busy to hear: in a busy early years setting, adults can become engrossed in the importance of the routines and adult duties relating to the operation of the setting and, therefore, miss important information and messages.
- It is not important: it may be that we sometimes do not hear the importance of certain information; it may be that some information is 'out of context' and therefore does not make sense; or it may be we feel it is not necessary to know everything.
- We cannot take it all in: in a large setting children are chatting and engaging energetically and perhaps our systems of observation do not permit us to grasp all the information we receive.
- Working with an agenda: there are increasing external pressures created by a host of demands – national curriculum frameworks, care standards, quality indicators and many others. Perhaps we become influenced by this agenda and can only hear information that relates to this.
- Have we forgotten? have we forgotten what is important to children, that children are people who feel and sense the world acutely?
- Are we afraid? Are we afraid of not knowing the answers, of being embarrassed, or out of control, or being challenged?

The information we now had from children meant for me that we needed to ask a different set of questions. Moss and Petrie (2002) have argued, in relation to children's services, "before we can arrive at the right answer, we have to decide the right question" (p 4). The process of asking questions, rather than looking immediately for answers, is an approach that we have been able to apply locally with significant consequences. We moved our thinking and began to ask:

- How can we be sure that we are *not missing* important messages?
- How *well* are we hearing, seeing and feeling children's voices?

The pedagogy of listening

Asking new questions encouraged further reflections and a new appreciation of the 'pedagogy of listening', outlined in Chapter Two. We began to contemplate and explore the multiple forms of listening, internal and external, and the complexities, both social and political, around what it means to listen and its impact. At the heart of our deliberations was Malaguzzi's theory of 'the hundred languages of children'. This process had a profound effect, helping us to reach new and more fundamental understandings of listening as a 'culture and as an approach to life'. We also understood that listening brought the responsibility to act on what we heard.

Taking action

Taking action takes courage. Taking action as a result of listening to children means sometimes having to change decisions already made. It sometimes shows up gaps in our adult thinking and understanding. Taking action means that we have to recognise and acknowledge this or admit that we were wrong and, perhaps more importantly, that we do not have all the knowledge.

As part of our programme to expand early childhood centres, we wanted to get children's views on the design of our new provision. We were keen to know what they liked doing in the nursery and what worked best for them. We consulted with a wide range of children attending centres and what they told us very powerfully was of their desire for and need to have outdoor play provision. This had also become evident in the two pilot centres – Park Drive and Croftamie – where the children frequently indicated their desire for outdoor play.

The level and detail of the children's views about outdoor play meant that we could not ignore this. I can remember the day that I was in my office and after reading all the information and evidence from children, I realised that making decisions about services for children would never be the same again. The perspectives that children brought to the process not only enhanced the possibilities but opened up areas that as adults we at times completed missed. The responsibility arising from this new knowledge and understanding about listening to children also felt daunting, professionally and personally.

As a result of the information from the children, our expansion programme changed. We introduced Grounds for Change, an initiative to promote new ways of developing outdoor play areas to extend and enrich children's learning and development. The outcome of this was:

- Equal consideration is given in all new provision to the development of outdoor as well as indoor areas.
- The establishment of a Grounds for Learning Fund, which brought together funding from children's services, environment services and Scottish Heritage to provide grant support to centres to develop outdoor areas.
- *Inside out and outside in*, guidance and accompanying staff development to support early childhood staff to develop, manage and design an outdoor area to enhance learning, and to change attitudes to the way in which outdoor play areas are used.

This has resulted in a major change in the way Stirling's early childhood provision is being developed. Almost all settings have an enhanced outdoor area, so that children can have access to a fully integrated curriculum that ensures their well being, development and learning opportunities both inside and outside. If we are serious about consulting with children and supporting their participation, this means that we need to be prepared to change as a result of the outcomes.

Children as partners

Our experience and new understandings as a result of consulting with young children were so exciting and insightful that we felt that we needed to share this more widely. *Children as partners* (Stirling Council, 2001), a guide to consulting with very young children and supporting them to participate effectively, was devised in order to support all early years staff in Stirling to embed the principles and process of consultation in practice. We also believed that as a process of democracy, consultation with children and encouraging their participation should be an integral part of the daily practice and general approach in all our early years settings.

It was evident that there needed to be an emphasis on adults taking responsibility to hear children and to listen to them more effectively and not to make children the problem by thinking that they must 'tell us' more clearly. This also required adults to have a better understanding of the power relationship between children and adults. A set of principles and values were devised by the centres that had been working on the initiative, in order to support others to work in this way (see below).

Children as partner's guidance: underpinning principles and values

- The rights of children should be respected: this includes the right to be heard and have views taken into account.
- Adults must listen and respond: children give us information in many different ways. It is important to ensure effective ways of supporting children to communicate their viewpoints.
- Participation takes time: children benefit from a consistent experience of the process of consultation and participation in order to understand fully both what is expected of them and of the outcomes.
- Consultation and participation is different from getting what you want: an important part of children learning about the process of consultation and participation is recognising other children's viewpoints. This can be difficult for some children and adults need to find ways of supporting them through this process.
- Consultation is not enough: what we do with the results of consultation and how our discoveries influence our practice is vitally important. It is also important to find effective ways of sharing the outcomes with children.

Effective consultation with children also recognises the importance of developing a culture and ethos of participation and acknowledging adult power and responsibilities within the adult–child relationship.

The power of children's voices

What we have learned in Stirling is the power of children's voices to change perspectives, to change adults' understandings about how and what children learn, to change our image of children. We can see more clearly their amazing potential, their richness, their talents, their understandings and workings of the world, their feelings about themselves and other children around them as well as the adults who engage with them.

Sam and Craig

Sam and Craig are two four-year-olds at Doune nursery. Sam's mother is Brazilian and he had just returned from his first family holiday in Brazil. Part of the holiday had included going on a safari. Sam was particularly interested in the safari animals and when he came to the nursery they provided opportunities for him to play and work with safari animals. This episode and conversation was recorded between Sam and Craig as they played with the safari animals in the nursery.

> Sam: "This is a herd. They are moving all the way from Alaska to Brazil. They have their heads down so they can hear the big boss."
>
> Craig: "The big boss is that cow in front."
>
> Sam: "This bit is Brazil. Brazil is a very important place. There's lots of grass there and a very important person – another queen. The queen is a mummy jaguar."
>
> Craig: "They need a lot more grass and there isn't much food here."
>
> Sam: "Alaska is very dry. Brazil is very hot and wet."
>
> Craig: "Lots of sweet grass."
>
> Sam: "Yes, 'cos of all the rain."
>
> Craig: "It fills the Amazon up."
>
> Sam: "The Amazon is a great big river."
>
> Craig: "Where alligators live."
>
> Sam: "And crocodiles called caymans."

Craig: "I've got an alligator book at home."

Sam: "The Amazon is very long and very deep. It's got lots of piranhas and eels, electric eels. It will take the animals one day and another day to get to Brazil."

Craig: "That's two days."

Sam: "Brazil is this big."

Craig: "They need their heads down to punch some little animals."

Sam: "No Craig, that's not it – they are listening to the big boss. These animals have to swim across the river to get to the good grass. Brazil is at the bottom of America, Alaska is at the top. The Amazon is the longest river in America, larger than another river in South America. Water buffaloes live in it."

Craig: "Brazil is a special place."

Sam: "Brazil are going to win the world cup. My mummy says so."

What this episode and many others that we have recorded told us in general terms has been set out above. But more specifically this small episode exemplified to early years staff:

- How well children listen both internally and externally and learn from each other.
- How effectively they communicate together.
- The very high level of respect for others as well as respect for places.
- Their awareness of their responsibilities.
- How young children are active citizens of the world now.

The implications of recording and sharing understandings of children's voices are overwhelming: "sharing documentation is in fact making visible the culture of childhood both inside and outside the school to become a participant in a true act of exchange and democracy" (Rinaldi, 2003). Among the implications for us in Stirling has been that we have reviewed and better understood:

- *The environment:* understanding the power of children's voices has meant paying attention to the environment in which children live and work, to ensure that it is welcoming, engaging, both inside and outside, that it can operate flexibly and is transparent (being open, both in terms of space and light as well as honest and trusting), and above all is inspiring.

- *Children's learning:* we are valuing more learning about children's learning, which means children's early learning and research is now recorded and documented more systematically, making this more visible, in order that there is debate, discussion and dialogue.
- *Adult interactions:* all of this has meant having a better understanding that children and adults can be learners and researchers together, listening to the 'hundred languages', and that adult interactions and relationships with children must, at all times, be respectful, meaningful, trusting and reflective.

Conclusion

From our earliest beginnings to our current position has been for me a life-changing journey, which still feels at an early stage. In Stirling we have become committed to actively seeking ways to engage in consultation with children, to consider and promote their participation, and to document this in a way that is meaningful.

There are many challenges in working in this way, not least the gap between our professional view of children as rich in potential with rights to be heard, and the wider view held of children in our society, which in the main continues to regard adult rights as paramount. Recognising that not all adults will be interested in listening to children in the way that we are, including some teachers and some residents of the communities in which children live, has led us to debate whether we are exposing children to the risk of adult hostility.

Encouraging children to use 'their voice' and supporting them to be heard, means that they are engaging in democratic practice. This brings with it the power to challenge adult authority. We remain thoughtful about the impact of this and believe the skills that children are developing are for life and will ultimately benefit them as individuals, as members of a group and society as a whole. However, we also accept another new responsibility: to work more closely with local communities and others to share and exchange views and understandings about children's participation.

The transition of children from early years to primary school has presented another challenge. Although the policy backdrop of promoting and supporting the culture of children's participation across all services in Stirling means that clear direction is being given to schools, and there are many good examples of children's participation happening, there are also factors that can inhibit it. These include the differences in adult:child ratios, for example between early childhood services and the early stages of primary school (and children in Scotland, as well as England, move into primary school at a relatively early age, by the time they are five years old); the impact of the national school curriculum; and differences in the pace of change in cultural attitudes and assumptions among some school teachers and managers.

This means that there can be gaps, and in some cases significant variations, between the way in which we view and work with children in different settings within the same Children's Service. There is a real commitment to change in Stirling and the way in which we are attempting to address this locally is through staff development and other initiatives involving educators in early childhood services and primary schools. This will take some time.

Supporting adults to work in this participatory way with young children requires a well thought through process of change, both in the theory of early learning and in practice. Some of our early years educators found it very difficult to engage in the process. For some there was a reluctance to change, for others it was the fear of not knowing what to do, or what to think.

Extensive and ongoing staff development continues to be an essential element of the success of this way of working. The core of our staff development programme is on facilitating and supporting staff to engage in reading and dialogue, as well as sharing practice. This is taking place among teams and groups working in early childhood centres. Alongside this is the opportunity for all staff to improve their skills and update their qualifications; for example, 10 out of the 12 staff in one centre are undertaking a degree course in early childhood. The aim is to encourage staff to become more critical thinkers and to be confident as 'researchers' alongside children.

With my colleague, Pat Wharton, we are now moving to the next stage. We are engaged in researching and developing what we call the Stirling Documentation Approach to Early Learning. This refers to our process of making visible how children explore and learn and how they make sense of the world, by recording and documenting experiences shared between the children and the staff who work with them. This has developed as a direct result of our process of consulting with children; as we began to record more systematically children's view and the outcomes of children's consultations, we could see more clearly the impact and importance of what we are hearing.

We have been intrigued and awakened to new possibilities by what children have told us. We are now being inspired and supported in developing this area of work by our connections with Reggio Children and Carlina Rinaldi. We are also making new international connections with colleagues from Scandinavia and New Zealand who are already engaged in this way of working, thinking and learning.

It has become clear that the way we are working provides really important evidence not only for us, the adults, but also for the children themselves. As a result of this we feel compelled to know more about children and ourselves, to observe more closely, to search for meaning and understandings, to document and to listen. We now feel that we are engaged, as Spagiari (2004) put it, in 'collecting parts' that are invisible in order to make that which is invisible, *the hidden potentials of children*, visible.

As a result of our experience of listening to children and hearing their voices, there has been a 'collective' change in our image of the child. We are beginning to shift our cultural assumptions and constructions of the child to recognise and acknowledge more the richness and potential of children and ourselves. This has had a significant impact on the way in which early years services in Stirling are being developed and designed; it has changed the thinking of staff who are working with children and those of us who devise policy. We are also just beginning to understand the potential impact of this on the wider community.

These new understandings about children and us have come not only from our readings or sharing inspirational thinking and practice from other colleagues. They have come about also because we were able to see it for ourselves, we heard it together and more importantly, we felt it – most powerfully. They open up endless possibilities.

Note

[1] In Stirling, we use the term 'educators' rather than 'practitioners' as we believe it more accurately reflects the increasing professionalism of early years workers, who bring together theory and practice to think critically about their role and responsibility in supporting children's early learning.

Further reading

Clark, A. and Moss, P. (2001) *Listening to young children: The Mosaic approach*, London/York: National Children's Bureau and Joseph Rowntree Foundation.
Giudici, C., Krechevsky, M. and Rinaldi, C. (eds) (2001) *Making learning visible: Children as individual and group learners*, Reggio Emilia: Reggio Children.
Hallett, C. and Prout, A. (2003) *Hearing the voices of children: Social policy for a new century*, London: RoutledgeFalmer.

References

Moss, P. and Petrie, P. (2002) *From children's services to children's spaces: Public policy, children and childhood*, London: RoutledgeFalmer.
Rinaldi, C. (2003) 'An audience with Carlina Rinaldi', MacRobert Arts Centre, Stirling University, September.
Spagiari, S. (2004) From a paper presented at Crossing Boundaries, an international conference in Reggio Emilia, Italy, February.
Stirling Council (2001) *Children as partners*, Stirling: Stirling Council Children's Service.

EIGHT

Beyond listening: can assessment practice play a part?

Margaret Carr, Carolyn Jones and Wendy Lee

In this chapter we turn from a local to a national experience, that of New Zealand. Since the late 1980s, New Zealand has engaged in a radical reform of its early childhood services. The reform movement has been led by a strong group of committed individuals and organisations and enriched by a broader national process of developing a new relationship between the indigenous Māori population and the non-Māori majority based on equality, reciprocity and respect. The reforms of early childhood services have in part been structural: all services have become the responsibility of the Ministry of Education; a common regulatory, curriculum and funding framework has been developed to encompass the many different types of services; and the workforce has been reformed, with a new qualification of early years teacher (which by 2012 will be required of all staff in most services) and an agreement to introduce pay parity across the whole teaching workforce (whether working with 18-month-olds or 18-year-olds).

But the reform movement has also been about rethinking early childhood services starting from a holistic concept of education – 'education in its broadest sense'. In the early 1990s a national early childhood curriculum was developed, based on understandings of learning as a process of reciprocal relationships and of the child as competent, both foregrounding the importance of children's voice. This chapter explores one of the issues to which the reform process has given rise: the dilemma of how to listen to children's voices while at the same time engaging in assessment practice.

When children are listened to, the power balance tips towards the child. Assessment practice, however, implies that the adult has a pre-set agenda, in which case the power balance tips dramatically the other way – towards the adult. Assessment practices are usually associated with normalisation, classification and categorisation; this chapter presents an alternative possibility and suggests some ways in which assessment practice might provide spaces for children's voices to be heard. It suggests that if we redefine the purpose of assessment, we can search for different ways of doing it that provide the conditions for really listening to children. Briefly, if we redefine the purpose of assessment as being to notice, recognise and respond to competent and confident learners and communicators, then children's voices will have a large part to play in defining and communicating that learning.

In addition to the central dilemma of how teachers can 'truly listen' to children when they have an educational agenda in (or on their) mind, the chapter discusses three other related issues: the image of the learner, and how it shapes how we define the 'educational agenda' and, hence, the rationale for listening to children; aligning assessment practice with the image of the learner, since assessment as a powerful practice can enable or disable the educational agenda; and the possible consequences of children contributing their voices to assessment – what happens when we go beyond listening.

The discussion is sited within two particular contexts. The first context is the New Zealand early childhood curriculum. The second context, a type of data collection, is an assessment resource prepared for the New Zealand Ministry of Education to support the national curriculum. Examples are drawn from these to illustrate the argument. These examples, of curriculum and assessment practice, are not deemed to be exemplary in the sense of a universal best practice. As Moss and Petrie have pointed out, providing examples immediately raises questions. It is our view too that:

> examples are best seen and used as provocations. They should surprise us, make us think, ask critical questions, appreciate the peculiarity of what we have taken for granted, illuminate implicit understandings and values, make narratives stutter, open us to new possibilities. (Moss and Petrie, 2002, p 148)

These authors explain what they mean by making narratives 'stutter', referring to Rose's discussion of critical thinking as:

> introducing a critical attitude towards those things that are given to our present experience as if they were timeless, natural, unquestionable.... It is a matter of introducing a kind of awkwardness into the fabric of one's experience, of interrupting the fluency of the narratives that encode that experience and making them stutter. (Rose, 1999, p 20; as cited in Moss and Petrie, 2002, p 148)

We believe strongly that documented examples of real children in real settings provide a venue for lively debate about theory and practice and an opportunity for interrupting the fluency of accepted narratives. The topic of assessment is a rich source of such debates and alternative readings. Furthermore, if we include children in the perspectives that define and communicate learning, then it is often children's voices that "surprise us, make us think, ask critical questions, appreciate the peculiarity of what we have taken for granted, illuminate implicit understandings and values, make narratives stutter, open us to new possibilities". The following is an example, from an early childhood centre (Carr, 2001b, p 67).

Rachel and Jason are four-year-olds. Alison (the teacher) was teaching Jason to write John's name, at his request. Rachel, who complained that someone was chasing her, interrupted them.

Rachel: "Alison."

Alison: "Yep."

Rachel: "Somebody want to chase us."

Alison: "Ooh. What do you need to do about that?"

Rachel: "I don't know."

Jason: "Run quickly and get away…."

Alison: "Is there anything you can say to them?"

Rachel: "Go away!"

Jason: "I, I, I trip; I trip them up and run."

Alison: "There's another, there's something else you can do instead. You can tell them to stop it and go away. That's another way."

Jason: "Yep."

It is unlikely that Jason has persuaded Alison that these are new and appropriate possibilities for dealing with unwanted behaviour; however, it was clear to the observer that this was a place where such radical and probably unacceptable alternatives could be expressed by the children and considered. Jason was, we think, attempting to make a normative narrative (about handling unwanted behaviour) 'stutter', and the teacher describes her own view as 'another way' rather than as 'the correct way'.

Listening to young children

"But I'm a robber. They don't drink tea."

"Peter is not a robber. Oh, no."

"He steals the lettuce, so he is a robber."

> "Mr McGregor is mean. So it's okay for Peter to do that. And I'm your mother. You can't be a robber if I'm waiting for you." (Paley, 2004, p 58)

It is very probable that in early childhood settings where teachers listen to the children, the children listen to each other – creating a general climate or disposition of 'multiple listening' (as Rinaldi terms it in Chapter Two of this book). Some of the descriptions of conversations with children in Vivian Paley's books are examples of this. The quote that begins this section comes from her book *A child's work*: Theresa has offered William a cup of tea, but William is currently playing the role of Peter Rabbit (from a book by Beatrix Potter) and maintains that robbers do not drink tea, and since Peter Rabbit stole a lettuce he is a robber. Paley is interested in such conversations. She adds:

> This has been a conversation of great merit. The logic is clear: robbers do not have mothers who wait for them and give them tea. As to whether or not it is acceptable to steal from a mean person, the issue will arise again now that the idea has been introduced, stimulating new conversations. (Paley, 2004, p 58)

The children in Paley's classroom know that she is listening carefully to them, and puzzling about the meaning. They know this because she revisits the conversations, and she writes them down. She has a purpose in mind: assisting children to communicate with each other on a range of topics that interest them in order to make sense of their worlds.

Teachers know that really listening to children is not an easy task, and it is especially difficult when we have a topic or some 'learning outcomes' to pursue. Lous Heshusius has written about exploring her own listening capacity. She describes her view of what happens when someone is truly listening: "There is a quietness, a stillness about the person. Nothing in her or his mind is weighing, evaluating, judging, or formulating unsolicited advice. Such encounters are rare, but lovely" (Heshusius, 1995, p 118).

From this perspective, 'truly listening' and evaluating or judging at the same time is impossible. Heshusius adds:

> It became clear that when I thought I was listening, most of my attention was with myself: I wondered how the other person's message applied to myself; I had vague images about what I should be saying, given my particular role (eg as teacher, mother); I thought about what I could say next to the person to steer the topic into another, more interesting direction. (Heshusius, 1995, p 118).

This chapter explores, but certainly does not solve, the dilemma of this balancing act between truly listening and our perceived role as teachers with an educational agenda in mind. Paley's work suggests that a balance is possible; however, she does not appear to see her role as a teacher to be to steer the topic into another direction or to concern herself with the sort of 'learning outcomes' that beset many teachers in this age of accountability via measurement. It seems to be an even greater dilemma if the teacher is assessing at the same time. Listening (in the sense that Heshusius means) and assessing seem to be very incompatible practices. As Rinaldi says in Chapter Two (see page 20, this book):

> Listening is not easy. It requires a deep awareness and at the same time a suspension of our judgements and above all our prejudices; it requires openness to change. It demands that we have clearly in mind the value of the unknown and that we are able to overcome the sense of emptiness and precariousness that we experience whenever our certainties are questioned.

The teacher who listens carefully to children's voices will have a particular image of children and of learners. Furthermore, the teacher who listens carefully to children and tries to 'assess' them at the same time will have a particular view of assessment. These images and views will have to accommodate uncertainty. "Development is an elusive underground process usually hidden from view" (Nelson, 1997a, p 101).

The image of the learner

> "'I'm really good at my letter signs … sometimes I forget that some go to the bottom and some go to the top. It's the unfairest thing that some letters start at the bottom' (Sarah, aged five)." (Duncan, 2004, p 14)

In an early childhood or school classroom setting, teachers listen to children for a purpose. Something happens beyond the listening. In Paley's case, the purpose is to interpret and assist the children's explorations of the meaning of life. Her view of the learner is that by playing out, revisiting and transforming their own and other people's stories learners can make sense of their lives. However, she is happy to live with ambiguity, accepting that "there are no certainties and no answers" (Paley, 1990, p 11).

Sometimes, however, the purpose has rather narrower objectives in mind, because the image of the learner is rather different. Two images of what literacy learning looks like and does might illustrate our point. For instance, with literacy learning in mind, the purpose of listening to children may be because we want to classify their ability with reference to a hierarchical framework of skills. Using this framework enables us to categorise the learner by level, and to provide sequenced activities for him or her to climb the ladder of accumulating skills in a particular sequence.

On the other hand, we may have in mind a framework of literacy practices, and a view of the learner as an increasingly competent user of those practices. We have suggested, for instance (adapting Luke and Freebody, 1999), that there are four literacy practices (Carr et al, 2005: forthcoming). We all use these practices at various times, and they do not appear in any particular order:

- *listening in* to and observing others using literacy (what Rogoff calls "*intent participation*" (Rogoff, 2003, p 317);
- *using* the systems and technologies for a purpose (including 'breaking the code': recognising and using the fundamental units, patterns and conventions of multiple literacies);
- *playing* around with the units and technologies of literacy;
- *critiquing*: being a critical analyst.

In our view, Sarah, whose comments begin this section, is being a critical analyst. This is her first year of school, and she is commenting on the inconsistency (and therefore the unfairness for the learner) of the way in which in her writing lessons it is a requirement that some of the letters start at the bottom and some at the top. Here is another example in which the teacher becomes aware, by listening to his comments, that Joshua has some alternative views about a storyline. (The teacher has documented this episode as a 'Learning Story', an assessment practice that is explained later in the chapter.) The teacher invites Joshua to be a critical analyst and to change the ending of the story.

Learning Story: a sticky end

Joshua peered over my shoulder as I read the book *The icky sticky frog*. The plot involves the frog spotting his hapless prey and then slurping them up with his long, sticky tongue. Near the end of the story, the frog spots a butterfly. However, this time, instead of the frog eating his quarry, a fish gulps down the frog. Joshua looked at the last picture for a while and then he said: "The butterfly is smiling".

"Mmm," I concurred. "Why do you think that is?"

"I think the frog should be smiling but he's inside the fish."

"Do you think the ending should be different?", I asked.

"Yes", said Josh.

"What do you think the ending should be?", I asked as we continued to look at the sorry state of affairs.

"I think the fish should eat the butterfly!", said Josh, his eyes lighting up with glee.

Short-term review (written by the teacher)

We often look at books and read stories around the tea table when the groups are small and receptive. Josh was itching to put his bag away and play outside, but the book captured his interest. I found his comment about the ending of the book very interesting as it has also touched upon a note of disappointment I feel when reading some stories. (*The gingerbread man* is one that comes to mind....) I found a handout that was supplied at a recent workshop I attended on literacy. The handout describes 'four roles of a literate person'. [*Later, in 1999 Luke and Freebody changed this descriptor to 'four literacy practices'; our comment.*] One of the roles is that of *text analyst* where the participant challenges the view represented in a particular text. And I guess Joshua did just that. We recognise that literacy involves so much, and that it is not only about reading and writing – it involves the ability to look critically at texts too.

The image of the learner usually includes a view of what it means to be a 'better' learner. Such a repertoire has (at least) three dimensions of strength (Luke and Freebody, 1999; Claxton and Carr, 2004). These are: the breadth of the repertoire (across a range of social activities); the degree of control or power or responsibility available to the learner; and the increasing flexibility and sophistication of use (including the extent to which there is some degree of critique, transformation and redesign). Immersion in a children's space (Moss and Petrie, 2002) where literacy practices are embedded in everyday explorations and purposes provides possibilities for children to strengthen their learning in this area. Immersion in a children's space where children are listened to, and their voices count, is a necessary condition for the latter two dimensions: control and critique.

Here is an example where the child became the teacher, a common variant of the child taking responsibility (see Chapter Three for another example). It is an entry in Erin's assessment record, written by one of her early years teachers.

Learning Story

When Stephanie arrived this morning she didn't have a locker with her name on it. I said I would fix the problem and wrote her name in the space.

Erin was watching all of this and when I announced that one of my 'e's wasn't very good, Erin informed me that she would teach me how to do proper 'e's.

She took the vivid [pen] off me and disappeared to a table.

A few minutes later she came back with a beautiful lower case 'e' formed by a series of dots. I carefully went over the dots and Erin seemed to think I had the hang of the 'e' problem.

She had a smile on her face that told me she had done her teaching for the day.

Short-term review

Erin took responsibility for my 'dilemma' and did something about it. She has obviously had letters taught to her in the same way and has learned well enough to pass this information on.

The more usual process of assessment and planning by the teacher, followed by a revised response from the child, was interrupted. Revisiting this written assessment in her portfolio is a reminder to Erin that she is frequently the expert, and that being able to teach others is a criterion for being a competent and confident learner. The teacher felt that it was worthwhile to comment on her own error or inadequacy, perhaps illustrating the notion that the process of being competent and confident includes making errors.

Te Whāriki

But our image of the learner is not just about how they become competent and confident participants in the culture's literacy practices. In the words of the New Zealand early childhood curriculum (New Zealand Ministry of Education, 1996), known to all of us by its shorter name as *Te Whāriki*, it is about the strands of well being, belonging, contribution, communication and exploration. *Te Whāriki* is a Māori word meaning a woven mat for all to stand on. The curriculum has weaving as a central metaphor (Carr and May, 1994). Each centre or other early childhood setting weaves its own programme from a framework of strands and principles: "There are many possible patterns for this. This is a curriculum without 'recipes' but more like a 'dictionary' providing signposts for individuals and centres to develop their own curriculum weaving through a process of talk, reflection, planning, evaluation, and assessment" (May and Carr, 2000, p 156).

Te Whāriki was developed at a time when government funding for early childhood centres was reaching an average of 50 per cent of operating costs and a national curriculum for schools was being written. The government saw that an early childhood curriculum could form the basis for accountability and hoped it would also contribute to a 'seamless' education system from birth to tertiary. However, the early childhood curriculum, as it finally emerged, turned out very different to the school curriculum that was framed around a traditional array of seven learning areas (Mathematics, Science, Language and Languages, Technology, Social Sciences, the Arts, and Health and Physical Education).

The unique characteristics of the early childhood curriculum were due to a number of features of the early childhood field and the curriculum development process. The early childhood field in New Zealand comprises a variety of different types of services, each with strong views about purpose and curriculum. These services include family- or *whānau*-based services: play centres and *nga kōhanga reo* (Māori immersion early childhood centres; *whānau* means extended family for Māori, the indigenous population), where connection with family and community is a foundation principle of curriculum. The curriculum was developed after lengthy discussion with practitioners from this wide range of services, and the development of its bicultural framework (strands and principles are expressed in Māori and English, but seen as parallel concepts rather than as translations) owed much to a consultative process that centrally included Māori participants on the development team. The concept of *mana* was central to the Māori participants – a concept that has no equivalent in English: it includes ideas of rights, integrity, status and empowerment. (See Nuttall, 2003, for more detail on the development and theoretical framework of *Te Whāriki*.)

The views in *Te Whāriki* of the learner, learning and assessment are of relevance to the question raised by his chapter: listening to young children – can assessment practice play a part? Examining the curriculum provides some clues as to the purpose of listening to children. *Te Whāriki* states that the curriculum will be locally woven, calling on the perspectives of families, community and the children themselves. Four principles set out the theoretical approach: curriculum is about reciprocal and responsive relationships (with people, places and things), connects with family and community, and is holistic and 'empowering'. The same principles have been attached to assessment practice.

The metaphor of *participation* (in a learning community) rather than *acquisition* (of a collection of skills and knowledge) is a theme that runs through the curriculum. Sfard (1998, p 11) sets out the implications for teaching of these two metaphors for learning. She concludes that each of these metaphors has a different purpose, but that if:

> ... one is concerned with educational issues – such as the mechanisms that enable successful learning or make its failure persistent, then the participatory approach may be more helpful as one that denies the traditional distinction between cognition and affect, brings social factors to the fore, and thus deals with an incomparably wider range of possible relevant aspects.

Sfard points out that acquisition and participation are not mutually exclusive. They may alternate within the same curriculum; sometimes acquisition of skill will be fore grounded even though participation is the overall principle. One of the strengths of an educational agenda that focuses on reciprocal and responsive relationships is that it encourages education to be explained in terms of the interactive process of teaching and learning rather than in terms of individual psychology. Lev Vygotsky, a key theorist within the arena of socio-cultural frames for education, had at his disposal the Russian word *obuchenie*, which means both teaching and learning (Mercer, 2001, p 152). In New Zealand, the Māori (indigenous) word *ako* also means teaching *and* learning. The curriculum includes the comment that the learner and the learning environment are closely connected, and the curriculum applies to both.

A child learns to talk in a setting where adults talk to children and to each other. A child learns to explore in a setting where exploration is valued and possible. (New Zealand Ministry of Education, 1996, p 19)

Learning as reciprocal and responsive relationships is a 'distributed' view (Perkins, 1993; Salomon, 1993): the notion that learning is 'stretched across' people, places and things. A view of the learner within a distributed or situative perspective focuses on:

> … engagement that maintains the person's interpersonal relations and identity in communities in which the individual has a significant personal investment. This view emphasises how people's very identities derive from their participatory relationships in communities. According to this view students can become engaged in learning by participating in communities where learning is valued. (Greeno et al, 1996, p 26)

In this view, learners become more adept at participating in distributed systems, increasingly able to recognise, respect, manage, develop and transform networks of support. The following comment is a parent's written response to a story in Dylan's assessment file in which he made a Thunderbirds 'block person' (a laminated picture, set into a stand, for use in block area play). During this process he decided to take a photograph of Jane, the teacher, using the glue gun to assist him. The

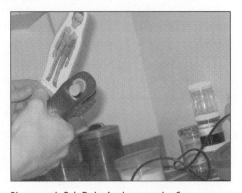

Photograph 8.1: Dylan's photograph of Jane helping

photograph was included in the story written about the episode. In a 'what next?' section of the assessment format, the teacher has written: "Let's ask Dylan!". His mother asks him, and she adds the following comment to the record:

> I asked Dylan 'what next?' and he said that we could make another block person of Shrek [*Shrek is the hero in a Disney film of the same name*] and he would take a picture of Jane doing it to put in his file. So I asked him where we would get the picture of Shrek? First he said 'from the Warehouse [*a department store*]'. Then I suggested that maybe his dad could get it for him on the computer and print it out.

Photograph 8.2: The completed

Dylan has contributed his understanding that support for learning in this particular enterprise (making a 'block person' of Shrek) will come from the teacher and the Warehouse. His mother adds a further suggestion: his father and the computer. Dylan is also preparing to take a further photograph of the teacher providing assistance.

Assessment practice will be aligned with the image of the learner

Hannah:"I'm really scared about the SATs [standard assessment tasks]. Mrs O'Brien [a teacher at the school] came and talked to us about our spelling and I'm no good at spelling and David [the class teacher] is giving us times tables so I'm frightened I'll do the SATs and I'll be a nothing."

Diane:"I don't understand, Hannah. You can't be a nothing."

Hannah:"Yes, you can 'cause you have to get a level like a level four or a level five and if you're no good at spelling and times tables you don't get those levels and so you're a nothing."

Diane:"I'm sure that's not right."

Hannah:"Yes it is 'cause that's what Mrs O'Brien was saying."

(Reay and Wiliam, 1999, p 345)

The above quote comes from a paper that outlines the construction of identity through assessment. It appears that for Hannah the assessment is not just about constructing a view of her as a learner, but as a person too. *Te Whāriki* also sets out a view of the person: that children will grow up:

… as competent and confident learners and communicators, healthy in mind, body and spirit, secure in their sense of belonging and in the knowledge that they make a valued contribution to society. (New Zealand Ministry of Education, 1996, p 9)

We interpret this as a view of children as competent and confident *in the here and now*, as well as in other places and times. We have no idea what environments and contexts the current generation of children will meet in the future, and a current resource on assessment practice in early childhood settings implementing *Te Whāriki* has been titled *Kei tua o te pae*, which means in English 'Beyond the horizon', reflecting this uncertainty (Carr et al, 2004). It seems reasonable to assume that assessment practices will be in alignment with that image of the learner. In *Te Whāriki*, assessment is described as a "two-way process" (New Zealand Ministry of Education, 1996), supportive of a "learning environment [that] should enable children to set and pursue their own goals within the boundaries necessary for safety and to reflect on whether they have achieved their goals" (p 30). Assessment practices will contribute to children's views of themselves as competent and confident learners and communicators.

Research on assessment and motivation indicates that those settings in which children can set and assess their own goals are rich sites for learning. Part of the reason for this is that children who contribute to their own (and others') assessments are being perceived as competent and confident learners. Involvement by the learner in the meaning making and goal setting that is part of the assessment process is a central feature of effective pedagogy and learning. Black and Wiliam (1998, pp 54-5), in a summary of their literature search on formative assessment, make the comment that "self-assessment by the student is not an interesting option or luxury; it has to be seen as essential". Claxton (1995, p 340) has suggested that assessment should:

> ... reflect those occasions when the goal is not clearly specified in advance, and include all the situations in which learners are developing their sense of what counts as 'good work' for them – where it is some inner sense of satisfaction, which is the touchstone of quality.

Te Whāriki includes a page of acknowledgement to Urie Bronfenbrenner. According to Bronfenbrenner (1979, pp 60, 212), learning and development are facilitated by the participation of the developing person in "progressively more complex activities and patterns of reciprocal activity" and by gradual "shifts in the balance of power" between the learner and the teacher (towards the learner). Such shifts in the balance of power reflect a shift towards the ability and the inclination of children to steer their own course, to set their own goals, to assess their own achievements, and to take some of the responsibility for learning in a number of ways. Traditionally, the balance of power between teacher and child or pupil during assessment has been very one-sided. The teacher writes the assessment, makes an interpretation, perhaps discusses it with other teachers and the family, but the child is not part of the equation.

As Rinaldi writes in Chapter Two of this book, documentation can be seen as 'visible listening'. A number of early childhood settings in New Zealand are now finding ways to include the children's voices in the documentation of their own learning. There have been two developments. First, assessment has been defined as 'noticing, recognising and responding' (Cowie and Carr, 2004). 'Noticing and recognising' includes listening to children's voices, and 'responding' takes the process beyond listening. Usually this noticing, recognising and responding is informal; teachers notice a comment perhaps, and recognise that this has connections with learning of interest. Paley's comment, quoted earlier, about Theresa and William's conversation is an example: "This has been a conversation of great merit ... the issue will arise again now that the idea has been introduced, stimulating new conversations". Teachers respond in many ways, and sometimes they will document the story.

Second, assessment practices in New Zealand have been exploring a narrative methodology for assessing children's learning: Learning Stories (Carr, 2001a; Hatherly and Sands, 2002). Here, as also described by Rinaldi in Chapter Two and Clark in Chapter Three, boundaries are crossed. Teachers are researchers, assessment is research, and we have borrowed many ideas from narrative-based research.

Learning Stories

By 1998, assessment had been mandated in early childhood centres receiving government funding (almost all centres) and the *Te Whāriki* strands and principles were set out as a framework for assessment as well as for curriculum. Assessment was required to be holistic, 'empowering', connected with family and community, and sited in reciprocal and responsive relationships (with people places and things). How was this to be done? Research with teachers developed a method of assessment that was called 'Learning Stories', and this narrative-based practice for assessing and documenting learning is now being trialled and adapted in many early childhood settings.

Learning Stories question a number of assumptions that as early childhood teachers in the 1980s, before *Te Whāriki*, we used to hold about assessment: the purpose, the outcomes of interest, the focus for intervention, validity, progress, value to practitioners – as well as the 'right' procedures (Carr, 2001a). Most of us recorded very little of the learning, perhaps an occasional checklist of 'school preparation'; so, unlike Reggio Emilia (see Chapter Two), there is not a long tradition of documentation.

Learning Stories are a method of documenting everyday interactions. Most of them include a learning episode, a 'short-term review' and a 'what next?'. The learning episode about constructing a block person in Dylan's assessment file was written as a Learning Story. That story included a photograph (taken by Dylan), and the 'what next?' was written by a parent after a discussion with Dylan. In this method, the assessments – and the notions of valuable knowledge and competence that they take as reference points – have called on multiple perspectives. Assessment records that include stories (that can be revisited) and photographs (that can be read by the children). Fasoli (2003) invites children (and their families) to make contributions: "I was holding the digital camera and Brittany asked me if I would take a photo of her, just the same as Hayley (a photograph in her older sister's portfolio, taken four years earlier), so she could have it in her folder. Brittany arranged herself and I took the photo" (teacher commentary, Carr et al, 2004).

Here is an excerpt from a teacher's log of progress towards a manageable and meaningful framework for assessment that is aligned to *Te Whāriki*.

> We were excited about the progress we were making and the positive feedback we were getting from parents when we shared their children's learning stories with them. We were finding that learning stories were allowing us to know the child at a much deeper level. We could see that this assessment framework was easy for all our families to understand, especially with the use of photos to illustrate the child's learning process. (Carr et al, 2003, p 198)

Teachers write Learning Stories in a range of ways, and address their comments to a range of audiences. In the Learning Story about Lachlan and the hula hoop (to be discussed later) the teacher is writing to his mother in the short-term review; frequently the comments in the short-term review and the 'what next?' will be addressed to the child. When the teacher wrote up the story of Dylan's construction (as previously discussed), she wrote: "Thank you for helping me Dylan. You have just documented your own learning".

Beyond listening: if children contribute their voices to assessment, what are the possible consequences?

> Damien loves to 'read' his portfolio. He is so enthusiastic in searching out the stories he loves the most that I have to hide away on my own to read the stories carefully and thoroughly, to make sure that I am not constantly interrupted and asked to look at the next one. When we look at it together he turns the pages over and over until he gets to his favourite story about the dinosaur T'Rex and 'Long Neck'. He reads out the words that are written about T'Rex eating 'Long Neck' as soon as he is made and he says, "Those are the exact words I said Mum, that is exactly what I said!".

Robyn, Damien's teacher, added:

> Damien left for school five weeks ago. His portfolio is still one of his most loved books.

Children have a right to have their voices heard in areas that matter to them. The United Nations Convention on the Rights of the Child includes (Article 12) the right to have a voice and to have it listened to and respected. "It is now more common to find acknowledgement that childhood should be regarded as a part of society and culture than a precursor to it; and that children should be seen as already social actors not beings in the process of becoming such" (James and

Prout, 1997, p ix). If we want to get close to recognising what learning is going on, then we will seek multiple perspectives. Sometimes the family will speak on behalf of the child, reflecting aspirations and knowledge from the community. But one of the multiple perspectives will be the children's. Clark and Moss (2001) used what they called a Mosaic approach (using a number of methods within a strength-based framework) to seek children's views on the quality of their childcare programmes (described in Chapter Three of this book). Assessment can do this too.

This is also a matter of social justice within the local context of the early childhood setting. A paper presented to the New Zealand Commissioner of Social Policy outlining fundamental changes that need to be considered in order to achieve a more just society (with particular reference to education for Māori) states that:

> There ought to be no doubt in the minds of teachers that children need to acquire, in the first instance, the relevant knowledge for their wellbeing. For children who wish to shape their own reality, who wish to have control over their own learning, teachers must facilitate and empower them, and there are no shortcuts to that. (Penetito, 1988, p 106)

Furthermore, respecting children's views also means that their views can make a difference. We suggest that the consequences of listening to children's views, and including them as part of assessment, can play out in three ways. It can make a difference to competence, continuity and community (Cowie and Carr, 2004). Here are some examples from *Kei tua o te pae* in which listening to the child has contributed to these three aspects of learning.

Competence

Assessment can make a difference to the child's view of her or himself as a competent learner. A number of writers have commented on the influence of assessment on identity (Gipps, 2002), and Hannah – "I'll be a nothing" – provided an example in the last section. Including children's voices, and revisiting them, is an effective way of using assessment as pedagogy for learning, with this in mind. A parent made the following comment in Charlotte's assessment folder: "Charlotte is very proud of her folder. She took it home and couldn't wait to show her sister as soon as she got out of school and then all the family who came to visit at the weekend. She wanted to talk us through every aspect!!".

The value of this revisiting, its contribution to what Rinaldi in Chapter Two calls 'interior listening', is supported by the research of Nelson (1996, 1997a, 1997b), who maintains that "children have individual episodic memories from infancy, but it is only in the light of *social sharing* that both the enduring form of narrative organisation, and the perceived value to self and others become apparent"

(Nelson, 1997a, p 111). One of the authors of this chapter (Margaret Carr) has interpreted an assessment in a home-based record with Nelson's research in mind. Nearly-three-year-old Jill has dictated the day's activities to her mother, and the mother has written them down in the Home-based Record Book (usually it's the other way around: the teacher, Georgie, writes them down for the family). Jill had described an adult as "getting cross". The interpretation is as follows:

> It cannot be discounted that this ability [to take another point of view in familiar circumstances] has been developed by [revisiting] the Record Book, for example by the documentation itself, which often commented not only on the children's feelings but also on the adult's (in one entry Georgie mentions that the gym teacher is 'sad' that they cannot keep going). (Carr, 2001b, p 131)

Photographs, especially digital images, which can be very quickly added to an assessment record, assist the revisiting: they can become part of the documentation on the same day as the learning episode, and they can be 'read' by the child. Here is a Learning Story in Lachlan's portfolio (Carr et al, 2004), which incorporates photographs. Lachlan is instructing his teacher to write the detailed strategies he has mastered in the art of hula hooping.

"Write about my moves. I keep wriggling to keep it moving."

"When it goes low I have to go faster, see?"

Lachlan shows me how fast he has to go to keep the hula hoop turning.

"See it's on my hips? When you start moving it goes faster. Sometimes it goes slow when I move my body fast and the hula hoop goes down."

Short-term review

Lachlan is so good at using the hula hoop, I can see why you got one at home Moira. It takes a lot of skill to get a hula hoop to move and I think Lachlan would have to be the 'King of the Hula Hoop' at kindergarten!

And, just look at the interest that was sparked for other children when Lachlan started to move!

Left: Photograph 8.3: Hula hooping
Above: Photograph 8.4: Hula hooping 2

Sometimes the children take their own photographs, documenting their own learning process, as in the example of Dylan's construction, described earlier in this chapter. Furthermore, photographs are a visual 'language' that children can use to register and develop their interest (Clark and Moss, 2001; Fasoli, 2003; see also Chapter Three of this volume).

Four-year-old Jason took the following photographs after he had become 'curious about the shadow' (the teacher's words) in a photograph taken of him by the teacher. She gives him the camera, and he takes a series of photographs of shadows: of his and the teachers', and of other shadows.

Photograph 8.5: Shadow 1

Then Jason begins to take photographs of the other children, and they take an interest in this. The teacher has interpreted these episodes as aspects of learning for Jason:

Photograph 8.6: Shadow 2

> Jason had not been at morning kindergarten long, and had been finding it all very overwhelming. As part of the process of settling in to a new situation, he had been looking for people who would be likely friends. Being behind the camera, he was not only able to take photos of what interested him, but also approach people that he would not otherwise [have] approached.

Photograph 8.7: Shadow 3

Jason may explore using the camera further, perhaps with shadows as a focus topic. He has used a visual language to express his interest. Children often use drawings in the same way.

Listening to very young children, who do not use oral language or construct images, includes interpreting gestures, sounds and facial expressions. One teacher wrote a Learning Story about a baby (perhaps eight months old) exploring two buckets of water on a wooden

Photograph 8.8: Shadow 4

deck, putting her hands into the water and rocking them from side to side. She inadvertently tipped one of the buckets over, then quickly righted the empty bucket, and the teacher described the 'look of astonishment' on her face when she could not find the water in the bucket or on the deck (it had quickly run out between the boards of the deck). She looked under the bucket. Then she carefully tipped the second bucket of water out, watching where the water went. She was apparently exploring, and trying to repeat and make sense of, a surprising encounter with tipping and disappearing.

It is typical practice for teachers in Reggio Emilia to document discussions among groups of children as they try to make sense of, and negotiate different viewpoints, about surprising encounters. Teachers in New Zealand occasionally do this: it can involve tape-recording and transcribing, and lengthy discussions with the children and/or teachers. However, having little or no 'non-contact' time and poor adult:child ratios mitigate against frequent use of this practice. The Bronfenbrenner model illustrates well the influence of funding and policy on the capacity for 'visible listening' (in schools as well). In response, a number of teachers are videoing episodes of collective negotiation and learning, and including these as part of children's records, sometimes on CD. These may be revisited and discussed, by families, teachers and children, but are not written down. This aspect of documentation is, as is all of current assessment practice, work in progress.

Continuity

Portfolios, files, or folios of stories about children's learning provide accessible artefacts for children to revisit and review their learning over time. Here is an example, where Alice is revisiting her file, and commenting on her progress in writing her name. The teacher writes the commentary.

Here is Alice and I taking a browse through her portfolio. "I know the words", Alice keeps saying to me. We look at each page. "In the family corner I like to play with my friends Finn and Taylor", says Alice running her finger along the line of words.

The next page is an old story of when Alice was beginning to write her name, "I do it now and I already have my birthday and I know how to do it".

Photograph 8.9: Alice reading

The next page is when Alice had been playing 'Doggy doggy who's got the bone'. On seeing this picture Alice begins to sing the song.

We are now at the end and Alice turns to me and says, "I need some more photographs of me, don't I?". Yes, I agree with you, Alice.

In another example, Alex reviewed an entry in her assessment folder, and noted that the photograph of a building construction was taken before the building was finished. She rebuilt the building, and a new photograph corrected the record.

Community

One of the purposes of developing a portfolio of assessment for learning is that these records will be shared with the wider community of family, including siblings and grandparents. The process is reciprocal. In the Exemplar Project we have collected examples of grandparents and siblings writing stories that they add to the assessment record. Hyoungjin's older sister wrote a Learning Story as a contribution to his portfolio:

> When Hyoungjin is bored or has nothing to do he sometimes plays with his golf set that we bought. It has three golf sticks. They are blue, yellow and red. There is a pocket stuck on the sides for about three balls. Hyoungjin then puts the ball where he wants it to be and holds the golf sticks his special way. Then he hits very hard. If he misses he tries again. He hits it so hard it flies all over the room. We are sometimes worried because it's like he broke a window. When visitors come he sometimes shows them how he hits them [the balls]. They be very surprised at how hard he hits them. He is a very good little golfer.

The point of relevance to this chapter is that when the portfolio goes home, the person who will interpret and add to the stories from the early childhood centre is the child. Damien and Charlotte were examples of this.

Conclusion

We earlier quoted Heshusius's observation that when an adult is truly listening "nothing in her or his mind is weighing, evaluating, judging, or formulating unsolicited advice". If this is so, then listening and assessment at the same time might be impossible. This chapter has introduced some ideas about how assessment can provide the conditions for listening, making it possible to combine the two. We have defined assessment as noticing, recognising and responding. Then, the Heshusius notion of 'weighing' might be seen as *noticing and interpreting* against an image of the child as competent and confident; 'evaluating and judging' might be seen as *interpreting* the learner's voice with reference to what the teacher already knows about the child and what has gone before. The examples in this chapter have illustrated that *responding* might not be confined to 'formulating unsolicited advice'. Documenting these episodes using stories and photographs has provided opportunities for children and their families to contribute, revisit, discuss and reinterpret the learning. In any event, we would argue that listening to children carefully is a central ingredient for assisting them to develop dispositions of responsibility or control and critique, and we have suggested that these are worthwhile aspirations for early childhood spaces, children and teachers.

Acknowledgements

This chapter includes work by the authors for the New Zealand Childhood Ministry of Education, Early Learning and Assessment (ECLA) Exemplar Project. The authors acknowledge funding for this project from the New Zealand Ministry of Education. We thank the families and teachers for their permissions, through the ECLA Exemplar Project, to include their quotes and stories.

Further reading

Carr, M. (2001) *Assessment in early childhood settings: Learning Stories*, London: Paul Chapman Publishing.

Paley, V. (1993) *You can't say you can't play*, Cambridge, MA: Harvard University Press.

Smith, A., Taylor, N. and Gollop, M. (eds) (2000) *Children's voices: Research, policy and practice*, Auckland: Pearson Education.

References

Black, P. and Wiliam, D. (1998) 'Assessment and classroom learning', *Assessment in Education*, vol 5, no 1, pp 7-74.

Bronfenbrenner, U. (1979) *The ecology of human development*, Cambridge, MA: Harvard University Press.

Carr, M. (2001a) 'A sociocultural approach to learning orientation in an early childhood setting', *Qualitative Studies in Education*, vol 14, no 4, pp 525-42.

Carr, M. (2001b) *Assessment in early childhood settings: Learning Stories*, London: Paul Chapman.

Carr, M. and May, H. (1994) 'Weaving patterns: developing national Early Childhood Curriculum guidelines in Aotearoa – New Zealand', *Australian Journal of Early Childhood*, vol 19, no 1, pp 25-33.

Carr, M., Jones, C. and Lee, W. (eds) (2004) *Kei tua o te pae: Assessment for learning, early childhood exemplars*, Wellington: Learning Media.

Carr, M., Hatherly, A., Jones, C. and Lee, W. (2005: forthcoming) 'Literacy: oral, visual and written', in Ministry of Education, *Kei tua o te pae: Assessment for learning, early childhood exemplars*, Wellington: Learning Media.

Carr, M., Hatherly, A., Lee, W. and Ramsey, K. (2003) '*Te Whāriki* and assessment: a case study of teacher change', in J. Nuttall (ed) *Weaving Te Whāriki*, Wellington, New Zealand: NZ CER, pp 187-214.

Clark, A. and Moss, P. (2001) *Listening to young children: The Mosaic approach*, London/York: National Children's Bureau for the Joseph Rowntree Foundation.

Claxton, G.L. (1995) 'What kind of learning does self-assessment drive? Developing a "nose" for quality: comments on Klenowski', *Assessment in Education*, vol 2, no 3, pp 339-43.

Claxton, G.L. and Carr, M. (2004) 'A framework for teaching learning: learning dispositions', *Early Years International Journal of Research and Development*, vol 24, no 1, pp 87-97.

Cowie, B. and Carr, M. (2004) 'The consequences of sociocultural assessment', in A. Anning, J. Cullen, and M. Fleer (eds) *Early childhood education: Society and culture*, London: Sage Publications, pp 95-106.

Duncan, J. (2004) '"She's always been, what I would think, a perfect day-care child": constructing the subjectivities of a New Zealand child', Paper presented to the 12th Reconceptualising Early Childhood Education Conference on Research, Theory and Practice: 'Troubling Identities', Oslo, May.

Fasoli, L. (2003) 'Reading photographs of young children: looking at practices', *Contemporary Issues in Early Childhood*, vol 4, no 1, pp 32-47.

Gipps, C. (2002) 'Sociocultural perspectives on assessment', in G. Wells and G. Claxton (eds) *Learning for life in the 21st century: Sociocultural perspectives on the future of education*, Oxford: Blackwell, pp 73-83.

Greeno, J.G., Collins, A.M. and Resnick, L.B. (1996) 'Cognition and learning', in D.C. Berliner and R.C. Calfee (eds) *Handbook of educational psychology*, New York, NY: Simon and Schuster, Macmillan and London: Prentice Hall, pp 15-46.

Hatherly, A. and Sands, L. (2002) 'So what is different about Learning Stories?', *The First Years: Nga Tau Tuatahi*, vol 4, no 1, pp 8-13.

Heshusius, L. (1995) 'Listening to children: "what could we possibly have in common?" from concerns with self to participatory consciousness', *Theory into Practice*, vol 34, no 2, pp 117-23.

James, A. and Prout, A. (1997) *Constructing and reconstructing childhood: Contemporary issues in the sociological study of childhood* (2nd edn), London: Falmer Press.

Luke, A. and Freebody, P. (1999) 'A map of possible practices: further notes on the four resources model', *Practically Primary*, vol 4, no 2, pp 5-8.

May, H. and Carr, M. (2000) 'National curriculum "empowering children to learn and grow": *Te Whāriki*, the New Zealand early childhood curriculum', in J. Hayden (ed) *Landscapes in early childhood education: cross-national perspectives on empowerment – A guide for the new millennium*, New York, NY: Peter Lang, pp 153-70.

Mercer, N. (2001) 'Developing dialogues', in G. Wells and G. Claxton (eds) *Learning for life in the 21st century: Sociocultural perspectives on the future of education*, Oxford: Blackwell, pp 141-53.

Moss, P. and Petrie, P. (2002) *From children's services to children's spaces: Public policy, children and childhood*, London: RoutledgeFalmer.

Nelson, K. (1996) *Language in cognitive development: The emergence of the mediated mind*, Cambridge: Cambridge University Press.

Nelson, K. (1997a) 'Cognitive change as collaborative construction', in E. Amsel and K.A. Renninger (eds) *Change and development: Issues of theory, method and application*, Mahwah, NJ: Lawrence Erlbaum, pp 99-115.

Nelson, K. (1997b) 'Event representations then now and next', in P.W. van den Broek, P.J. Bauer and T. Bourg (eds) *Developmental spans in event comprehension and representation: Bridging fictional and actual events*, Mahwah, NJ: Lawrence Erlbaum, pp 1-26.

New Zealand Ministry of Education (1996) *Te Whāriki. Te Whāriki Mātauranga mō ngā Mokopuna o Aotearoa: Early childhood curriculum*, Wellington: Learning Media.

Nuttall, J. (ed) (2003) *Weaving Te Whāriki*, Wellington: New Zealand Council for Educational Research.

Paley, V.G. (1990) *The boy who would be a helicopter*, Cambridge, MA: Cambridge University Press.

Paley, V.G. (2004) *A child's work: The importance of fantasy play*, Chicago, IL and London: Chicago University Press.

Penetito, W. (1988) 'Maori education for a just society', *Social Perspectives: Report of the Royal Commission on Social Policy*, April Report Vol IV, Wellington: Royal Commission on Social Policy, pp 89-114.

Perkins, D.N. (1993) 'Person-plus: a distributed view of thinking and learning', in G. Salomon (ed) *Distributed cognitions: Psychological and educational considerations*, Cambridge: Cambridge University Press, pp 88-110.

Reay, D. and Wiliam, D. (1999) '"I'll be a nothing": structure, agency and the construction of identity through assessment', *British Educational Research Journal*, vol 25, no 3, pp 343-54.

Rogoff, B. (2003) *The cultural nature of human development*, Oxford: Oxford University Press.

Rose, N. (1999) *Powers of freedom: Reframing political thought*, Cambridge: Cambridge University Press.

Salomon, G. (ed) (1993) *Distributed cognitions: Psychological and educational considerations*, Cambridge: Cambridge University Press.

Sfard, A. (1998) 'On two metaphors for learning and the dangers of choosing just one', *Educational Researcher*, vol 27, no 2, pp 4-13.

NINE

The competent child and 'the right to be oneself': reflections on children as fellow citizens in an early childhood centre

Anne Trine Kjørholt

Alongside the most extensive early childhood services in the world, the Scandinavian countries have developed a strong discourse about childhood and children's rights, in which practices of participation, giving voice and listening are prominent. Starting from a Danish report called *Listening to children: A book about children as fellow citizens* (Ried Larsen and Larsen, 1992), this chapter makes a critical analysis of the values and assumptions underlying such increasingly widespread practices within Scandinavian early childhood centres. In particular, it examines how they may constitute the child as a particular subject, an autonomous subject to be supported in the exercise of free choice, at the expense of other possibilities such as a relational perspective emphasising care, interdependence and solidarity that links children as individuals to a wider network of relationships.

The chapter confronts us with the possibility that well-meaning initiatives, such as listening to children, can be dangerous not least because they can become means for the more effective governing of children and because behind an apparently neutral surface they may be inscribed with particular moral ideals that should be the subject of critical study and public contestation.

> In the Anthill nursery, no adults pick the toddlers up and carry them, screaming and wriggling, to the bathroom to put on a new nappy. Here the toddlers have the right to continue their play, until they themselves decide to have a new nappy. (Ried Larsen and Larsen, 1992, p 31)

These two sentences introduce the article 'Vuggestuebørn har også ret' ('Toddlers in nurseries have rights, too') in the book *Listening to children: A book about children as fellow citizens*. The project 'Children as Fellow Citizens' was initiated and supported financially by the Danish Ministries of Social Affairs and Culture in the early 1990s. It is one of many participatory projects for children and young people that have been initiated by public authorities in the Nordic countries, as well as in many other countries, since the early 1990s. As the title of the book indicates, listening to children is seen as an important part of recognising their citizenship.

The aim of the Danish project was to empower children as citizens and increase their ability to influence their daily lives. As in Norway and elsewhere, the emphasis on listening to children's voices is part of discourses constructing children as social participants in society that have flourished during the past 15 years in both child policy and child research (Kjørholt, 2001, 2004). The increasing number of participatory projects in this period should be viewed in the context of international discourses on children as social actors with certain rights to participation on the basis of their human rights, as manifested in the United Nations Convention on the Rights of the Child. These discourses on children as citizens are closely related to the concept of 'the competent child' (Kjørholt, 2001; Mortier, 2002), which is often presented as a paradigm shift, replacing earlier concepts of children as vulnerable, dependent and in need of care.

These new discourses, along with the variety of participatory projects, obviously represent new opportunities for children and young people to be listened to, to influence decision-making processes in different contexts, and to be participants in social, political and cultural life in new ways. On the other hand, discourses constructing children as subjects with rights to participation in society are not unproblematic. They often suffer from lack of conceptual clarity and ambiguity related to ideas of both participation and the child subject.

In this chapter I shall present two particular texts that stem from a publication produced by the Danish project Children as Fellow Citizens. My aim is to examine the potential dangers of listening, by discussing the particular notion of young children as 'fellow citizens' represented in these texts. An important task is to show how the practice of listening and the particular construction of children as fellow citizens that are presented in the texts are connoted with specific ideological and moral values. I argue that the construction of the child subject in these texts is related on the one hand to processes of individualisation[1] and the construction of the autonomous, self-determining subject in late modern societies in the Western world in general; and on the other hand to particular cultural notions of 'the free child' that were current in Denmark and Norway during the 1990s. I stress that my intention here is to discuss a particular position existing in the discursive field[2] of children and participation and represented by the two texts, not to present a complete analysis of discourses and ongoing practices in Nordic early childhood institutions as such.

Theoretically I shall relate the discussion to Charles Taylor's theories of individualism and self-realisation in modern societies (Taylor, 1978, 1985, 1991). However, my approach to these texts will also be related to the concepts of discourse and governmentality (Foucault, 1991; Rose, 1996; Neumann, 2000; Hultqvist, 2001).

After the introduction, I will present a short section on methodology, and a brief introduction of the two texts. The analysis of the texts starts with a presentation of a narrative I call 'The right to be oneself', followed by a section discussing the texts' position in the discursive field. After this, I shall continue with a discussion of the texts relating to Charles Taylor's theoretical perspectives on negative liberty, individualisation and self-realisation, as well as perspectives on self-determination as new forms of governmentality, thus questioning the autonomous subject (Foucault, 1991; Rose, 1996; Hultqvist, 2001). Finally I conclude with a critical discussion of both the emerging practices in day care centres and the extreme individualism that the practices described seem to reflect.

Methodological approaches

In my analysis of these texts, I am drawing on the concepts of discourse and narrative. The term 'discourse' is used here as an analytical tool to explore how children are constituted as particular types of subjects through certain ways of speaking in the texts. Foucault refers to discourse as "the general domain of all statements, sometimes as an individualisable group of statements, and sometimes as a regulated practice that accounts for a number of statements" (Foucault, 1972, p 80). This definition leads to a broad view of 'texts', in principle covering both material features such as the physical environment and social practices. The concept of discourse can be used to shed light on how a certain text is culturally constructed in a particular time in history, serving certain interests and representing a specific 'regime of truth' that treats certain assumptions as if they were self-evident and defines what can and cannot be said and practised (Foucault, 1972; Kaarhus, 1992).

The concept of discourse, used as an analytical tool, opens the possibility to explore critically political discourses that subjects are placed in, and thus to offer ideological criticism. According to the anthropologists Crispin Shore and Susan Wright, who use the concept of discourse to analyse the field of policy, discourses are "configurations of ideas which provide the threads from which ideologies are woven" (Shore and Wright, 1997, p 18). Inspired by this thinking, I focus on identifying characteristics of the construction of young children as fellow citizens in the texts, together with related ideas and 'regimes of truth' that seem to be taken for granted.

The texts will also be read as narratives. The concept of 'narrative', taken from literary criticism, is also adopted within the human and social sciences to understand how human life and experience are organised in narrative structures and constituted as narratives. Children's everyday lives are constituted through a variety of different narratives on childhood that exist in a particular society at a certain time. Policies can be read as narratives that serve to justify or condemn the present or legitimise new political visions and practices. Margaret Somers uses the concept of 'political or public narratives', which are "those narratives attached to cultural and institutional formations larger than the single individual, to intersubjective networks or institutions, however local or grand, micro or macro stories" (Somers, 1994, p 619).

As this quotation stresses, cultural narratives are important because they are used as frames of reference for social practices, for instance in early childhood centres: frames of reference that, like regimes of truth, are often taken for granted. Both children and adults are positioned within cultural narratives, which open the way for certain forms of action and meaning making while prohibiting others (Davies, 1993). Narratives or storylines are collective, but they are changed through the different ways in which individuals interpret them and develop their own narratives (Søndergaard, 1999). In other words, cultural narratives represent constraints and possibilities for how subjects narrate themselves and 'do' different positions (Søndergaard, 1999). By reading a certain political or cultural text as a narrative, dominant representations and lines of development in the text often stand out as more evident and visible.

My own position as a reader of the two texts is influenced by theoretical and methodological understandings anchored in childhood as a social construction, cultural analytical approaches that take discourse theory as a starting point, and philosophical theory on individualisation and self-determination (Foucault, 1972; Taylor, 1985; Mills, 1997; Lee, 1998; Neumann, 2000). I am also influenced by my position as a practitioner, in that I draw on my own earlier experiences as a pedagogue in Norwegian *barnehager* (kindergartens).

'Listening to children': a presentation of two selected texts

The written texts that I have chosen come from a publication produced by the Ministry of Culture in connection with the project Children as Fellow Citizens. The two texts are entitled 'Toddlers in nurseries have rights, too', and 'The play is more intensive: no fixed meals and enforcing activities'. The book from which the texts are taken – a report on the project, entitled *Listening to children: A book about children as fellow citizens*, which includes several short articles (Ried Larsen and Larsen, 1992) – can be described as popular in form and aimed at convincing and persuading readers of the value of giving children rights to participate in decision making in day care centres. The authors are journalists by profession and 6,000-8,000 copies have been sold by the Danish Ministry of Culture to a variety of readers, for instance practitioners in early childhood services, local authorities, policy makers, and so on. Requests for the report peaked during the 1990s, but it has also been in demand during the past few years (personal communication from the Danish Ministry of Culture).

The texts are of particular interest because of their rhetorical form. This highlights certain representations of children, freedom and self-realisation in discourses on children's participation. Also evident are the relationships between constructions of children as active social participants in these texts and similar constructions in discourses on children and participation in Norway in 1990s (see, for example, Kjørholt, 2001).

Text one: Toddlers in nurseries have rights, too

Children's rights to be listened to within early childhood institutions are central in this text. Two institutions in a local community have formed part of the Children as Fellow Citizens project: Vuggestuen Myretuen, a nursery for children under three years of age; and Børnehaven Grantoften, a kindergarten for children from two to six years of age. The authors of the book from which the two selected texts are taken, Hanne Ried Larsen and Maria Larsen (Ried Larsen and Larsen, 1992) describe everyday life in these centres and the new practices implemented by the staff as part of the project. The ongoing theme in this text is how toddlers are being empowered and emancipated from adult control by these new practices.

The quotation about toddlers' rights to decide when they are going to have their nappies changed, presented at the start of this chapter, is taken from this text. This quotation illustrates how toddlers are constructed as autonomous subjects with the right to make their own decisions in everyday life within the institutional context. The rhetorical style of the text, which is aimed at convincing the reader of the value of the new practices, is also mirrored in the thematic approaches. One of the themes discussed is parental attitude towards the changes in the institution. Some parents are presented as being negative and sceptical – asking the staff whether the children are going to decide everything by themselves. As part of the argument of the superiority of these new practices, the staff in Vuggestuen Myretuen are described as being successful in changing the attitudes of the parents at special meetings with them. The negative attitudes of parents are explained as resulting from a lack of knowledge and information; so, the authors argue that, when parents are informed and become used to the changes, their negative attitudes disappear.

The authors continue by describing what the professional caretakers do if the toddlers refuse to change their nappy even after being asked ten times: "In order to avoid them [the toddlers] going too far, we make an agreement with them. When they have finished playing, their nappies will be changed".

In the text about Vuggestuen Myretuen, we see the toddlers being constructed as a particular type of subject – rights claimers. The former practice of putting on a new nappy without listening to the toddlers' voices is described as a form of coercion exercised by adults over the toddlers. The new discourse constructing the toddlers as subjects with rights of participation allows no room for this kind of practice on the part of the adults, which, within a different discourse of care and child development, would be defined as an inevitable act or duty of care associated with professional work in early childhood institutions. The children's rights to have 'poo' in their nappies is only one of the rights the children have obtained after the staff started to reflect critically on their rules and listen more to the children.

In the opening quotation we see that children are constructed as belonging to a 'child community' of equals, indicating that power relationships between children seem to be absent. This point is evident in another theme that is discussed in the text, dealing with the toddlers' rights to solve their own conflicts. Conflicts between adults and children are seen to be a result of adult control, which represents a threat to the children's possibilities for self-realisation within the institution. Conversely, conflicts between children do not seem to be an impediment to the individual child's right to self-determination. The quotation below underscores this point:

> The adults' respect for children saying 'no' results in fewer conflicts between children and adults. They do not scream when they are going to get a new nappy. They do not scream when they are going to have their rainwear put on.... But there are more conflicts among the children themselves, a right they have also obtained. Earlier, the adults intervened more. Now the children are allowed to find solutions by themselves. (Ried Larsen and Larsen, 1992, p 31)

The fact that the new cultural practices in this institution result in more conflicts among the children themselves is therefore accepted, since they open up new possibilities for the children to practise another aspect of the right to influence their daily lives – the right to solve their own conflicts without adult intervention. However, the text is completely silent about how different children manage to solve these conflicts.

The authors of 'Toddlers in nurseries have rights, too' also raise the following question: Are there any limits to the children's rights to be listened to and to decide for themselves in the daily life of Vuggestuen Myretuen? The answer, from the staff's points of view, is that "there has to be a certain framework, otherwise the toddlers will feel insecure. But many rules seem to exist for the sake of the rules themselves. All rules have to be discussed" (Ried Larsen and Larsen, 1992, p 31). Two of these rules concern the meals and the sleeping routines in the nursery: the toddlers are not allowed to decide if and when they eat their meals and sleep during the day.

Text two: The play is more intensive

The right of children to decide when to eat their meals, however, is a central theme in the second text, which describes the new practices and daily life in Børnehaven Grantoften. The subtitle of this text indicates the main theme of this short article: 'No fixed meals and enforcing activities'. As in the previous text, the main theme is a description of the improved quality of life for children after the changes in the practices within the institution. As part of the introduction, the author refers to the staff, saying: "Two schoolchildren attended the day care centre [for two days], and then we started to discuss our daily routines and practices. The children made observations, and they inspired us to break with many of our habits" (Ried Larsen and Larsen, 1992, p 27).

The schoolchildren, from the local primary school, were given the task of expressing their views about the ability of the younger children to decide for themselves. Based on the pupils' advice and their own reflections, the staff changed their practices in certain ways to endorse children as fellow citizens. Daily routines, for instance a meal for everybody at a particular time, is one practice that is seen as being forced on children by adults and it has therefore been abolished. The overall argument is that the abolition of rules and the practice of adults deciding timetables and activities mean a better life for children.

The ability of children to decide when to eat seems to be an important part of the right to self-determination, according to the ideas in the Children as Fellow Citizens project. I quote from the text:

> Now the children can eat their lunch when they are hungry.... The fruit meal at two o'clock is also eliminated. It was not the children who needed to stop playing and sit together, eating fruit and listening to fairy tales. The fruit is ready at two o'clock, but the children decide by themselves when they want to eat it. Now the staff only arrange meetings with the whole group (*samlingsstunder*) when it is somebody's birthday, or a group of children have prepared a hot meal for everyone. In other words, when there is a reason for the whole group to be together. (Ried Larsen and Larsen, 1992, p 29)

This text illustrates how different arrangements, such as common meals for everybody (prepared by adults) and fairy tales with the whole group have been eliminated in order to promote children's rights to make their own decisions. As the last sentence indicates, these activities are not seen as a good enough reason for the collective group of children to be together. However, a child's birthday or a hot meal prepared for everybody by a group of children is seen as a reason to be together as a collective group. The paradox that these reasons also seem to be the result of adult opinions and evaluations is not mentioned in the text.

As in the text 'Toddlers in nurseries have rights, too', reactions from parents are also a theme in the second text. The authors report the staff referring to rumours saying that children are allowed to do whatever they want, for instance bring snakes to the centre from their homes. A paragraph in the text adds the following argument to this, under the subtitle 'The world is not created free'. One of the staff members says: "We have not made the whole world free. The children are not allowed to shout or to run up and down the corridors or create a disturbance. It is our responsibility to teach the children ordinary manners" (Ried Larsen and Larsen, 1992, p 28). And she continues: "Excursions, rhythm and music practice and common meals once a week are among the few obligatory activities in Grantoften. It is not up to children to decide whether they want to participate in these activities. The adults see it as their responsibility to give children experiences outside the institution".

The rhetorical form of the text provides no room for discussion or critical argument. Critical voices opposed to the new practices are explained as being caused by a lack of information. The quotation above also underlines certain ambiguities and paradoxes embedded in the text. On the one hand, adult control and decision making on behalf of the children is presented as an evil that has to be abolished. On the other hand, the staff members have in fact made many decisions about structure, rules and the organisation of time and space within these institutions. Another paradox concerns an additional theme presented in the text, namely that the adults need to have a certain structure: "When old habits are broken, one has to have something to stick to" (Ried Larsen and Larsen, 1992, p 28).

In the beginning, the staff drew up a form that organised the adults' activities according to time, space and responsibilities with regard to the new situations. It is remarkable that, whereas a certain structure of time and space during the day is presented as a threat to children's rights to participation, this is presented as a need of the adults working in the centre.

A public narrative about children: 'the right to be oneself'

I read the two texts from Children as Fellow Citizens as a public narrative about children that I have entitled 'The right to be oneself'. As already noted in the methodological section, 'public narratives' are "attached to cultural or institutional formations larger than the single individual" (Somers, 1994, p 619). This public narrative is first and foremost a story about the right of children to decide for themselves and to realise themselves in 'free activities' with other children. In the texts, the fellow citizenship of children is constructed as the individual's right to be free and make her or his own decisions. Freedom for the individual child is connected with notions of 'free choice', a core value in the new practices that the staff are implementing. Children are presented as a weak group in contrast to the adults, who are in a position of power. Intervention from the group in power, the adults, represents an obstacle to the children's ability to be free and to decide for themselves.

The particular way in which children are constituted as rights-claiming subjects from an early age in the two texts is, to me, an illustration of how universalising discourses on children's rights in this context are connected to particular moral values that are hidden in the discourse – in particular valuing the ability of children to make their own individual choices. In this particular narrative, time is a structuring element dividing the story of childhood into two phases: 'the past', characterised by a patriarchy controlling children's well being in a negative way; and the present, which also points towards future visions of equality for all, including children. The new practices that are being implemented are seen as an inevitable step in progress towards democracy for all human beings. The authors take the view that the practices of the past must be left behind because they are oppressive to children and deny them their rights. As such, the narrative is also about the development of egalitarian democratic societies, a development treated as politically and ideologically neutral, something to which one has to adapt.

In the texts, the young children are placed within discourses on children who belong to a group of peers within an age-related social order. This group is described as having a right to play without being interrupted by adults, young children being constructed as, first and foremost, 'playing subjects'. Citizenship is then related to individual choice and rights to play. Children are presented as autonomous and recognised as *equal* to adults in certain respects, but on the basis of being *different*; they are seen as human beings belonging to a particular cultural group whose aim is to realise play. Discourses that construct children as vulnerable and in need of the care and protection of adults are rejected.

The texts also illuminate the tension between, and dualistic nature of, two opposing discourses on children as subjects in early childhood centres. The narrative evokes prevailing discourses in Danish early childhood institutions that situate adults as authoritarian subjects who force young children to perform certain practices without respecting the children's own desires and will. In discourses on children as fellow citizens the daily practice of pedagogues in providing toddlers with a new nappy is given a meaning that differs from the same practice constructed in other discourses on professional care and children's needs. The toddlers and children in the narrative 'The right to be oneself' are constructed as autonomous, competent, rational subjects from an early age, exhibiting the competence not only to make their own decisions, but also to express these decisions verbally.

Common meals: a threat to children's self-realisation

The public narrative is a story about the relationships between citizenship and individual freedom. In my view, the narrative illustrates how this particular position in the discursive field of children's rights to participation means excluding certain kinds of meaning making and cultural practices while promoting others. Whereas a weekly excursion for everybody outside the institution is highly valued and is seen as obligatory for all children, common meals for everybody, which are organised at a certain time every day, are seen as obstructing the exercise of children's rights.

This challenges prevailing discourses in traditional *barnehagepedagogikk* (early childhood pedagogy) and professional care, both in Denmark and Norway, in which collective meals for everybody are valued. Such collective meals can be characterised as a time-structuring, ritual activity, affirming a particular cultural fellowship and making visible each and everybody's belonging to a specific community of children – *barnefellesskap*. These traditional discourses emphasise a homelike, cosy atmosphere in the construction of the meal as a cultural practice (Korsvold, 1998). Flowers and candles create an aesthetic framework around a community of children in which cultural values are both reproduced and created. Common meals can be characterised as both a central site for social interaction, friendship, care and humour, and an affirmation of belonging to this community of children. Participation in common meals has significant symbolic value as an assertion of belonging to a particular culture (Douglas, 2002). The meal is seen as a highly structured and ritualised action, and it obviously also represents discipline and socialisation into certain norms and values in the surrounding culture.

It is interesting to note that the changes in cultural practices that are being implemented by the staff within the institution are mainly spoken into existence within a rights discourse: children's universal rights in general and their right to participate in particular. In the public narrative 'The right to be oneself', common meals are constructed merely as a way of exercising adult power and controlling the children. Other aspects of a common meal, such as those I have described above, are totally absent in the narrative. A collective meal decided by adults is seen as being inconsistent with children's right to choose for themselves. This particular construction of the child subject in the narrative – as an individual human being with the right to decide for him/herself – leaves room for certain types of behaviour and freedom, while closing the door on other possible forms of meaning making and social practices within the institution, like a common meal. The new practices that are being implemented can be interpreted as being part of individualisation processes, in that they eliminate certain forms of collective practices when the whole group is participating together in the same activities.

But the public narrative conveys other possible subject positions for the 'child' and other forms of promoting 'participation rights'. In the text from the Children as Fellow Citizens project, the 'competent child with the right to decide for him/herself' is spoken into existence *as if* there were only one way for the staff to act to fulfil children's rights. In the chosen texts, the particular construction of 'the competent autonomous child' is in a position of hegemony, which effectively excludes alternative subject positions.

The narrative is also a story about the dualistic nature of children and adults as belonging to two different and opposite groups. Relationships between adults and children are constructed only in terms of perspectives of power, which itself seems to be understood as an individual property possessed and exercised above all by adults, while being absent as a force among children.

The position of the texts in the discursive field

As described in the introduction, I shall now place the two texts from the publication *Listening to children: A book about children as fellow citizens* in the discursive field of children as social participants in early childhood services in Denmark and Norway. A central question is whether the particular construction of children and toddlers as fellow citizens in the two texts represents dominant and hegemonic positions in the discursive field, or reflects a marginal position.

In order to answer this, I shall refer to recent discussions in professional and research literature on children as social participants within the field of early childhood education and care. There is a huge amount of literature in this field, and my intention is not to present a complete review of it all. However, I have selected some texts that I find to be of particular interest for my discussion.

In a book published by the Danish National Institute for Educational Research (Denmarks Pædagogiske Universitet) in 1998, the authors discuss pedagogical theory and practice in early childhood centres in Denmark. In a chapter of this book entitled 'Participation or reactive pedagogy' (Hviid, 1998), Hviid characterises ongoing practices in these institutions as a 'what do you want pedagogy', emphasising children's freedom of choice and 'free play'. This pedagogy takes as its starting point the individual child's perspective and refers to particular notions of 'freedom', 'desire', 'self-determination', 'diversity' and 'free choice'. Self-determination, Hviid argues, is mainly understood as the individual's ability to 'decide for her/himself', and to have as many possibilities for individual choice as possible. This understanding prevails in different institutions for children, from toddlers up to schoolchildren.

Hviid is critical of this practice for a variety of reasons. One of her arguments is that this kind of pedagogical practice places the children overwhelmingly in a position where they must take responsibility for their own lives and development. The implication of this, she argues, is that the right to make a choice of one's own includes being responsible for this choice. She points out that this particular practice of encouraging individualism was introduced in the 1990s, representing a change from pedagogical practices during the 1970s and 1980s. Writing at the end of the 1990s, she concludes, "the Danish day care institution probably stands at the threshold of another kind of pedagogy, which places more emphasis on the social and learning aspects" (Hviid, 1998, p 208).

In the discursive field, Hviid's voice confirms the pervasiveness of representations of self-determination and freedom in Danish institutions for children in the cultural texts that I have discussed. However, hers is also a critical voice in the discursive field, since it reveals the emergence of a different construction of the child subject and individualism at the dawn of the 21st century. The hegemonic position of the particular child subject in the two texts I have discussed is thus challenged.

I have also identified similar notions of self-determination and free choice operating in the discursive field in Norway. In many *barnehager* (kindergartens) and *skolefritidsordninger* (school-age free time centres), the practice of eating a meal together has been eliminated since the end of the 1990s as part of the intention of giving children more time for 'free play' and to decide when (and even if, in some institutions) they want to eat their lunch. The head of the state network for *skolefritidsordninger* in Norway reports: "I travel all over the country and hold courses where one of the issues I address is the meal. When, talking into the microphone, I speak warmly of free eating in tall trees with one's mates,

I get icy looks from wise women in their prime in the audience" (SFO, 1999, p 4).

We can see, therefore, that the construction of children as social participants in institutions in Norway is emphasised in various ways. But there has been no state-initiated project on children as fellow citizens in early childhood centres, as there has been in Denmark. However, in some parts of the country some public authorities have recently initiated more systematic approaches to implementing practices connected to 'children's participation rights' in *barnehager*.

The child's right to choose activities, and the children with whom she/he wants to play, is stressed in institutions both for young and school-age children in both Norway and Denmark. Contemporary discussions concerning early childhood institutions in Denmark are characterised by "moral assumptions and evaluations on individual autonomy, social coherence and perceptions of the welfare society and citizenship" (Gulløv, 2001, p 2). Research in Danish *skolefritidsordninger* shows that the staff strongly emphasise children's abilities to decide and manage themselves. Susanne Højlund relates a story concerning one of the staff members in an institution in Denmark where she was doing fieldwork. While closing the door to a particular room where children were playing together without adult intervention, she enthusiastically stated, "in that room the children can be themselves completely and utterly" (Højlund, 2000, p 7). This quotation illustrates how notions of freedom and self-realisation within institutional contexts are associated with the absence of adult control and intervention.

These particular cultural notions of 'being oneself' also correspond to the anthropologist Marianne Gullestad's analyses of changes in relationships between the generations in Norway during the past five to six decades. Whereas children in the 1950s were brought up to be useful, children in contemporary Norway are brought up to 'be themselves' (Gullestad, 1997). There is, however, as Prout (2000) has pointed out, a certain tension between different contemporary discourses: between discourses of children as autonomous social actors with an emphasis on self-realisation on the one hand, and discourses of children as beings in need of more control on the other. The ambiguities between contemporary discourses illustrate a situation characterised by a new blurring of borders between adults and children.

The texts presented about children as fellow citizens in Danish early childhood centres form part of contemporary discourses on children's rights and their place in society. Thoughts, reflections and ways of reasoning about children that are presented in the texts affect the social practices being developed within the institutions, as well as how the generational order is constructed. Locating the child subject in discourses on children's rights in these two early childhood institutions universalises a particular subject position for children, and by so doing contributes to making a shift in discursive practices in early childhood centres authoritative (Shore and Wright, 1997).

Negative liberty, individualisation and self-realisation

From this background, I draw the conclusion that the two texts in the Danish report *Listening to children*, represent a position that is not on the periphery of the discursive field of children and participation. However, researchers have not empirically documented how far the practices described in the two selected texts have spread in Danish and Norwegian centres. The texts document a certain position in the discursive field that it is important to make visible and discuss.

One important question is how such public texts on children as fellow citizens can acquire validity by being produced in universal children's rights discourses. I shall approach this question by referring to the philosopher Charles Taylor, for whom individualism is a major malaise of modernity. Taylor, like many other contemporary philosophers and social scientists, stresses that individualism can take various forms and assume several facets that can be approached from different perspectives. In my discussion I shall tentatively look at particular forms of modern individualism as moral discourses on human life that characterise Western societies. Children and adults are both placed in particular discourses representing moral ideas and values that form the subject in such a way as to affect possible ways of acting and thinking. Particular storylines or narratives on individualism can be identified in these discourses. Taylor argues that "modern freedom and autonomy centres us on ourselves, and the ideal of authenticity requires that we discover and articulate our own identity" (Taylor, 1991, p 81).

Taylor's theories on individualism in modern Western societies are useful in understanding powerful discourses and storylines that affect the construction of modern subjects – children as well as adults. In earlier times and a different social order, individual life was to a large degree determined by 'fate' and by inhabiting particular positions serving the interests of a community grounded in the order of things or the will of God. Today, new moral positions hold that everyone has the right to have their own values and to develop their own ways of life grounded in individual choices about what is important. Taylor claims further that "this individualism involves a centring on the self and a concomitant shutting out, or even unawareness, of the greater issues or concerns that transcend the self, be they religious, political, historical. As a consequence, life is narrowed or flattened" (Taylor, 1991, p 14).

This centring on individual self-fulfilment is connected with a moral idea of being 'true to oneself', which can be described as a culture of authenticity that points to a better or 'higher' mode of life. Subjects who are true to the 'inner voice' by which they are constituted reach the higher mode of life. In order to act correctly, one has to listen to one's own nature and feelings 'deep inside'. Taylor is critical of the fact that the force of subjectivism and the contemporary culture of authenticity are not openly discussed as a moral ideal, but are rather explained in terms of "recent changes in the mode of production, or new patterns of youth consumption, or the security of affluence" (Taylor, 1991, p 21).

Closely related to the contemporary culture of authenticity are Rousseau's ideas about freedom. Taylor argues that freedom is often conceptualised as 'self-determining freedom', referring to the idea that individual freedom means individual independence from others, being free from external influences. This concept of freedom is connected with traditions of 'negative freedom'. Whereas theories of negative freedom are connected with individual choice and notions of freedom as doing what one wants, another tradition of 'positive freedom' stresses the subject's actual ability to control and shape his/her own life (Taylor, 1985).

Although children are not a specific focus of his theoretical approach, I find Taylor's perspectives to be of great relevance in discussing children as subjects in modern Western societies. He claims that the ideal of authenticity in Western culture in the past two centuries has "identified one of the important potentialities in human life" (Taylor, 1991, p 74). However, he also argues that it is important to explore contemporary discourses critically in order to reveal negative forms of the ideal of authenticity that are connected with notions of freedom as self-determining freedom. Taylor's standpoint is that practices linked with contemporary ideals of individual self-realisation and authenticity must be defined and discussed in relation to the moral ideas and ethics to which these practices subscribe (Taylor, 1991).

From this perspective, implementing children's rights to be active participants in early childhood or other institutions entails continuous critical evaluation: of the dynamic relationships between each child subject's expression, wishes and needs on the one hand, and the particular moral and cultural space in which these expressions are developed on the other. I agree with Taylor that we cannot reject the ideals of self-realisation and authenticity that are connected with the construction of human subjects in modern societies. The ability to be active participants by developing individuality and self-realisation within the early childhood centre are, I suggest, of great importance. However, individual self-realisation and the right to be an active social participant in everyday life must be evaluated in accordance with the social practices that are constructed and the social and moral space within which these practices are constituted. Human relationships, intergenerational as well as age-related, are part of the social and moral space of these institutions.

In the public texts I have presented, the moral space in which children are placed seems to be a space that constructs self-determination and negative freedom as overarching values. This is problematic for many reasons. Taylor argues that "the subject himself cannot be the final authority on the question whether he is free; for he cannot be the final authority on the question whether his desires are authentic, whether they do or do not frustrate his purposes" (Taylor, 1985, p 216). According to Taylor, individual self-realisation is always closely connected with participation in and belonging to a human community. The subject's individual autonomy is closely intertwined with dependency since it is constructed within a web of social relationships (Lee, 1998).

The values and moral standards in human communities constitute a basis for individual choice, values and preferences. Rather than a focus on individual choice to liberate children from external control – that is, adult power – the main focus should be discourses and social practices in early childhood centres. It is most important to explore critically what kind of choices each child has. These choices can be evaluated by being related to analysis of the complexities of the cultural context, constituting a social space for children as citizens.

Social processes of inclusion and marginalisation during 'free play' are one important aspect of this space. Can each child choose to be included in different groups of child communities and to form close friendships? Is there a variety of different positions available related to play, or are some children constantly placed in marginal positions such as, for example, that of being a dog in a symbolic play about family life? Is individual self-realisation and autonomy related to caring relationships? What kind of subjectivities and social practices are available in the social space within which the child is placed? Children's voices in some ways always mirror the moral and social space of which they are part. Listening to children, therefore, also means to examine critically the social practices that are constituted by adults in the institutional context.

Discourses on children as fellow citizens in early childhood centres have to link children as individuals to a wider network of relationships, a network consisting of both children and adults. Within any one institution there is likely to be a fluid network of different and shifting relationships, characterised by diversity related to ongoing social processes and social practices. These relationships may represent different communities – *fellesskap* – that expose children to certain moral and cultural values and standards. Degrees of inclusion, exclusion and belonging to such groups of friends – or communities – will be a core issue in relation to understanding children's expressions and choices. These are not 'free choices'; rather they are choices developed within the particular social and moral space to which each child relates.

Self-determination as new forms of governmentality: questioning the autonomous subject

The particular construction of children as fellow citizens in early childhood centres can also be examined from another angle. Foucault's concept of governmentality questions notions of individual freedom and power as an individual possession, as revealed in the public texts on citizenship in Danish centres that have been analysed earlier in this chapter. Subjects, Foucault argues, are situated and constituted within discourses, "practices that systematically form the objects of which they speak" (Foucault, 1972, p 49). The fact that discourses 'design' subjects in particular ways implies that individual autonomy and freedom are always related to a particular subject positions. From a discourse theoretical point of view, one might argue that these particular forms of individualism – which, according to Taylor, may legitimate 'the worst forms of subjectivism' –

represent 'regimes of truth' to which subjects in modern Western societies are subjugated.

Foucault highlights an apparent paradox of present-day life: "Never, I think in the history of human sciences – even in the old Chinese society – has there been such a tricky combination in the same political structures of *individualisation* techniques and of *totalisation* procedures" (Foucault, 1982, p 213; emphasis added). Without going further into this short text by Foucault, we can see that the quotation underlines the oppressive power of contemporary discourses that place human beings in positions that promote new forms of subjectivity: in this context, individualism is an imperative, not a choice.

Foucault regarded practices of government in contemporary Western societies as troubling (Gordon, 1991). He coined the concept of 'governmentality' to describe the way in which individuals are regulated not through external coercion but by the creation of subjectivity and self-discipline, which in turn regulate choices. In modern societies, regimes of truth 'design' subjects – adults as well as children – in particular ways, creating new forms of subjectivity, for example as self-determining rational subjects. Thus constituted, subjects then govern themselves: governmentality, as Foucault pithily put it, is "the conduct of conduct".

New forms of subjectivity relate to changes in economy and political life and the development of decentralised forms of governing. Liberal principles of governing emphasise the autonomous and self-regulated subject. Building on the theories of Foucault and Rose, Hultqvist's analysis of early childhood centres (*forskola* or preschools) and primary schools in Sweden shows that, since the 1970s, there has been an increasing emphasis on the child as a responsible subject.

> [Children] have become a subject that is 'guaranteed' a certain freedom to act on their own, to be autonomous and self-reliant. This idea of freedom inscribed within the practices of childhood is the vantage point for the new decentralised rationales for governance. Freedom is the result as well as the prerequisite of such decentralised forms of governing. (Hultqvist, 1997, p 409)

In his analysis of the history of Swedish preschools, Hultqvist asserts that the particular construction of the child subject in contemporary preschool discourses can be traced back to a period of transition between 1920 and 1940. The child was seen as a renewer of society, as a hope for creating a better society in the future. In order to make a more humane society and recreate social life, the child had to realise his or her full potential.

> Inherent in this vision is the liberal idea to set the child free. The child must be released from the restraints of the old order, for example from the traditions and conventions of the adult society, in order for the child to be able to realise their (and the person's) full potential. (Hultqvist, 1997, p 419)

The quotation also illustrates how contemporary notions of children and self-realisation in Nordic countries are related to the concept of negative freedom that I presented earlier. According to Hultqvist, freedom is a principle through which children are governed. On the basis of this, one may assume that contemporary discourses on children as fellow citizens linked to notions of freedom as negative freedom restrict children's possibilities to act and think, rather than broadening their horizons for a variety of possible actions, thoughts, expressions and emotional feelings of freedom and belonging. One might argue that young children's verbal expressions of their desires and choices in the two Danish centres, Myretuen and Grantoften, mirror discourses on extreme forms of individualism in the institutional context. In other words, the children choose and express wishes and desires from a limited repertoire of subject positions made available to them within particular discursive practices that are constructed by the adults in the institutions. Placing young children in early childhood institutions in a position to take their own decisions in this way can thus be interpreted as an example of new forms of governmentality in modern societies.

The early childhood centre as a space for children as citizens

I have argued that it is important to realise that the space created for children to construct themselves as fellow citizens and competent individuals with the right 'to be themselves', reflected in the texts about the two Danish centres, is in fact an ideological and moral space suggesting particular notions of what it means to be a child. But this is not openly discussed in the texts. Likewise, the fact that adults construct the space created for children's rights of participation as a rather limited space for action and meaning making is hidden. There are some paradoxes in this particular construction of the social and 'free' space, for placed within these discourses there are many areas of choice denied children.

The space is designed in a particular architectural style, with particular toys and furniture representing values and norms concerning how to behave as a child in the institution. They are placed in this limited material space together with groups of other children of roughly their own age. Placing children in this age-related social order clearly imposes many restrictions on the choices that are available to them. For example, they are not able to choose to participate in an intergenerational relationship and interact with age groups other than preschool children; they cannot participate in working activities, or decide to engage in activities together with their parents or older siblings; nor can they choose to go outside the institution. It is important to bear in mind, therefore, that the children's voices that the discourse requires staff to listen to are produced within this particular social and ideological space. Other voices would have appeared within other cultural contexts.

The two texts about children as citizens in early childhood institutions can, I have argued, be read as a narrative of the construction of children as rational subjects realising ultimate moral values: of self-determining freedom and individual choice. The new practices empowering children to decide for themselves, being freed from external (adult) control, are obviously connected with notions of negative freedom. The representations of children and the new social practices that are described in the texts 'The play is more intensive: no fixed meals and enforcing activities' and 'Toddlers in nurseries have rights, too', certainly serve to substantiate Taylor's argument. Based on his theoretical perspectives, it is important to view children's social participation in such institutions in the light of a broader cultural context – first and foremost, as he assumes, within the moral space of which individual choice and freedom form a part. This concerns both the individual level and the group level. For each individual, choices have different meanings and significance, some being of great importance while others count less according to the situation and the more overarching values to which the individual subscribes. Chapter Four in this book by Hanne Warming also illustrates this point.

In the text 'The play is more intensive', conflicts between children were seen as promoting a new right: to solve conflicts by themselves. Whereas the staff in the institution aimed to avoid conflicts between adults and children, since they saw these as an expression of adult power and control, the new practices were seen as promoting this new right among children. This example clearly shows that the overriding moral value here is self-determination for the individual child. Ways of resolving conflicts are neither differentiated nor evaluated according to any form of ethical standard of good and bad. If two children are involved in a conflict between each other, and the children are forced to find their own solutions to this conflict, children (like adults) will obviously choose a variety of different ways to solve such conflicts. Some children may then be placed in positions as winners, whereas others become losers. Some children might suffer by being placed in a subordinate position as victims of injustice, which is legitimated by discourses on 'children's rights to solve conflicts on their own'. Such discourses also imply leaving the responsibility to children for their own social life, as well as for making moral decisions on their own. One may ask whether this practice represents adults' abdication from a caring relationship with children.

In my view, Taylor's critique of self-determination and 'free choice' as guiding moral values can be related to this example. Some ways of solving conflicts are better than others, according to moral standards of justice. To avoid placing children in positions of perverted individualism, it is necessary to discriminate and reflect on different ways of solving conflicts in relation to these standards, and to make such moral standards superior to the individual's free choice. When groups of children are together – as in an early childhood centre – reflections and evaluations about whose interests count must be made repeatedly.

Seeing the particular form of individual freedom that is described in the texts as a way of governing children – and thus as being an inherent part of power relations – makes possible reflections on children's participation within institutional contexts other than the particular rights discourse represented in the analysed text. So from a Foucauldian perspective, it can be argued that, by being placed in discourses constructing human beings as autonomous and self-determining subjects, children are being placed in positions that are oppressive in new ways. Subjects are constructed as having the intentions and the 'free will' to decide for themselves and create their own 'way of life'. The agency associated with this child subject implies, in certain contexts, a subject with an almost absolute power to influence and change the circumstances of life.

This perspective also opens up the possibility of questioning the role of language and speech acts as constitutive of the subject as a social participant, as seen in the Danish texts about the two institutions, Myretuen and Grantoften. It has been argued that universalistic notions of the human being, such as rights discourses, can be connected with particularistic notions of the human being that recognise individuals as rights claimers based exclusively on cognitive and linguistic competence (Vetlesen, 1996). An alternative view is to link rights and human dignity not to individual competence, but to the assumption that individuals who can be offended and humiliated and exposed to vulnerability of any kind have rights (Vetlesen, 1996). An implication of this is to open up for notions of children as sensitive and emotional subjects who express their experiences in a variety of different ways. This argument is of particular relevance, I think, for discussions of children's rights to be listened to in formal institutions like an early childhood centre.

Conclusion

The aim of this chapter has been to discuss and contextualise universal children's rights discourses and practices connected with children's rights to be listened to and be active participants, which have been widespread in Nordic countries in recent years. The narrative of children's rights to participation within Danish early childhood centres is a narrative of particular forms of individualism in a modern Western society that constructs certain ideas of individual autonomy and self-realisation as overarching moral values. Self-realisation is conceptualised as the individual's right to make her or his own choices and decisions; and children's self-realisation is seen, first and foremost, as an individual project that can be realised within an age-related social order. As such, the narrative I have entitled 'The right to be oneself' is also a public narrative that conceptualises an age-related social order as a moral ideal, constructed as a relationship between equal individual child subjects. Play is seen as a core activity of the subjects belonging to a 'community of children', reflecting particular cultural notions of what it means to be a child in the Danish context.

This particular construction of children and childhood is in line with constructions of children as social participants and fellow citizens in Norway (Kjørholt, 2001). The toddlers in the Myretuen centre were constructed as 'fellow citizens' by obtaining the new 'right' in their daily life in the institution "to have poo in their nappy" (Ried Larsen and Larsen, 1992, p 31). This example clearly illustrates the need to challenge such positions within discourses on 'children and participation' in different ways, to destabilise it by making visible truths that are taken for granted, and to 'speak into existence' important issues and perspectives that until now have been excluded from the discourse.

I have also argued that there is a need to replace the notion of the autonomous subject with a relational perspective emphasising care and solidarity, based on the assumption that all subjects, whether adults or children, move between different and shifting positions of dependence and independence, competence and incompetence. The construction of children as social participants – or citizens – in early childhood centres represents important challenges for policy and research, as well as for the field of early childhood education and care. The ability of children and toddlers to be active social participants influencing everyday life and realising themselves are today preferred goals. However, individual self-realisation and rights of participation must be critically explored in relation to the complexities of the moral and cultural space children inhabit. A core need is to obtain insights into children's own constructions of identities and communities in these institutions, and to explore how they position themselves within contemporary discourses on individualisation and children as citizens.

Acknowledgements

I warmly thank Eva Gulløv, Hansjörg Hohr, Chris Jenks, Karen Fog Olwig and Jens Qvortrup for valuable comments on an earlier version of this chapter.

Notes

[1] The concept of 'individualisation' is often used in different ways without further clarification. Näsman, referring to Turner (1986), distinguishes between three forms of individualism: a political doctrine of individual rights; an expression of individual autonomy; and the process of individuation, which points to integrative processes connecting the individual to social forms (Näsman, 1994). It is the first two forms that are of particular relevance for my discussion here.

[2] The concept 'discursive field' refers to the variety of different possible interpretations of meaning existing in the discourse, *before* certain articulations and positions are fixed in the discourse – a process that Laclau and Mouffe refer to as "the partial fixation of meaning within discourses" (Torfing, 1999).

Further reading

Gullestad, M. (1997) 'From being of use to being oneself: dilemmas of value transmission between the generations in Norway', in M. Gullestad and M. Segalen (eds) *Family and kinship in Europe*, London: Pinter, pp 202-18.
Hultqvist, K. (2001) 'Bringing the Gods and the angels back? A modern pedagogical saga about excess in moderation', in K. Hultqvist and G. Dahlberg (eds) *Governing the child in the new millennium*, London: Routledge, pp 143-71.

References

Danmarks Pædagogiske Universitet (Danish National Institute for Educational Research) (1998) *Pedagogisk faglighed i dagistitusjoner (Pedagogy in day care centres)*, Copenhagen: Danmark's Paedagogiske Universitet.

Davies, B. (1993) *Shards of glass: Children reading and writing beyond gendered identities*, NSW, Australia: Allen & Unwin.

Douglas, M. (2002) *Purity and danger: An analysis of the concepts of pollution and taboo*, London: Routledge.

Foucault, M. (1972) *The archaeology of knowledge*, London: Routledge.

Foucault, M. (1982) 'The subject and power', in H.L. Dreyfus and P. Rabinow (eds) *Michel Foucault: Beyond structuralism and hermeneutics*, Brighton: Harvester Press, pp 208-26.

Foucault, M. (1991) 'Governmentality', in G. Burchell, C. Gordon and P. Miller (eds) *The Foucault effect: Studies in governmentality*, Chicago, IL: University of Chicago Press, pp 87-104.

Gordon, C. (1991) 'Governmental rationality: an introduction', in G. Burchell, C. Gordon and P. Miller (eds) *The Foucault effect: Studies in governmentality*, Chicago, IL: University of Chicago Press, pp 1-51.

Gullestad, M. (1997) 'From being of use to being oneself: dilemmas of value transmission between the generations in Norway', in M. Gullestad and M. Segalen (eds) *Family and kinship in Europe*, London: Pinter, pp 202-18.

Gulløv, E. (2001) 'Placing children', Paper presented at the research seminar 'Children, Generation and Place: Cross-cultural Approaches to an Anthropology of Children', Network for Cross-Cultural Child Research, University of Copenhagen, 19-21 May.

Højlund, S. (2000) 'Childhood as a social space: positions of children in different institutional contexts', Paper presented at the conference 'From Development to Open-ended Processes of Change', Institute of Anthropology, University of Copenhagen, 6-7 April.

Hultqvist, K. (1997) 'Changing rationales for governing the child: a historical perspective on the emergence of the psychological child in the context of preschool – notes on a study in progress', *Childhood*, vol 4, no 4, pp 405-24.

Hultqvist, K. (2001) 'Bringing the gods and the angels back? A modern pedagogical saga about excess in moderation', in K. Hultqvist and G. Dahlberg (eds) *Governing the child in the new millennium*, London: Routledge, pp 143-71.

Hviid, P. (1998) 'Deltakelse eller reaktiv pædagogik' ('Participation or reactive pedagogy'), in U. Brinkkjær, I.M. Bruderop, V.R. Hansen, P. Hviid, J.C. Jørgensen, C. Palludan and S. Thyssen (eds) *Pedagogisk faglighed i dagistitusjoner (Pedagogy in day care centres)*, Rapport 34, Copenhagen: Danmarks Pædagogiske Universitet, pp 207-26.

Kaarhus, R. (1992) 'Diskurs som analytisk begrep' ('Discourse as an analytical concept'), *Norsk Antropologisk Tidsskrift*, vol 3, no 2, pp 105-17.

Kjørholt, A.T. (2001) '"The participating child" – a vital pillar in this century?', *Nordisk Pedagogikk*, vol 21, no 2, pp 65-81.

Kjørholt, A.T. (2004) 'Childhood as a social and symbolic space: discussions on children as social participants in society', Doctoral thesis 152, Trondheim: Department of Education/Norwegian Centre for Child Research, Norwegian University of Science and Technology.

Korsvold, T. (1998) *For alle barn! Barnehagens framvekst i velferdsstaten (For all children! The progress of kindergarten in the welfare state)*, Oslo: Abstrakt Forlag As, Utdanningsvitenskapelig Serie.

Lee, N. (1998) 'Towards an immature sociology', *Sociological Theory*, vol 46, no 3, pp 458-82.

Mills, S. (1997) *Discourse*, London: Routledge.

Mortier, F. (2002) 'The meaning of individualization for children's citizenship', in F. Mouritsen and J. Qvortrup (eds) *Childhood and children's culture*, Odense: University Press of Southern Denmark, pp 79-102.

Näsman, E. (1994) 'Individualization and institutionalization of childhood in today's Europe', in J. Qvortrup, M. Bardy and H. Wintersberger (eds) *Childhood matters: Social theory, practice and politics*, Aldershot: Avebury, pp 165-88.

Neumann, I. (2000) *Mening, materialitet, makt: En innføring i diskursanalyse (Meaning, power and materiality: An introduction to discourse analyses)*, Oslo: Fagbokforlaget.

Prout, A. (2000) 'Children's participation: control and self-realisation in British late modernity', *Children and Society*, vol 14, no 4, pp 304-15.

Ried Larsen, H. and Larsen, M. (1992) *Lyt til børn: En bok om børn som medborgere (Listening to children: A book about children as fellow citizens)*, Copenhagen: Det Tværministerielle Børneudvalg og Kulturministeriets Arbejdsgruppe om Børn og Kultur.

Rose, N. (1996) 'The death of the social? Re-figuring the territory of government', *Economy and Society*, vol 23, no 3, pp 327-56.

SFO (Skolefritidsordninger) (1999) *SFO-Nytt no 7*, Oslo: Norwegian Ministry of Education.

Shore, C. and Wright, S. (1997) 'Policy: a new field of anthropology', in C. Shore and S. Wright (eds) *Anthropology of policy: Critical perspectives on governance and power*, London: Routledge, pp 3-42.

Somers, M. (1994) 'The narrative constitution of identity: a relational and network approach', *Theory and Society*, vol 23, no 6, pp 605-49.

Søndergaard, D.M. (1999) *Destabilising discourse analyses: Approaches to poststructuralist empirical* research, Working Paper 7, Køn i den akademiske organsisasjon, Copenhagen: København Universitet, Institutt for Statskundskab.

Taylor, C. (1978) *Sources of the self: The making of the modern identity*, Cambridge: Cambridge University Press.

Taylor, C. (1985) *Philosophy and the human sciences*, Philosophical Papers 2, Cambridge: Cambridge University Press.

Taylor, C. (1991) *The ethics of authenticity*, Cambridge, MA: Harvard University Press.

Torfing, J. (1999) *New theories of discourse: Laclau, Mouffe and Zizek*, Oxford: Blackwell.

Turner, B.S. (1986) 'Personhood and citizenship', *Theory, Culture and Society*, vol 3, no 1, pp 1-16.

Vetlesen, A.J. (1996) 'Om menneskers likeverd i spenningsfeltet mellom universalistiske og kommunitaristiske perspektiver' ('Equality among human beings in the intersection between universal and communitarian perspectives'), *Norsk Filosofisk Tidsskrift*, vol 31, no 1-2, pp 19-38.

TEN

Beyond listening: future prospects

Anne Trine Kjørholt, Peter Moss and Alison Clark

In our opening chapter we discussed the choice of *Beyond listening* as the title for this book as reflecting certain ambivalence towards the term. But as we come to the end of the book, we can see our ambivalence goes deeper and concerns some of the reasons why listening has become so prominent. Listening to children today is often inscribed in rights discourses, constructing children as competent social actors with rights to be listened to and to have a say in matters that affect their lives (Kjørholt, 2001, 2004). These rights discourses are based on the Anglo-American liberal tradition, which constructs human beings as legal subjects capable of speaking for themselves and acting in their own interests. The subject is constructed as a rational autonomous individual, with the consciousness to formulate his or her own needs and wishes. Within these discourses, it has been argued that children are "deemed to possess the autonomy and self-consciousness sufficient to be able to make rights claims" (Diduck, 1999, p 128).

From our perspective, this relationship between listening and rights can be problematised for a number of reasons. First, it creates two opposing or dichotomous images of the child: as either vulnerable and dependent *or* as autonomous and competent. In rights discourses, competence is used as a legal concept, related to psychological understanding; the attribution of incompetence in children, both legally and psychologically, is often used to deny children rights to participate and to be listened to (Flekkøy, 1993; Mortier, 2002). Today's liberal-based rights discourses on listening to children produces new visions of childhood, empowering a disenfranchised group in society by replacing one essentialist image of child – 'the vulnerable and dependant child' – with another – 'the autonomous omnipotent competent child' (Kjørholt, 2001, 2004) who is given the right to have a voice. Neoliberal and market-oriented discourses on consumerism also constructing young children as customers and consumers contribute to strengthening this particular image of the competent autonomous child.

This dichotomy is also to be seen in the so-called new sociology of childhood with its criticism of what are called pre-sociological perspectives on children and childhood, closely associated with a developmental paradigm. These perspectives, mainly involving actors from psychology, pedagogy and health science, have been characterised as constructing the child as a 'human becoming', an incomplete human being compared to an adult and/or mature person, vulnerable, dependent and, first and foremost, in need of care. The new childhood researchers have replaced this construction with the child as a 'being', a competent social actor on a par with adults (Qvortrup, 1994).

This dichotomous construction – opposing images of children as either autonomous and competent or vulnerable and dependent – relies on particular notions of what it means to be a human being, anchored in Western-oriented and Kantian notions of maturity related to individual autonomy and rational thinking (Kjørholt, 2004). It pays no attention to the alternative possibility: that human worth may be rooted in care, interdependence and mutual needs (Diduck, 1999). Instead, the quasi-legal discourse of the autonomous, rational child subject creates a new form of oppressive subject position for children.

In order to create liberating discourses, it is important to avoid placing children in dichotomous constructions of subjectivity as either dependent or independent, either mature or immature, either vulnerable or competent, either equal or unequal to adults. The culture of relationship and listening, as elaborated in this book, represents a break with such dichotomous constructions, accentuating communities and belonging and subjectivities that are relational, connected and interdependent or, as Lee (1998) argues, constantly moving in relations with others between positions of dependence and independence. Such subjectivities are "difficult for liberal notions of justice to accommodate, based as they are on abstracted autonomy, independence and disconnection from other subjects and social conditions" (Diduck, 1999, pp 124-5).

Second, rights discourses are prone to exclude the embodied subject and thus the embodied expressions that are vital in order to understand and recognise children as human beings. This perspective is of particular relevance in relation to toddlers and other children in early childhood centres. It is highly important to be aware of the 'unspoken words', the huge complexity of bodily movements and emotional expressions, by which children construct their identities and social practices in everyday life (for example, illustrated in the account of a Learning Story about a baby in Chapter Eight). It has been argued that there are some "needs that are not easily expressed in rights claims – like the need to be loved, to receive emotional support and so on" (Mortier, 2002, p 83). Emotional support and close and caring relationships with both adults and other children are significant in order for children to become active participants in everyday life within early childhood centres (Kjørholt, 2004).

Third, a rights-based approach can give rise to an over-simplified idea and unambiguous view of the child and listening. Competence is conceptualised as a static, immanent and individual characteristic. 'Children's voices' are essentially authentic spoken by individual and autonomous subjects. There is no element of relationship and emotion and, therefore, of interpretation involved: simply the direct, unmediated and authentic expression and reception of views, requirements or choices.

Nor, in the universal liberal discourse, is there any room for diversity. The increasingly rhetorical power of 'children's voices', and the hegemonic position of global rights discourses and neoliberal, market-oriented consumer discourses, make it pertinent to critically examine and explore the local contexts and the social practices related to terms like 'listening' and 'participation'. Theoretical reflections and critical discussion of different 'listening practices' – such as those outlined in the preceding chapters – are crucial in order to avoid 'surfing on the surface of the wave' of the increasingly rhetorical power of contemporary discourses on 'the competent child' and related terms such as listening, participation rights, children's voice(s) and children's perspective(s).

Beyond rights to ethics

The critique of universal rights discourses for being connected to particularistic notions of the human being – recognising individuals as right claimers based exclusively on cognitive and linguistic competence – convinces us of the need to go beyond these discourses when listening to young children (or indeed any person of whatever age). However, it is important to underline that going beyond rights discourses does not mean rejecting these discourses. We recognise that the prominence given to rights as a rationale for listening will vary between people and organisations; some will consider it the main rationale, and we can respect that position. We have problemetised the rationale, not opposed it.

In our view, rights have their place, and an important one, in improving the lives of children and reconstructing their position in society from that of passive dependants to that of active subjects and citizens. We agree with Burman's pragmatic view on rights, "that we should recognise the tactical character of our engagement with the discourse of individualism via rights approaches and work alongside this towards formulating more genuinely interpersonal and intersubjective approaches to development and education" (Burman, 2001, pp 14-15). From this perspective, rights need to be seen as part of political processes in the global society of negotiations between different groups; in other words, as part of the currency of democratic politics rather than as truth claims professing to stand outside such messy exchanges.

They also need to be supplemented with more nuanced and interpersonal ideas of what it means to be a human being, including what it means to be a child. The human beings involved in the social processes of listening, whether they be children or adults, are not simply rational beings with cognitive competence only, but sensitive, emotional, embodied beings. Valerie Driscoll and Caron Rudge underline this in Chapter Six, where they insist that children's emotional well being is an important part of the culture of listening in Fortune Park. Similarly, Carlina Rinaldi in Chapter Two insists that "listening is emotion", and "involves interpretation" as well as "sensitivity to the patterns that connect us" (see pages 19-20, this book).

If we want to go beyond rights, as the sole or even main rationale for listening, where do we head? The preceding chapters can be interpreted as opening up to another approach to listening, related to a more nuanced idea of the child and a different paradigm for understanding the world and our relationships to it, which has profound implications for theories and practices: listening as an ethic. As Dahlberg and Moss (2005) have discussed, listening can be understood as a value in the ethics of an encounter, with its attention to otherness that cannot be 'grasped', resisting attempts to make the other into the same. This ethics of an encounter or 'culture of listening' can be seen as promoting different competences by encouraging children's active participation and exploration of their environment together with other children and adults. The different chapters in the book rely on the assumption that a caring community of mutual recognition and listening is crucial for the individual child's feeling of competence, individuality and belonging to a wider community of human beings.

An approach to listening based on a relational ethics – such as the ethics of an encounter – accommodates greater complexity. It understands children's voices and perspectives as multifaceted, changing and conceptualised. Rather than authentic, 'children's voices' are spoken from particular positions within an intricate web of relationships with others. Competence is no longer seen as an essential, generalised or 'natural' trait ascribed by birth, but as a dynamic concept referring to specific and differentiated forms of practices and skills. There are huge individual variations according to degrees of competence and of skill in a particular field. Different competences are, like identities, continually changing and developing, dependent on individual and social experiences and the elaboration of particular practices in a specific context (Kjørholt, 2004);"children and adults can be moved in and out of competence, in and out of maturity" (Lee, 1998, p 474). Given this understanding, to ascribe an essential 'competence' to children and young people can be interpreted as a barrier to recognising them as human beings with diversified and differentiated skills and competencies on a par with adults. Competence can be seen as dynamic and relational, constituted by engaging in specific social practices, including a culture of listening, within a complex web of relationships to others.

If listening is first and foremost about an ethic of openness to and respect for the other, then we have to question a notion of listening that requires the expression of views and experiences in a rational way, primarily through the medium of one language: speech. (We are aware that Article 13 of the United Nations Convention on the Rights of the Child does advocate for the use of variety of means of expression.) However, a fundamental question concerning 'children's voices' and the philosophy of listening can be formulated like this: To what degree and in which ways can human beings, whether they be children or adults, express their experiences? Or put in another way: Can human experiences and meaning be grasped through interpretation of language? And if so, which kind of language(s)?

These questions are also fundamental in research. Discussing methodological approaches to qualitative research, the researcher van Manen argues that "meaning is multi-dimensional and multi-layered. Language is a cognitive apparatus.... What we try to do in phenomenological research is to evoke understandings through language that in a curious way seem to be non-cognitive" (van Manen, 2001, p xviii). The quotation underlines the need to be aware of the limitations of oral language to generate knowledge of social life. By asking how we capture our experiences in language, and what the relationship is between language and experience, van Manen further argues that:

> ... experience is always more immediate, more enigmatic, more complex, more ambiguous than any description can do justice to. The human science researcher is a scholar-author who must be able to maintain an almost unreasonable faith in the power of language to make intelligible and understandable what always seem to lie beyond language. (van Manen, 2001, p xviii)

Although addressing research, this point is highly relevant also for the philosophy of listening to human beings in general, and to young children in particular, illustrating some of the tremendous challenges that practitioners and researchers are faced with in the processes of listening and interpretation, as well as in relation to the different aspects of the processes of social interaction.

The philosophy of listening understood as an 'ethic of an encounter' represents a broad approach to listening far beyond the scope of human experiences limited only to cognitive abilities and oral language. Participant observation as a method to listen to and interpret children's experiences and perspectives, discussed by Hanne Warming in Chapter Four, clearly illustrates how human experiences and perspectives are embedded in and expressed through the social practices in which they engage. Studies of children within peer-cultural contexts, such as early childhood centres, underline the importance of studying children from their perspectives by using ethnographic approaches, and by a focus on children's agency (Åm, 1989; James, 1993; Strandell, 1994; Gulløv, 1999; Nilsen, 2000; Corsaro, 2003).

Observation and participation in children's daily life in early childhood centres is then a valuable tool to get deeper insight into the 'unspoken words' and the complexities of different meaning-making processes in such institutions. It also opens for interpretation of emotions and embodied experiences that are not necessarily conscious for the individual mind. Malaguzzi's theory that a child has a hundred languages, referred to in many chapters of this book, underlines the need to listen to children's experiences as expressed in a variety of different ways, far beyond spoken words only (given further weight by Malaguzzi's contention that children lose most of these languages through adult neglect of them). As underlined by Carlina Rinaldi in Chapter Two, listening to young children in early childhood centres also implies stimulating children to creative and various ways of expressing their experiences and exploring their ideas and theories together with adults, trying to prevent the loss of languages. Her statement that the act of listening is always emotion, a metaphor for having the openness and sensitivity to listen and be listened to, and engages all the senses can be related to a phenomenological understanding of the human being. A hermeneutic phenomenology is both descriptive, in that it tries to grasp things as they appear, and interpretive, because uninterpreted phenomena do not exist (van Manen, 2001).

To see 'listening as time', embracing silences and interior listening, as elaborated by Carlina Rinaldi in Chapter Two, illustrates the ultimate openness to self and others, including what it means to be a human being. We will present a short narrative, taken from a Norwegian kindergarten where the author once worked, to give an example of what listening to young children with sensitivity to the 'unspoken words' and silences can mean:

> A group of 18 active children aged between three and five are sitting on the floor. The theme for today's assembly is 'from grain to bread'. Golden grain is collected from the fields and two stones for grinding are ready for use. A bag of flour is on the table, and afterwards everyone will make their very own bread. The children are eagerly watching Tone, who is an excellent storyteller with the ability to create the right atmosphere. Everyone except for Ronny; he is a restless little fellow aged four, who cannot concentrate either on the harvested grain or on the dialogue about the process of going from grain to bread. He twists and turns and tries to get the other children's attention by making faces. After a while, he starts crawling around. Eventually, the preschool teacher, Karen, intervenes. She doesn't say 'no'. She doesn't scold. Smiling, she takes Ronny's hand, and walking softly out of the room, whispers into his ear: "I think you and I need to go for a run". Ronny was 'seen' by Karen, who took care of his needs without him expressing them verbally. The image of a panting, sweating four-year-old, rather on the plump side with red cheeks, running back and forth along the long corridor, with an equally sweating, red-cheeked Karen, some 50 years his senior and also on the plump side, is still vivid. Ronny was glowing with happiness, and after a while he sunk down relaxed on Karen's lap and listened to the fairy tale about 'the little red hen' during the rest of the assembly.

This glimpse into daily life in an early childhood centre in the 1970s reveals a different construction of children as subjects than represented in the Danish texts in Chapter Nine about children as citizens in centres in the 1990s. With care and sensitivity, Karen listened to and interpreted Ronny's bodily movements and 'unspoken words' with all her senses, gave him a joyful experience of 'running together' and, we could say, by this contributed to developing his self-esteem as a competent social participant in the day-care centre within a culture of listening (Kjørholt, 2004).

In our view, listening as an ethic does not reject discussion of the 'competent child'. Rather, it is related to a notion of 'the competent child' that is far beyond the self-determining autonomous child described in Chapter Nine. It is a notion, which understands competence not as a finished state related to independence, but as an ability to relate, captured in this discussion by Carlina Rinaldi:

> I think that all of you, by now, are familiar with the image of a competent child, on which our educational experience in Reggio is based. But competent in what? In relating with the world. Children do not know the world, but they have all the tools they need to know it, and they want to know it. Within this relationship with the world, children come to know it and to know themselves.

> I said a competent child. Competent because he has a body, a body that knows how to speak and listen, that gives him an identity, and with which he identifies things. A body equipped with senses that can perceive the surrounding environment. A body that risks being increasingly estranged from cognitive processes if its cognitive potential is not recognised and enhanced. A body that is inseparable from the mind. Mind and body, it is increasingly clear, cannot be separated, but form a single unit with reciprocal qualification. (Rinaldi, 2005, pp 91-2)

Beyond the responsible child?

Rights-based discourses of listening and participation raise questions about responsibility. The texts about Danish kindergartens analysed in Chapter Nine gave to young children a high degree of responsibility for their own choices and everyday life. But others criticise children's social participation in a variety of different contexts in society on the grounds that they place too heavy a burden on children's shoulders by giving them too much responsibility and exposing them to inadequate care and protection (Nijnatten, 1993). It has further been argued that adults have the overall responsibility for creating environments ensuring children a high quality of life, representing contexts for children's participation (Mollenhauer, 1986).

Others have emphasised children's rights to be children (Veerman, 1992). This argument often accentuates the *difference* of the child subject as compared with adults. And the different child subject means, first and foremost, a subject with rights and possibilities to play, connected to notions of children as innocent and close to nature. On the other hand, it has been argued that listening to children's voices and giving them rights as fellow citizens is a tool to integrate children in the social structure of society, strengthen their influence and agency in society and educate them as future adult citizens (de Winter, 1997).

Once again we have to move beyond dichotomous images, to find a more nuanced and complex view, such as that presented below by Martin Woodhead, a critic of developmental psychology for producing notions of the universal, global child without taking variations and cultural context into consideration (Woodhead, 1999).

> Displacing an image of the needy child with an image of the competent child must not result in the neglect of differences between younger and older human beings. We must not throw out the baby with the developmental bath water. The difference is that a children's rights paradigm alters the status of children as social actors. Respect for their competence, as rights bearing citizens does not diminish adult responsibilities. It places new responsibilities on the adult community to structure children's environment, guide their behaviour and enable their social participation in ways consistent with their understanding, interests and ways of communicating, especially in the issues that most directly affect their lives. (Woodhead, 2000, p 124)

This view resonates, we think, with the perspectives of the contributors to this book. As we read the different chapters, listening to children does not imply an abdication from adult responsibility. Rather it presupposes adults being responsible for the construction of the culture of listening, for example through attention to caring relations and emotional well being, and designing spaces (physical, social, cultural, discursive) that promote listening and democracy. But does this mean that a culture of listening, inscribed with an ethics of an encounter, implies asymmetrical relationships between children and adults?

As outlined in the introductory chapter, an ethics of an encounter is related to Emmanuel Levinas's philosophy of relationship to 'the Other'. To Levinas, subjectivity means responsibility. He argues "the knot of subjectivity consists in going to the other without concerning oneself with his movement towards me" (Levinas, 1991, quoted in Vetlesen, 1995, p 36). Previous to freedom and choice is the face of the other, and the responsibility for him/her. The relation to the other is a necessary condition for subjectivity in the way that subjectivity is constituted as the fulfilment of a movement between I and you, the 'you' being the axis of the constitution of the I. Levinas argues that this relation that constitutes the subject is not a symmetrical relation based on mutual recognition. Responsibility rests in subjectivity, being "the response to the imperative addressed in the concrete act of facing" (Levinas, 1991, p 39).

The practice of a 'culture of listening' in early childhood services as discussed in the different chapters in this book rests on an underlying assumption of a moral obligation of responsibility to the other. However, since this is a fundamental claim in Levinas's philosophy concerning the constitution of subjectivity, we might argue that the child subject is faced with the same imperative addressed in the concrete act of facing otherness. In this respect, the relations between adults and children can be described as symmetrical, since both are equally touched by the face of the other. This argument makes the construction of early childhood services as spaces for 'cultures of listening' even more pertinent.

The many possibilities of listening

If we can get beyond – although not reject – the rights-based discourse of listening, we can open up to listening as a concept of many possibilities that applies not just to young children, but to older children and adults of all ages: listening as an important part of ethical and democratic political practice; listening as the expression of cultural values; listening as a way of relating; listening as a space for critique; listening as a means of inclusion and participation. For example, the inclusion of parents and politicians in processes of participation as seen in Stirling, described by Linda Kinney in Chapter Seven, opens for a new ethos of democracy.

The preceding chapters have shown the role of listening in enabling children's participation in decision making (Chapters Three and Seven), but also in many other practices and activities: learning (Chapter Two), assessment (Chapter Eight), relationships between centres and families (Chapter Six), policy making (Chapter Eight), research (Chapters Three, Four and Five). We would like to add another example: listening as a means to enable identity formation via narratives.

The daily reports in the profile books used in Fortune Park (Chapter Six) can be seen as short stories or narratives about children's everyday life. The texts create possibilities for children, practitioners and parents together or separately to look at and reflect on the different narratives again and again, contributing to making sense of the world and one's place in it. The text made by Hans, six years old, presented in the introduction to Chapter Five, also illustrates how children construct their identities in narrative structures: "First I stayed in a playground, then in a childcare institution, now I am in kindergarten and then I will go to school and then to work, and then I will stop working, and I will be free all day because I am growing old". This young boy demonstrates awareness of different experiences in a whole life-phase perspective, systematised through chronological time as a structuring element.

During the past 20 years, there has been an increasing emphasis on seeing life experiences and social life as narratives (Bruner, 1987; Taylor, 1978; Gudmundsdottir, 1996; van Manen, 2001). Post-structuralists define narrative and narrativity as concepts through which we understand and make sense of the social world (Somers, 1994; Søndergaard, 1999). The philosopher Charles Taylor also claims that the continuing process of identity formation, or making sense of oneself, has a narrative form. By this he means that in order to understand and make sense of the complexities of our life experiences and our place in the world, we grasp our lives in narrative forms. He argues that "it has often been remarked that making sense of one's life as a story is also, like orientation to the good, not an optional extra; that our lives exist also in this space of questions, which only a coherent narrative can answer" (Taylor, 1978, p 47).

Taylor's concept of narrative here refers to interpretations of experiences that can be consciously grasped by the subject herself. As we have seen, the child subject – as well as the adult subject – is an embodied subject. The culture of listening, as elaborated in the different chapters of this book, can be seen as a facilitator of identity processes. The work of Vivian Paley referred to by Margaret Carr and her colleagues in Chapter Eight gives a concrete example of the practitioner's role in using stories to assist children's exploration of the meaning of life. By telling and listening to different narratives, listening practices may gradually contribute to increased consciousness of what it means to be *that particular embodied child* in the particular context. Emotional as well as cognitive experiences are thereby recognised and made visible.

As referred to in Chapter Five, children as well as adults in modern societies are constructing their own identities by being faced with complexity and diversity and a 'loss of the taken for granted'. Brit Johanne Eide and Nina Winger in Chapter Five say that "to be heard and listened to may be important for children's self-reflective processes and identity constructions both at a personal and collective level" (see page 77, this book). Children are co-constructors of their childhoods and active participants in the constructions of their identities in everyday lives and in establishing relationships with adults and other children (Dahlberg et al, 1999). They are caring subjects, who contribute emotionally to their own and others' quality of life.

The Mosaic approach, presented by Alison Clark in Chapter Three, represents an interesting tool to promote children's own constructions of identities together with other children and adults within early childhood settings. Children, practitioners and parents are engaged in reflexive practices related to interpretations of events, phenomena and 'lived lives' in everyday life, by using a variety of different methods. The question addressed in so doing is ultimately about identity: what does it mean to be in this place and, perhaps more importantly, what does it mean *to be me* here? Learning Stories, as described in Chapter Eight, represent another possibility for exploring listening as narrative. This narrative means of assessing learning allows space for the perspectives of families, community and the children themselves to join those of practitioners in this task of listening.

The concept of listening as narrative reaffirms the theme running through this book that listening is not limited to written or spoken text. Narrative can be bodily represented and communicated. Bodies may be read as narratives, communicated through bodily movements. Life experiences are embodied as feelings and knowledge that can be consciously expressed and reflected upon by the subject. But as the narrative about Ronny illustrates, there are also bodily experiences, unconscious cues that cannot be represented in any written or spoken language, or any form of conscious, intentional bodily communication and meaning making. To interpret bodies as narratives is, therefore, a complex and complicated matter, both from within, for the embodied subject herself, as well as for a researcher and a practitioner trying to comprehend it from outside.

Listening and the creation of children's spaces

We have adopted a critical perspective to listening. We have argued that both the concept and its practice are contentious and potentially problematic, dangerous and full of risks. We have expressed our concerns with the rights and consumer discourses that have contributed so much to the present-day high profile of listening to children.

Yet we reach the end of this book convinced that listening is of the utmost importance. Viewed as an ethical and political concept, an important value in relationships and democracy, it resists many of the normative methods ('human technologies' as Rose [1999] describes them) that increasingly govern children (and adults) today through seeking to make the other into the same; the early childhood field is increasingly filled by such technologies as governments seek to realise the redemptive potential of the young child.

But listening also opens up to a whole range of visions and hopes related to new practices, learning and assessment within institutions, as well as new ways of living together as human beings. By so doing, listening affects how we conceptualise and envision institutions for young (or older) children, and the relationship of children to these institutions. They can be seen as children's spaces, where technical practice is subordinated to ethical and political practice, places where children live their childhoods in communities with other children and adults, learning and exploring their environment with a 'hundred languages' and in relationship to others, competent within a social milieu that enables them to construct identity, values and knowledge with others. In services understood in this way, listening can be understood, as we argued at the start of the book, as "a pedagogy and a way of researching life, a culture and an ethic, a continuous process and relationship" (see page 13, this book).

References

Åm, E. (1989) *På jakt etter barneperspektivet (In search of the child perspective)*, Oslo: Universitetsforlaget.

Bruner, J. (1987) 'Life as narrative', *Social Research*, vol 54, no 1, pp 11-33.

Burman, E. (2001) 'Beyond the baby and the bathwater: post dualistic developmental psychologies for diverse childhoods', *European Early Childhood Education Research Journal*, vol 9, no 1, pp 5-22.

Corsaro, W. (2003) *We're friends, right? Inside kids' culture*, Washington, DC: Joseph Henry.

Dahlberg, G. and Moss, P. (2005) *Ethics and politics in early childhood education*, London: RoutledgeFalmer.

Dahlberg, G., Moss, P. and Pence, A. (1999) *Beyond quality in early childhood education and care: Post modern perspectives*, London: Falmer Press.

de Winter, M. (1997) *Children as fellow citizens: Participation and commitment*, Oxford/ New York, NY: Radcliffe Medical Press.

Diduck, A. (1999) 'Justice and childhood: reflections on refashioned boundaries', in M. King (ed) *Moral agendas for children's welfare*, London: Routledge, pp 120-38.

Flekkøy, M.G. (1993) *Children's rights: Reflections on and consequences of the use of developmental psychology in working for the interest of children. The Norwegian Ombudsman for Children: A practical experience*, Ghent: University of Ghent.

Gudmundsdottir, S. (1996) 'The teller, the tale and the one being told: the narrative nature of research interview', *Curriculum Inquiry*, vol 26, no 3, pp 239-306.

Gulløv, E. (1999) *Betydningsdannelse blant born* (*Meaning making processes among children*), Copenhagen: Gyldendal Socialpædagogiske Bibliotek.

James, A. (1993) *Childhood identities: Self and social relationships in the experience of the child*, Edinburgh: Edinburgh University Press.

Kjørholt, A.T. (2001) '"The participating child" – a vital pillar in this century?', *Nordisk Pedagogikk*, vol 21, no 2, pp 65-81.

Kjørholt, A.T (2004) 'Childhood as a social and symbolic space: discourses on children as social participants in society', PhD thesis, Trondheim: Faculty of Social Sciences and Technology Management, Norwegian Centre for Child Research/Department of Education, NTNU.

Lee, N. (1998) 'Towards an immature sociology', *Sociological Theory*, vol 46, no 3, pp 458-82.

Levinas, E. (ed) (1991) *Totality and infinity*, Pittsburgh, PA: Duquesne University Press.

Mollenhauer, K. (1986) *Vergeten samenhang: Over cultuur en opvoeding* (*Forgotten context: About culture and upbringing*), Meppel: Boom.

Mortier, F. (2002) 'The meaning of individualisation for children's citizenship', in F. Mouritsen and J. Qvortrup (eds) *Childhood and children's culture*, Odense: University Press of Southern Denmark, pp 79-102.

Nijnatten, C.H.C. (1993) *Kinderrechten in discussie* (*Children's rights – a discussion*), Meppel: Boom.

Nilsen, R.D. (2000) 'Livet i barnehagen: en etnografisk studie av sosialiseringsprosessen' ('Life in kindergarten: an ethnographic study of the socialisation process'), PhD thesis, Trondheim: Faculty of Social Sciences and Technology Management, Norwegian Centre for Child Research/Department of Education, NTNU.

Qvortrup, J. (1994) 'Childhood matters: an introduction', in J. Qvortrup (ed) *Childhood matters: Social theory, practice and politics*, Aldershot: Avebury, pp 1-23.

Rinaldi, C. (2005) *In dialogue with Reggio Emilia*, London: RoutledgeFalmer.

Rose, N. (1999) *Powers of freedom: Reframing political thought*, Cambridge: Cambridge University Press.

Somers, M. (1994) 'The narrative constitution of identity: a relational and network approach', *Theory and Society*, vol 23, no 6, pp 605-49.

Søndergaard, D.M. (1999) *Destabilising discourse analyses: Approaches to poststructuralist empirical research*, Working Paper 7, Køn i den akademiske organsisasjon, Copenhagen: København Universitet, Institutt for Statskundskab.

Strandell, H. (1994) *Sociala mötesplatser för barn* (*Social meeting places for children*), Helsinki: Gaudeamus.

Taylor, C. (1978) *Sources of the self: The making of the modern identity*, Cambridge: Cambridge University Press.

van Manen, M. (2001) *Researching lived experience: Human science for an action sensitive pedagogy*, London, Ontario, Canada: Althouse Press.

Veerman, P.E. (1992) *The rights of the child and the changing image of childhood*, Dordrecht: Martinus Nijhoff Publishers.

Vetlesen, A.J. (1995) 'Levinas – en ny etikk' ('Levinas – a new ethics'), in H. Kolstad, H. Bjørnstad and A. Aarnes (eds) *I sporet av det uendelige* (*In the step of infinity*), Oslo: Aschehoug og Co.

Woodhead, M. (1999) 'Reconstructing developmental psychology: some first steps', *Children and Society*, vol 13, no 1, pp 3-19.

Woodhead, M. (2000) 'Children's rights and children's development: rethinking the paradigm', *Ghent Papers on Children's Rights*, no 6, Ghent: Children's Rights Centre.

Index

A new deal for children?
Re-forming education and care in England, Scotland and Sweden
Bronwen Cohen, Peter Moss, Pat Petrie and Jennifer Wallace

"... a thought provoking, informed and instructive account, and an important point of reference for those who wish an analytic grip of many of the new concepts of governance around child care. Well worth reading whether you are an academic, policy maker, practitioner, student or anyone else interested in child care policies." *Journal of Social Policy*

Important reforms are taking place in children's services in the UK, with a move towards greater integration. In England, Scotland and Sweden, early childhood education and care, childcare for older children, and schools are now the responsibility of education departments. This book is the first to examine, cross-nationally, this major shift in policy.

Paperback £19.99 US$35.00
ISBN 1 86134 528 3
234 x 156mm 256 pages June 2004

Children of the 21st century
From birth to nine months
Edited by Shirley Dex and Heather Joshi

This book documents the early lives of almost 19,000 children born in the UK at the start of the 21st century, and their families. It is the first time that analysis of data from the hugely important Millennium Cohort Study, a longitudinal study following the progress of the children and their families, has been drawn together in a single volume. The unrivalled data is examined here to address important policy and scientific issues.

Paperback £24.99 US$39.95
ISBN 1 86134 688 3
Hardback £55.00 US$85.00
ISBN 1 86134 689 1
234 x 156mm 296 pages October 2005
The UK Millennium Cohort Study series

Child welfare and social policy

An essential reader

Edited by Harry Hendrick

"This groundbreaking selection of seminal writings puts the subject of children and social policy in 21st-century Britain firmly on the map. Immense value is added by Harry Hendrick's introduction and trenchant critique, which locates every contribution within its specific policy context. This book is bound to become required reading for any under- and postgraduate social science student in the UK." *Eva Lloyd, Senior Lecturer in Early Childhood Studies, School for Policy Studies, University of Bristol*

This book provides an essential one-stop introduction to the key concepts, issues, policies and practices affecting child welfare, with particular emphasis on the changing nature of the relationship between child welfare and social policy. No other book brings together such a wide selection of material to form an attractive and indispensable teaching and learning resource.

Paperback £25.00 US$39.95
ISBN 1 86134 566 6
Hardback £55.00 US$85.00
ISBN 1 86134 567 4
240 x 172mm 576 pages March 2005

Children, family and the state

Decision-making and child participation

Nigel Thomas

"This book makes a welcome contribution to our understanding of looked after children's experiences of participation in decision-making. The author's findings contain important messages for social workers, managers and policy makers ... It should be essential reading on all courses for those working with looked after children at both undergraduate and postqualifying level. It is a must for anyone committed to understanding and promoting children's rights." *Social Work Education*

Children, family and the state examines different theories of childhood, children's rights and the relationship between children, parents and the state. Focusing on children who are looked after by the state, it reviews the changing objectives of the care system and the extent to which children have been involved in decisions about their care.

Paperback £18.99 US$29.95
ISBN 1 86134 448 1
234 x 156mm 256 pages October 2002